Dress
Sense

Joanne, daughters, and friends, Nigeria, 1965.

Dress
Sense

*Emotional
and Sensory
Experiences of the
Body and Clothes*

Edited by
Donald Clay Johnson
and
Helen Bradley Foster

Oxford • New York

English edition
First published in 2007 by
Berg
Editorial offices:
First Floor, Angel Court, 81 St Clements Street, Oxford OX4 1AW, UK
175 Fifth Avenue, New York, NY 10010, USA

Berg is the imprint of Oxford International Publishers Ltd.

Library of Congress Cataloging-in-Publication Data

Dress sense : emotional and sensory experiences of the body and clothes / edited by Donald Clay
Johnson and Helen Bradley Foster. — English ed.
    p. cm.
    Includes bibliographical references and index.
    ISBN-13: 978-1-84520-692-5 (cloth)
    ISBN-10: 1-84520-692-4 (cloth)
    ISBN-13: 978-1-84520-693-2 (pbk.)
    ISBN-10: 1-84520-693-2 (pbk.)
  1. Clothing and dress—Psychological aspects. 2. Clothing and dress—History. 3. Emotions.
4. Senses and sensation. I. Johnson, Donald Clay, 1940- II. Foster, Helen Bradley.

GT524.D76 2007
391.009—dc22

                                                                                            2007033131

British Library Cataloguing-in-Publication Data

A catalogue record for this book is available from the British Library.

ISBN   978 1 84520 692 5 (Cloth)
       978 1 84520 693 2 (Paper)

Typeset by JS Typesetting Ltd, Porthcawl, Mid Glamorgan
Printed in the United Kingdom by Biddles Ltd, King's Lynn

www.bergpublishers.com

CONTENTS

TABLES AND ILLUSTRATIONS

TABLES

FIGURES

CONTRIBUTORS

Sarah Adams (Assistant Professor, School of Art and Art History, University of Iowa) has undertaken research on ephemeral women's body and mural painting in southeastern Nigeria. Her work explores the construction of art historical knowledge in the absence of an archive of objects.

Heather Marie Akou (Assistant Professor, Apparel Merchandising Department, Indiana University) currently investigates generational changes in Somali children's dress. Joanne Eicher directed Akou's master's thesis, "Re-thinking 'fashion' the Case of Somali Women's Dress in Minneapolis-St. Paul as an Evaluation of Herbert Blumer's Theory on Fashion" (2001) and her PhD dissertation, "Macrocultures, Migration, and Somali Malls: A Social History of Somali Dress and Aesthetics" (2005).

Susan P. Ashdown (Helen G. Canoyer Professor, Department of Textiles and Apparel, Cornell University) studies functional apparel design, the sizing and fit of apparel, anthropometrics for design, the perception of fit, and the development and use of the 3-D body scanner and other new technologies in the apparel industry. She teaches classes on draping, product development, computer-aided design, apparel sizing and fit, and the relationships among materials and design choices.

Cynthia Becker (Assistant Professor, Art History Department, Boston University) concentrates on African arts with particular attention on the Amazigh (Berbers) in northwestern Africa. She published *Amazigh Arts in Morocco: Women Shaping Berber Identity* (University of Texas Press 2006). Her current enquiry concentrates on identifying art historical connections across the Sahara due to the trans-Saharan caravan trade.

Marlene R. Breu (Professor, Textile and Apparel Studies Program, Family and Consumer Sciences Department, Western Michigan University) has conducted fieldwork in Turkey since 1990. Her published works include articles and book chapters on traditional Turkish dress. Two forthcoming books deal with sacred historical textiles and other artifacts in the Armenian Orthodox Churches of Istanbul.

Sandra Lee Evenson (Associate Professor of Clothing, Textiles, and Design, Margaret Ritchie School of Family and Consumer Sciences, University of Idaho) did her PhD dissertation, "A History of Indian Madras Manufacture and Trade: Shifting Patterns of Exchange" (1994), and her MA thesis "The Manufacture of Madras in South India and its export to West Africa: A Case Study" (1991), under Joanne Eicher. She co-authored *The Visible Self: Global Perspectives on Dress, Culture and Society* (Fairchild 2000) with Joanne B. Eicher and Hazel A. Lutz. Her teaching concentrates on cross-cultural aspects of dress, production, and globalization and her research examines relationships between world cultures and the history of dress.

Helen Bradley Foster (Instructor, Department of African and African American Studies, and Department of Art History, University of Minnesota) centers her investigations on material culture. Her publications include articles on American and Greek folklife. In 1997, she published *New Raiments of Self: African American Clothing in the Antebellum South* (Berg); in 2003, *Wedding Dress Across Cultures* (Berg), co-edited with Donald Clay Johnson.

Suzanne Gott (Assistant Professor, Department of Visual and Aboriginal Art, Brandon University) concentrates her scholarly investigations upon women and urban visual culture in the Ashanti region of central Ghana. She presently is working on a forthcoming book on women and the dynamics of heightened display and performance among contemporary Asante.

Jane E. Hegland (Professor and Head, Apparel Merchandising and Interior Design Department, South Dakota State University) utilizes the qualitative research paradigm, particularly interpretive methodologies, to study and to teach ways dress constructs gender and identity within a specific cultural context. This includes cross-dressing, the relationship between rape and dress, the high-school prom in American culture, the aesthetics of dress, and the application of material culture analysis. Joanne Eicher directed her MA thesis "Drag Queens, Transvestites, Transsexuals: A Visual Typology and Analysis of Male-to-Female Cross-Dressing" (1991), and her PhD dissertation, "The High School Prom: A Case Study of Expectations and Dress for an American Ritual" (1995).

Nancy Nelson Hodges (Associate Professor and Director of Graduate Studies, Department of Consumer, Apparel, and Retail Studies, University of North Carolina at Greensboro) teaches courses on gender issues in relation to social, cultural, and historic aspects of dress. She undertakes qualitative research using feminist and ethnographic methods on approaches to dress and lived experience, women and creative expression, cross-cultural exploration of women, education and apparel industry employment.

Donald Clay Johnson (Curator, Ames Library of South Asia, University of Minnesota) compiled *Agile Hands and Creative Minds: A Bibliography of the Textile Traditions of Afghanistan, Bangladesh, Bhutan, India, Nepal, Pakistan, and Sri Lanka* (Orchid Press 2000) and actively writes on aspects of the textile and dress traditions of India. He and Helen Bradley Foster jointly edited *Wedding Dress Across Cultures* (Berg 2003).

Mary A. Littrell (Professor and Head, Design and Merchandising Department, Colorado State University) has concentrated her work on business social responsibility, sustainable artisan enterprise, and cultural analysis of dress and textiles. For the past decade she has conducted enquiries on artisan enterprises in India. Her co-authored book, *Social Responsibility in the Global Market: Fair Trade of Cultural Products* (Sage Publications 1999), describes nonexploitive and humanizing ways to conduct global business fostering artisan employment, cultural integrity, and business sustainability.

Suzanne Loker (J. Thomas Clark Professor of Entrepreneurship, Department of Textiles and Apparel, Cornell University) actively undertakes enquiries analyzing innovative business strategies and technologies in the apparel industry, including body scanning, mass customization, radio frequency identification, socially responsible practices, and economic development through creative economy initiatives.

Annette Lynch (Associate Professor, Textiles and Apparel Department, University of Northern Iowa) did her dissertation, "Hmong-American Dress for the New Year: A Material Cultural Approach" (1992), under Joanne Eicher. In 1999, Lynch published *Dress, Gender and Cultural Change* (Berg) and in 2007 Berg will publish her book on fashion change theory in the new millennium. Her investigations concentrate on cultural construction and transformation of gender through dress and appearance.

Katalin Medvedev (Assistant Professor, Textiles, Merchandising and Interiors Department, University of Georgia) teaches classes on the cultural perspectives of dress. Joanne Eicher served as advisor for her PhD dissertation, "If this Dress Could Speak: Sartorial Resistance of the Hungarian Socialist Woman 1948–1968" (2006).

Jennifer Paff Ogle (Associate Professor, Design and Merchandising Department and member, Women's Studies Program, Colorado State University) works on ways in which meanings about appearances and bodies form within sociocultural contexts and through interpersonal interactions. Recent enquiry includes exploration into media, family, and peer influences upon body image, the media's construction of the Columbine shootings as a dress-related social problem, and feminist readings of the body.

M. Elise Radina (Assistant Professor, Department of Family Studies and Social Work, Miami University) directs her research on the roles of women in familial and social relationships within their own, family members', or friends' illness experiences. Using qualitative methods, she studies the ways breast cancer survivors renegotiate their social roles. A secondary area of exploration investigates adult children's experiences in caring for aging parents.

Victoria L. Rovine (Assistant Professor, Art History Department and African Studies Department, University of Florida) conducted extensive research in Mali on the revival of traditional textiles within the contemporary art and fashion markets. The Smithsonian Institution Press published her book *Bogolan: Shaping Culture through Cloth in Contemporary Mali* (2001). Currently she studies African fashion designers in the global economy for which she received a Getty Foundation Curatorial Research Grant and a Rockefeller Foundation Bellagio Study Center residency to pursue this project.

Marybeth C. Stalp (Assistant Professor, Sociology Department, University of Northern Iowa) uses qualitative methodology techniques, including visual sociology, in her investigation of the intersection of gender and culture in the United States. In addition to her work on the emergence of the Red Hat Society, she studies contemporary American women's quilting as a gendered form of cultural production, with specific attention to family tensions resulting from midlife women developing quilting interests.

Linda Welters (Professor and Chairperson, Textiles, Fashion Merchandising and Design Department, University of Rhode Island) conducted numerous field studies in Greece from 1983 to 1995, the results of which are published in journal articles and books. She also investigates New England material culture and twentieth-century fashion and publishes widely on these topics. Joanne Eicher served as co-advisor for her dissertation, "Analysis of Greek Women's Chemises in American Collections" (1981).

INTRODUCTION

Helen Bradley Foster and Donald Clay Johnson

This volume emanates from a retirement symposium held at the University of Minnesota in 2005. That meeting and this book honor the career of Joanne Bubolz Eicher, Regents' Professor Emerita.

After a dual graduate major in sociology and anthropology at Michigan State University, Eicher taught at her alma mater from 1961 to 1977 in the Department of Human Environment and Design. In 1977, the University of Minnesota invited her to establish and serve as chair of the Department of Textiles and Clothing in the College of Home Economics. Eicher headed the department through its reorganization in 1983 when it became the Department of Design, Housing, and Apparel under the new College of Human Ecology. She remained chair of the restructured department until 1987. During the same years, Eicher, as director of the Goldstein Gallery, established the international reputation of this university design museum through inaugurating its exceptional exhibition and lecture programs.

During the course of her teaching career at the University of Minnesota, Eicher served as major advisor for fifteen Ph.D. dissertations, as co-advisor for six PhD dissertations, and as major advisor for twelve Master of Art degrees. In retirement, Eicher continues as major advisor for five students seeking their PhD, as co-advisor for three other PhD students, and as major advisor for two Master of Art students.

Eicher's fieldwork research began in Nigeria. Over the years her research, teaching, lecturing, and honorary awards have taken her to Canada, Cote d'Ivoire, Egypt, England, Ethiopia, Ghana, India, Italy, Korea, Mali, People's Republic of China, and the Republic of Benin. Such diverse international work on design within diverse human communities allows her to focus her attention on dress in specific cultural and cross-cultural contexts.

Much of this work involves collaboration with people of other nationalities, American academic colleagues or graduate students. A striking characteristic of Eicher – her generosity to other professionals and to her students – becomes evident when viewing her extensive publication record. Thus far, this includes thirteen books, twenty-five chapters in books and catalogs, forty-eight journal articles, and extensive entries in eight dictionaries and encyclopedias including, among others: *Encyclopedia of Clothing and Fashion* (2005), *Routledge International Encyclopedia of Women: Global Women's Issues and Knowledge* (2000), and *The Dictionary of Art* (1996). With her well-deserved prestige in several academic fields, she easily might have published solely in her own name. Instead, there are an amazingly high number of publications she co-authored and co-edited with others. Of important note when recognizing academic unselfishness – Joanne B. Eicher does not insist that her name always come first in co-written works!

Eicher never looks back; as soon as she completes one project, she is already hard at work on the next. Her colleague at the University of Minnesota, Marilyn Delong, observed this characteristic when she told this story. When Delong shared with Eicher that her first book had just been published, she received Eicher's congratulations along with the question: "And what will your next book be?" Such an approach illustrates Eicher's own productivity and why she plays such an important role in the work of so many other scholars on so many aspects of dress.

Words such as clothing, clothes, costume, garb, garment, raiment, outfit, uniform, attire, apparel, ensemble, and so on, usually denote generalized material items put *on* the body. In 1992, Eicher and her long-time colleague, Mary Ellen Roach-Higgins, chose "dress" as the term that, besides clothing, also encompasses cosmetics, tattoos, jewelry, nail polish, hairdos, scarification, etc. As defined by Eicher and Roach-Higgins, "dress" became the standard term to use for the ways in which anyone, anywhere covers or uncovers, adds to or subtracts from, her or his body. In its briefest definition: "dress of an individual is an assemblage of modifications of the body and/or supplements to the body" (Eicher & Roach-Higgins 1992). With that one word – "dress" – they broadened the definition from only what is attached to the body to include what is taken from the body. With the adaptation of a single word to encompass a more formidable way of looking at the human body, Eicher and Roach-Higgins greatly expanded the means by which material culture scholars examine the human body.

To extend nuanced searches about how we choose to decorate our bodies under the broad definition of "dress," Eicher suggested the theme for the 2005 symposium: The Senses and Sentiments of Dress. Earlier, Eicher had already begun to think about expanding on the senses (see Eicher *et al.* 2000 [1973]: Chapter 1). For the symposium, she challenged other scholars to find instances in which the remaining four senses – touch, smell, hearing, and taste – inform perceptions of dress, instead of the more usual sense of sight which we first use when assessing another's dress and until now the sense most often used to study dress. By including "sentiments" in the theme, Eicher also wanted another meaning of "sense" to be examined: the feelings, emotions, memories, impressions, responses, and sensations we associate with dress.

Page limitations forced us to select just fifteen of the thirty-three papers and ten poster sessions presented at the symposium. Once we made these hard decisions, we divided the essays into the four parts that became the book. Although several chapters could easily fit into more than one part, the arrangement provides discussions of senses and sentiments that occurred in our pasts, that continue to exist, contemporary evaluations or challenges to their significance, and concludes with chapters that analyze the current and future influence of online technology on our perceptions of dress.

The chapters cover historical, geographical, and cultural values and how these shape attitudes and approaches toward dress. The authors come from a variety of disciplines: African studies, art history, Asian studies, design, family studies, fashion merchandising, folklore, sociology, textiles and clothing, and women's studies. The chapters cross spatial boundaries – Africa, Asia, Europe, North America – and take us from our pasts to our presents and into our futures.

HISTORICAL PERSPECTIVES

In her work, Eicher often gives a historical background to present-day research. In the first three chapters of this part, the authors, likewise, explore the meanings and memories of nineteenth- and twentieth-century dress among communities still with us.

Part I begins with Linda Welters drawing from her long-term study of Greek regional dress, worn in villages in the eastern Peloponnesus from the nineteenth century until about the 1950s. The actual dress objects worn at weddings and festivals often remain, as do the memories about them. Welters finds that, along with visual recognition, people especially remember the sounds once made by objects in village dress.

The continent of Africa is Eicher's own earliest and foremost region of study. Significantly, and a reflection of Eicher's intellectual influence in the study of dress, Africa is the continent most covered in this book. Heather Marie Akou begins our sojourn in Africa with her study among Somalis living in Minneapolis and St. Paul, MN, the cities with the highest concentration of refugees from Somalia in the United States. Her study took her to the collection of Somali objects at the Museum of Natural History, part of the system of national museums in Washington, DC. The objects she discovered there dated to precolonial times, but Somalis continue to use similar items. While the objects are not textiles, the material we generally associate with attire, they nonetheless all fall under the heading "dress" as defined by Eicher.

Dress as a form of resistance in Hungary during the period of socialist rule becomes the theme by which Katalin Medvedev gains access to the memories of two women who lived under that not-too-distant regime. The women's narratives reveal the solutions they forged in order to wear what they wanted, flouting totalitarian dogma as to what should be worn.

Going further back in time, Donald Clay Johnson explores the often humorous lengths British men, and the women who accompanied them, went to in order to remain recognizably British in imperial India during the eighteenth through twentieth centuries. Johnson draws from contemporary accounts to describe the woolens, flannels, pith helmets, and other items of attire worn at the time in the tropical Indian climate by those from the temperate British Isles.

The narratives of another group of people from the nineteenth century give voice to far more perilous and heroic circumstances associated with dress. Helen Bradley Foster draws from the stories told by and about enslaved African Americans who dared to escape from captivity to gain their own freedom. In the cases described, three approaches to this daring task proved successful; in each, the means of escape entailed dressing in disguise.

LIVING TRADITIONS

What people feel, literally in terms of physical senses, and also emotionally, about dress is the focus of the next two sections. This comes about because of the recent phenomenon of mixing cultures, which thereby introduces differences in dress, followed by how we think about others because of their appearance. From this, meaningful questions arise: How do we feel about the dress of others? How do we learn to understand the various habits, fashions, and feelings others have for their own dress?

Marlene Breu begins by describing the physiology of smell and discusses how community worldview in several regions of the world creates very different reactions to natural bodily scents and odors and applied fragrances. She then narrows her study to reveal how some rural Turks exhibit the sense of smell in particular as an important way in which to enjoy the bodies of others.

Cynthia Becker returns us to Africa with her work among the Amazigh, Berber people of Morocco. She explores how Berbers use each of the senses when judging their community dress. Becker also demonstrates the protective features of Berber items of dress, especially during rites of passage.

Moving to the African west coast, Suzanne Gott explores the sense of touch in the waist beads still worn by many Asante girls and women in Ghana. From a very early age, girls also wear strings of beads around other body parts in the belief that the touch of these beads ensures curves in the aesthetically correct places. As adults, women wear several strands of beads around their waists, the most private and sexually attractive part of the Ghanaian female body.

Moving down the west coast we arrive in Nigeria, the nation where Eicher began her fieldwork more than forty years ago. Sandra Evenson takes us to the Kalabari, among whom the world-famous Indian fabric madras is known as "Real India." Since British traders introduced it in the nineteenth century, the Kalabari have given the cotton, plaid cloth both material and social significance. Along the way, textile manufacturers and traders have attempted to pass off imitation madras, but always unsuccessfully because, among the Kalabari, the visual takes second place to the way Real India feels, smells, and even tastes.

Sarah Adams introduces us to another community in Nigeria, the Igbo. Adams analyzes Igbo body painting as another methodological approach for art historians to employ: the body becomes an active not merely a passive object of study. Adams applies Pierre Bourdieu's 1977 theory of *habitus* as a new model for examining the active body within its culture.

CHALLENGING TRADITIONS

Still examining the present day, the authors in this part confront the contemporary entanglements we all experience as technology disperses the material cultures of diverse communities all over the planet. The globalization of world economies gives rise to a recent surge in popularity of dress fashions labeled "ethnic," "authentic," and "traditional."

Eicher's exploration of East Indian dress has been ongoing for a number of years, particularly the link between certain Indian textiles and West African communities. In Part III, the first chapter observes Indian dress, but within contexts in the United States. The second chapter extends into an examination of the use of "traditional" imagery in creating African haute couture. The third chapter looks at the response of a group of older women to a society that traditionally counts them out as they age.

Mary A. Littrell and Jennifer Paff Ogle scrutinize the "experience of dress" among East Indian-born women resident in the United States. Drawing on interviews with these women, the authors discuss the women's ability to intermingle their indigenous dress with Western dress and test "traditional" dress in terms of nationality. Further, they discover that three important themes emerge which focus on perceptions of traditional dress in new environments.

Victoria L. Rovine clearly illustrates the various sensual components of Westerners' assessments of whether a traditional item of dress from another culture is "authentic." The merchandising of these imported articles of attire becomes of prime importance in how Westerners make their judgments. Rovine shows this first by deconstructing an advertisement for Indian tunic blouses in *The New York Times*. She then analyzes the ways high-fashion designers from Mali, Senegal, and South Africa skillfully blend the past with the present in constructing their "authentic" creations.

In American society, the Cary Grant syndrome is still going strong: older men only get better looking; older women only get older looking. Annette Lynch, Elise Radina, and Marybeth Stalp examine how older women experience aging in the United States. Interviews with Midwestern members of the ten-year-old phenomenon, "the Red Hat Society," explore why these women wear such flamboyant dress items as large, decorated red hats and frilly purple stoles. The authors find that the older women publicly flaunt themselves in the red hats and accessories as positive ways to negate society's view of them.

THE FUTURE

In the final part, the authors deal with future dress sense as it already transpires in the electronic age. Jane E. Hegland and Nancy Nelson Hodges read, peer at, and analyze websites of male-to-female cross-dressers. These men set up individual websites that contain personal histories and photos of themselves "dressed" and in which they discuss both their sensory reactions to dress and their sentiments associated with dress. Analysis of these sites leads the authors to offer interesting functions for cyberspace now and in the future.

Along with other virtual realities that computers continue to bring us comes "virtual dress." This system allows a person's virtual body to be dressed with scanned images. Suzanne Loker and Susan Ashdown describe research efforts being made on sites that focus on each of the senses. The authors interview people and analyze their reactions to images of their own dressed body scans. By this method, Loker and Ashdown suggest the symbolic sense of dress experience in virtual reality applications.

Joanne Bubolz Eicher bases her cross-cultural scholarship and teaching on dress and textiles as nonverbal communication. Sharing her specialization with so many others on an international level, Eicher influences them to think deeper about how we represent ourselves and how we judge the appearance of others. In this book, the authors follow Eicher's lead to explore the nuances and more obvious ways in which people use their physical and emotional senses to evaluate themselves and others. Although the fifteen studies in this book contain temporal observations on a variety of cultures, paramount to the findings is that how we use our senses about dress is not always universal. Nonetheless, how we use our senses becomes of utmost concern as we relate to the world today.

REFERENCES

Eicher, J. B. and Roach-Higgins, M. E. (1992), "Definition and Classification of Dress," in R. Barnes and J. B. Eicher (eds), *Dress and Gender: Making and Meaning in Cultural Context*, Oxford: Berg.

Eicher, J. B., Evenson, S. L. and Lutz, H. A. (eds). (2000 [1973]), *The Visible Self*, New York: Fairchild Publications.

1 SIGHT, SOUND, AND SENTIMENT IN GREEK VILLAGE DRESS

Linda Welters

In Europe, as in other parts of the world, folk dress communicates facts about an individual's identity. First and foremost, it locates the wearer in a specific community, typically a group of villages, but occasionally a region where a nomadic people roams (Frater 1996). Second, in an area of multiple ethnicities, it signals ethnic heritage, often along with linguistic differences (Welters 1995). Third, it signifies a person's socioeconomic standing through a code that only members of the community may comprehend. Gender is a fourth aspect of identity clearly projected by folk dress. Sentiment, however, is not so apparent in an individual's appearance. Yet the notion of sentiment, as acquired through the senses, helps explain how individuals employ dress and appearance to create an identity for themselves. This notion is not articulated in the literature on Greek folk dress. Cultural anthropologists who work in Greece, however, have begun to explore the senses as they affect memories of food (Seremetakis 1994; Sutton 2001).

Elsewhere I have argued that dress represents a geographical *place* through one or more of the following five principles: (1) use of locally available materials to make clothing, (2) emergence of a specific style based on collective physical and social needs of a region's inhabitants, (3) use of unique local or regional words to name an item of dress, (4) use of dress by an individual to express identity with a community and (5) use of dress to symbolize place through memory and representation (Welters 2004: 131).

Here I focus on Greek women's folk dress as an expression of community sentiment, and the role the senses play in building that sentiment. I concentrate on two of the five senses: sight and sound.

My observations are based on fieldwork conducted in Greek villages from 1983 to 1995.[1] Over that twelve-year period I studied dress in the provinces of Attica, Argolida, Corinthia, Boeotia, Fokida, and Euboea. (Attica, Boeotia, and Fokida are located on the Greek mainland; Argolida and Corinthia lie across the Gulf of Corinth on the Peloponnesian peninsula; and Euboea is a large island situated parallel to the mainland across from Boeotia.) These provinces form a ring with Athens at its center. They are home to several different ethnic groups: Greeks, Greek-Albanians, Vlachs, Sarakatsani, and Greek refugees from Turkey.[2] Each province has its own local folk dress (Benaki 1948; Papantoniou 2000).

Greece endured almost 400 years of occupation by Ottoman Turkey (1453–1821). This circumstance of history brought Turkish influence to many regions, aligning the country more with the Near East than with Europe. It also limited Greece's participation in Europe's industrialization during the nineteenth century. As a consequence, mainland Greece retained its agricultural economy along with the conservative customs and beliefs associated with people who work the land. In the islands and main towns, folk dress (also termed traditional dress, regional dress, or ethnic dress) began to disappear in the late nineteenth century as transportation and trade improved, and as larger pan-European clothing concepts emerged. On the mainland, the agricultural villages changed more slowly than the towns and cities, thus preserving the folk dress. Dress customs altered with every generation as commercial products were introduced and adopted by the young people. Around the time of the First World War, fashionable dress started to replace the traditional styles, creating a kind of hybrid attire. This gradual transition from folk to fashion continued until the onset of the Second World War when the German occupation and the ensuing civil war eclipsed normal life. After the war, television and the advent of tourism brought rapid development to Greece. By 1990, elderly women in just a few rural villages wore folk dress on a daily basis. One of these places was the Aghia Anna villages on the island of Euboea, which I studied.

Working first in museums to gain an understanding of the components that made up local folk dresses, I developed an album of photographs that illustrated different dress items from specific regions. Then I visited villages to interview people who remembered the making and wearing of the local folk dress. In total, I interviewed more than 400 people and photographed their extant material culture, mostly costumes and old photographs. The research focused on women's dress rather than on men's dress for two reasons. First, men's village dress is not as nuanced in meaning as women's dress. Second, it changed more rapidly to Westernized attire (e.g., suits, trousers, and shirts).

During the course of the interviews, it became apparent that the entire community valued the clothing worn by village women on special occasions. This was evident in their memories of folk dress as something special, which they described as "pretty" or "beautiful." The characteristics that made the outfits so attractive in the eyes of the villagers varied from district to district. In Sofiko, Corinthia, Fani Martelou thought the young women in their white dresses, colorfully embroidered jackets and aprons "looked like dolls" (interview, November 8, 1986). In Kamaria on Euboea, it was the *siguni* (sleeveless jacket) that made the girls look so good (Evmorphia Lykou, interview, June 12, 1990). Husbands, too, appreciated the women dressed up in their finery. One elderly man claimed: "The Greek costume was beautiful, but a great expense and difficult to preserve" (Panayiotis Kaparellou, interview, December 3, 1986).

Often, villagers boasted about their local folk dress, claiming it was the best in the region. Eleni Alexiou of Kastaniotissa, Euboea, bragged: "Our costume was the proudest one. The other villages didn't have such nice ones" (interview, June 12, 1990). In Attica, several of the larger villages laid claim to having the "best" embroidery designs for chemises. One woman said: "I can tell you that the whole of Messoghia had designs from Markopoulo" (Welters 1988: 74). Yet the women of neighboring Koropi made the same claim about their embroideries, which were nearly identical to those of Markopoulo.

Women who wore such clothes in their youth emphasized the communal aspects of the style rather than their own individual beauty. They identified the clothing in the photo albums as "ours" rather than "mine." Objects they did not recognize were "not from here," "from another place," or "foreign." The expression "foreign" could refer to a village just a few kilometers away on the other side of a geographical boundary, such as a mountain. The community that identified with a particular costume, then, was a cluster of villages in the same area.

Figure 1.1   Giannoula Krikou and her daughter at a celebration in Delphi in 1930.

Part of the charm of the special occasion attire was its elegance compared to everyday dress (Figure 1.1). For everyday wear, village women donned simple clothing in long-wearing fabrics and covered their hair with scarves. These dull-colored, unembellished clothes suited the everyday lives of these women. Thus, when the young women of the village dressed up in their finery – delicate fabrics, embroideries, jewelry, with hair dressed and visible under pretty scarves – it was a treat for everyone's eyes. As Eleni Karatzouli of Krioneri, Corinthia, who wore hand-woven clothes on a daily basis, but festive wear on special occasions, stated: "the whole place was becoming white when we wore them" (interview, November 20, 1986).

A woman's day was filled with chores: cooking, cleaning, washing, caring for children and older relatives, feeding animals, fetching water from the community spring, and tending to fields located some distance from the village. Women were also responsible for clothing preparation and care. Before imported factory-made goods found their way to the villages, women orchestrated every aspect of cloth making, a very time-consuming activity.

People did not own many clothes. A young woman typically received a cache of clothing and other household textiles as part of her dowry when she married. This was expected to last a lifetime. Upon marriage, a woman moved to her husband's familial home. Often animals shared the same dwelling, either on the ground floor of a two-story house or in a stable adjacent to the living quarters (du Boulay 1974). Village houses were crowded, with several generations living together under the same roof. It was a challenge for a housewife to keep a clean house in such an environment. Being a good housekeeper was an important attribute for a Greek woman then as well as now (Friedl 1965).

Clothes storage posed a challenge. Everyday clothes were hung on hooks, while good clothes rested in trunks where they could be accessed for intermittent use. In the provinces I visited, there was no room for large wardrobes in the typical village house. To compensate, some families carefully layered clothes and household textiles in the corners of rooms; sometimes these stacks reached to the ceiling.

The wearing of festival dress was age and status specific. Only young women, either engaged or newly married, wore the decorative ensembles. Centuries-old beliefs dictated the design of the wedding outfits; brides were expected to have specific colors and embroidery motifs, as well as to display fringes, on their clothes. The colors red and black are common to the oldest costumes studied. These are primal colors tied to fertility and the earth (Welters 1999: 9). Embroidery designs often included geometric motifs that are recognized fertility signs in prehistoric cultures (ibid.: 8). Fringe, an analog for women's hair and, by association, sexual maturity (Barber 1994), appeared on jackets, sleeves, aprons, chemises, and headscarves. The wedding ensembles worn in each of the districts I studied incorporated one or more of the colors, motifs, or fringes associated with fertility.

Strict local customs did not allow women to wear the wedding ensembles until the day of their wedding, although in some areas engaged girls signified their new status by wearing some of the components accorded to married women. All stops were pulled out for the wedding day. Brides wore elaborately embroidered outfits and copious amounts of jewelry. They had assistance getting dressed from older women, who knew the local customs regarding wedding dress. Other young women who had married recently also wore their bridal attire to the wedding. This participation by older women in preparing the bride and the younger women in the bride's age group wearing their own outfits further reinforced the community sentiment for the festival dress.

Some exceptional wedding ensembles gained near-legendary status among villagers. In the Messoghia villages of Attica, older residents still remembered one bride's elaborate gold *foundi* (local name for the chemise) eighty-three years after the wedding. It was covered with gold thread (Welters 1988: 52).

The wedding outfit was worn for a designated time period after the wedding, which varied from place to place: fifteen days in Attica, forty days in Euboea, and so on. New brides even went to the fields in their wedding outfits. At the end of the period, the bride accompanied her mother-in-law to church, then put away her wedding dress, which became her festival dress. Well-off peasant communities had several levels of festival dress. Bridal dress was always the most elaborate, followed by a "second" festival dress.

A newly married woman could wear the "good" dress on festive occasions, including other women's weddings, until the birth of one or two children. Having proved its success as a good luck charm to render the married woman fecund, the dress was packed away for use by daughters or future daughters-in-law. The customs were quite rigid on this issue. It simply was not appropriate to wear the wedding dress as a festival dress after the birth of several children. In addition, it was strictly taboo for widows and women past menopause to wear clothes with elaborate embroideries or fringes. These women were relegated to wearing plain, undecorated dress even on festive occasions (Figure 1.1). The customs were enforced through ridicule. Women told us stories of making fun of those women who broke the rules. We met an older woman on the island of Euboea who had covered the embroidered hem of her chemise with plain white cotton because she was "ashamed" to be wearing embroideries at her age (Yanula Georgatzi, interview, June 6, 1990).

When was it appropriate to wear festival dress? Which days counted as "festive"? Such occasions included Sundays, Easter, Christmas, New Year's, weddings (which often took place after the harvest), national holidays such as March 25 (Greek Independence Day), Carnival (the days before Lent), and local celebrations such as the village church's saint's day. Church was the most frequent venue for wearing festive dress. Villagers belonged to the Greek Orthodox faith and attended services every Sunday and on holy days. On special days, the services were followed with music and food.

Dance is central to community celebrations in every Greek village. Like dress, dance varies from region to region. Dancing took place on a large flat space, often the village square in front of the church. In smaller villages, the local threshing floor sufficed. Evgenia Spilioti of Klimenti, Corinthia, remembered: "When the holiday came about, they were going to the threshing floor all dressed up. They were dancing on the threshing floor wearing nice

Figure 1.2   Musicians and young women in festive dress on St. George's Day in Arachova, Boeotia, ca. 1930.

aprons and embroidered jackets" (interview, November 29, 1986). Throughout Greece, girls danced together in a line. Everyone knew the dances. When the musicians started playing, all the girls, dressed in their local festive dresses, fell in line (Figure 1.2). The young village women in their finery were a *sight* to behold for the villagers. Everyone valued this sight and cherished memories of the whirl of gauzy white skirts and the blur of colorful embroideries as the young women danced. Inappropriate attire was shamed out of the line as the following story attests:

> Outside the church . . . the musicians gathered and the girls congregated. The boys were coming in *foustanella* [man's pleated skirt], and the dance was getting white completely. If someone was wearing a regular dress, they wouldn't let them get in the dance. And the old women would shout from behind: "You are shaming them, get out of line, you are destroying the beauty of the dance." We were dancing until night. (Georgia Oikonomou, interview, November 6, 1986)

The clothes had to be appropriately embroidered in the local tradition. A 98-year-old woman told us: "If it was plain, it wouldn't be decent to go dancing at the Church. We needed to show off" (Sirmo Serafim, interview, July 1, 1988).

The *sound* made by the jewelry was also an important component of bridal and festival attire. Types of jewelry worn as part of festival dress included bracelets, necklaces, chest decorations, earrings, buckles, ornaments for braided hair, and gilded coins attached to clothing. The coins especially were characteristic of women's festive dress (Figure 1.3). They appeared on caps, headdresses, scarves, and chains. The wedding ensembles of Attica incorporated large amounts of jewelry, with the bride's head and chest entirely covered with coins. Other regions of Greece had more modest jewelry.

The coins, in particular, made clinking noises when worn. Brides, for instance, when dressed in their finery, left their natal homes mounted on a horse or donkey and were led to the home of the groom, every move of the hoof echoed by the jangling jewelry. One person recalled that the villagers could hear a young bride coming down the village path before she could be seen. Likewise, the noise made by women dancing reinforced the festival dress as something special for the community. The sound of the coins clinking together echoed the rhythms of the music.

The sense of *touch* must have contributed to the sensory experience of wearing festival dress, although this was not articulated in the interviews. The difference in the tactile

Figure 1.3   Young girls in festival dress in Orchomenos, Boeotia, ca. 1980.

qualities of "best" dress – soft silks, delicate trims, and textured embroideries – contrasted sharply with the rough, coarse textures of everyday dress. These sensations were experienced by the individuals wearing the clothes, remembered by older women who had once worn the outfits, but only imagined by observers.

People loved these celebrations. The elderly women recalled the hours of dancing as tiring, but fun. One woman thought the old-time celebrations were much better than the modern ones. Dances were among the few activities where young women could mix with members of the opposite sex in honor-bound Greek village society. Unmarried women were under the constant scrutiny of family. On festival days the young men and women could inspect each other even though they could not dance together one-on-one.[3]

Wedding and festival dress live on in the memories of Greek villagers long after they ceased to be worn. This is also true of certain local foods that are no longer available (Seremetakis 1994), and for meals eaten long ago (Sutton 2001). Memories of food are often linked to ritual, as they are with folk dress. The memory of material objects "form the historicity of a culture, items that create and sustain our relationship to the historical as a sensory dimension" (Seremetakis 1994: 3). Instead of the smell and taste of remembered foods, it is the recollections of sight and sound of dress and its associated customs that link the individual to the culture. The material object occasionally survives and becomes the center of sentiment.

For many Greek villagers, the extant components of folk dress serve as a shrine to the past and to the solidarity of a community to which the individual belongs. Thus, it is not unusual to see village homes decorated with parts of grandmother's wedding dress. In Attica, especially, families go to great lengths to display parts of ancestors' wedding costumes. Framed embroidery fragments from sleeves or hems decorate many a wall. Entire garments are framed and placed as centerpieces in front parlors. Glass display cases show the components of a mother's wedding outfit, artfully arranged on each shelf. In one home, a fashion mannequin under glass is attired in grandmother's bridal dress. For some families who no longer have the actual wedding dress, a photograph of the ancestral bridal couple substitutes. Many families sold the embroidered pieces to peddlers in leaner times, an action subsequently deeply regretted.

Devoid of an actual dress or photograph, folk dress is reproduced in other forms, which links the user to the place from which the costume derived. For example, children wear reproduction costumes on national holidays both in Greece and abroad (Figure 1.3). Every March 25, they take part in parades to celebrate Greek Independence Day. While some of these costumes are "national" dresses concocted from the 1840s attire of Greece's first queen, others draw inspiration from authentic village dress. Souvenirs, such as dolls dressed in regional costumes, or painted figurines, are another manifestation of the use of dress to signify place. Images of women dressed in folk costume even appeared on matchbooks manufactured by the Greek state monopoly in the 1970s, and on ouzo bottles in the 1990s. These images are drawn from well-known sources, namely the collection of the Lyceum of

Greek Women and the Benaki Museum's two volumes of costume plates published in 1948 and 1954. Women dressed in regional costumes show up on postcards in every region. Five of the official pins designed for the Athens 2004 Olympics consisted of women in folk dress from the various regions of Greece.

In all these images, the representation of the costume evokes Greece, the place, whether it is an emigrant's familial home or a country where visitors enjoy a great vacation. Either way, the warm sentiments attached to the image of the folk dress extend to the country of Greece, fusing the many meanings of village folk dress in the past into affection for the country itself.

NOTES

1. Thanks are due to Earthwatch, the Peloponnesian Folklore Foundation, the Pasold Research Fund, the American Philosophical Society, and the University of Rhode Island for providing support for these projects. I am also grateful to the volunteers who accompanied me on the three projects funded by Earthwatch, and to my Greek-born interpreters.
2. Here I define "ethnic group" as "any group of people who set themselves apart and are set apart from other groups with whom they interact or coexist in terms of some distinctive criterion or criteria which may be linguistic, racial or cultural" (Seymour-Smith 1986).
3. Most marriages were arranged. Occasionally couples eloped; this typically occurred when a family could not offer a sufficient dowry.

REFERENCES

Barber, E. W. (1994), *Women's Work: The First 20,000 Years: Women, Cloth, and Society in Early Times*, New York: Norton.
Benaki, A. (ed.). (1948), *Hellenic National Costumes*, Vol. 1, Athens: Benaki Museum. Text by A. Hatzimichali.
du Boulay, J. (1974), *Portrait of a Greek Mountain Village*, Oxford: Clarendon Press.
Frater, J. (1996), *Threads of Identity: Embroidery and Adornment of the Nomadic Rabaris*, Ahmedabad, India: Mapin.
Friedl, E. (1965), *Vasilika: a Village in Modern Greece*, New York: Holt, Rinehart and Winston.
Papantoniou, I. (2000), *Greek Dress From Ancient Times to the Early 20th Century*, Athens: Commercial Bank of Greece.
Seremetakis, C. N. (1994), "The Memory of the Senses, Part I: Marks of the Transitory," in C. N. Seremetakis (ed.), *The Senses Still: Perception and Memory as Material Culture in Modernity*, Boulder, CO: Westview Press.
Seymour-Smith, C. (1986), *Macmillan Dictionary of Anthropology*, London: Macmillan Press.
Sutton, D. (2001), *Remembrance of Repasts: An Anthropology of Food and Memory*, Oxford: Berg.
Welters, L. (1988), *Women's Traditional Costume in Attica, Greece*, Nafplion: Peloponnesian Folklore Foundation.
Welters, L. (1995), "Ethnicity in Greek Dress," in M. E. E. Roach-Higgins, J. Eicher and K. K. P. Johnson (eds), *Dress and Ethnicity*, New York and Oxford: Berg Publishers, pp. 17–30.
Welters, L. (ed.). (1999), *Folk Dress in Europe and Anatolia: Beliefs in Protection and Fertility*, Oxford: Berg.
Welters, L. (2004), "Fashion," in M. Sletcher (ed.), *New England: The Greenwood Encyclopedia of American Regional Cultures*, Westport, CT: Greenwood Press, pp. 131–64.

2 MORE THAN COSTUME HISTORY: DRESS IN SOMALI CULTURE

Heather Marie Akou

In the twenty-first century, immigration has become a major concern around the world. What happens when a country like Iraq or Somalia breaks down? Who should be able to migrate from one place to another? Does the West need to take in every refugee or immigrant looking for a better life? And how should they behave, think, and dress when they get there?

For Somali refugees in the United States, these concerns are a central part of their daily lives. To outsiders, it looks like many Somalis, especially women, are not assimilating into American culture, but continuing to wear their "traditional" dress. Ironically, many of these "traditional" styles did not exist in Somalia until the 1970s. Tensions over Somalis and their dress could improve with public education, but until I started my dissertation there was no research being conducted on this topic. After an overview of Somali dress practices in the nineteenth and early twentieth centuries, this essay analyzes how Somali refugees in the Twin Cities of St. Paul and Minneapolis, MN, are keeping their culture and traditions alive through dress, particularly through modifying their bodies.

The simplicity of clothing in Somali history partially accounts for a lack of prior research on this topic. Somalis are not known for their weaving, jewelry making, or embroidery; hence it might seem there is nothing very appealing about a study of their methods of adornment. A closer look, however, at practices designed to change the color, smell, and texture of the body, reveals a much more complex situation.[1]

In the nineteenth century Somali nomads made a living primarily by herding camels and sheep between water sources along the coastline of the Horn of Africa and the rich interior grasslands. Animals provided most of their food and carried their belongings. They also provided leather for clothing until their owners began trading it to Europeans who wanted it for shoe manufacturing. In exchange for leather and other local goods, such as ostrich feathers, tortoiseshell, and frankincense, Somalis received cloth, glass beads, and exotic foods such as spaghetti and bananas from the Europeans. Some Somalis became wealthy trading ivory and slaves, while others developed plantations with forced labor and grew crops of sesame seeds and orchella weed, a natural dyestuff, for the European market. Men and women in these wealthier communities often wore expensive clothing made of cotton or silk imported from the Middle East or South Asia. Intermarriage with Arab and Persian settlers had a strong influence on styles of garments among the well-to-do.

Figure 2.1 Somali men, women, and children photographed in the early twentieth century for *The Standard Library of Natural History* (1911).

Somali nomads wore more simple and practical clothing made from long pieces of plain white cotton cloth known as "merikani" that was imported from India, Great Britain, and especially the United States (Figure 2.1). Men wore two pieces of cloth sewn together in a large square that, depending on the weather and social situation, could be wrapped around the midsection or the whole body. Women wore a single piece of cloth that ranged from four- to twenty-yards long. They knotted this cloth at the right shoulder and secured it around the midsection with a series of tucks and pleats held in place by a piece of handmade rope. By the nineteenth century, most Somali nomads considered themselves Muslims; even so, nomadic women did not wear "veils" or head coverings for religious purposes. Also, until the mid-twentieth century, very few Somalis wore European-style clothing.

Nomads carried everything they owned, either personally or on their pack animals. Men often carried spears or small shields and wore daggers tucked into the folds of their clothing. Men also carried tools like camel whips made of braided leather, and spears used for walking sticks as well as for battle and hunting. A caste of artisans known as the *Midgan* made the shields. While most Somalis considered hunting a dirty and spiritually dangerous practice that should only be done if necessary (for instance, to kill a lion that was threatening the herd), *Midgan* men hunted hippopotami, oryx, and giraffes for their very tough and durable skins. After curing, an artisan would incise a piece of leather with a decorative pattern

Figure 2.2   Close-up view of leather sandals made for a wedding.

of dots and attach it to a wooden base, creating a shield approximately 10–12 inches in diameter. The reverse side was then painted with a geometric pattern.

The *Midgan* also made sandals from pieces of leather by piercing them with an awl and sewing them together in a stack until they formed a layer of leather up to one-inch thick (Figure 2.2). Sandals usually were not as decorative as the pair in Figure 2.2; but this pair, made for a wedding, was enhanced by cutting triangular notches into the leather and painting the insteps with a geometric pattern. When not being worn, the shoes could be tied to a leather strap and slung over one shoulder.

Although they did not make elaborate metal jewelry, Somali nomads did make some decorative pieces out of natural materials such as shells or palm kernels, the latter being easy to incise with patterns of dots. The *Midgan* also made simple pieces of metal jewelry such as iron bracelets. Although Europeans traded glass beads, more precious jewelry made of silver, amber, and coral came from the Middle East and South Asia. Jewelry, a woman's most important and valuable personal property, served as a portable bank account. Any Somali woman who could afford it wore a large crescent-shaped pendant with dangling silver bells called an *audulli*, usually strung with chunks of amber, coral, and beads made of glass and silver. Other groups in the Horn of Africa wore silver jewelry, amber and glass beads, but this particular configuration was unique to Somalis. Since men could accumulate wealth through animals, they wore accessories primarily for religious or decorative purposes: objects such as wooden prayer beads and leather amulets containing verses from the Qu'ran.

Leather amulets were not strictly Islamic, but reflected pre-Islamic dress practices. In 1912, the British explorer Ralph Drake-Brockman recorded a story about an amulet worn by Mohammed Abdullah Hassan, a famous nomad who led an armed rebellion against the British in the early twentieth century:

> Among the many curious stories connected with Mohammed Abdullah is one concerning the small amulet in which is said to be a complete copy of the Koran, and which he carries on his person day and night; he is said to wear it suspended and hidden from view in his left armpit … [having been warned by a lizard] that he must wear it day and night, and never let anyone lay a hand on it, and that if he did this, not one of his enemies could injure him. (1912: 183–5)

Drake-Brockman's account may have been an exaggeration, but this reference to protective amulets and animal spirits was not out of character for Somali nomads.

In addition to wearing material objects, Somalis also modified the texture, color, and scent of their hair, skin, mouths, and clothing. Frankincense, a tree resin, is native to the Horn of Africa. Somalis gathered it for trade, but it also had a number of uses in their dress practices: chewing it as a breath freshener, adding it to water as a kind of laundry soap, and burning it to scent their clothing and bodies with the resulting smoke. In Europe, frankincense was compressed to make imitation amber beads, which made their way back into Somali dress as objects of trade. Henna was another product with multiple uses. Women used it to dye their fingertips and apply decorative patterns to the palms of their hands. Men, after bleaching their hair with a mixture of ashes, camel butter, and clay, used henna to dye their beards and hair bright orange. In addition, they used red and yellow ochre clay as a hair colorant and styling aid; both men and women used ochre to stain their clothing.

Hairstyles indicated status for Somalis of both genders. Small children had their hair shaved in patterns. As girls became adults, they let their hair grow out and arranged it in hundreds of tiny braids to show they were ready for marriage (Figure 2.3). As married women, they took the braids out and pulled their hair back at the nape of the neck in two bundles, covering their hair with a piece of black or indigo-colored cloth (*shash*) to symbolize their new status. Adult men created elaborate hairstyles by applying camel butter to their hair and teasing it with a comb. To keep a hairstyle from being ruined at night, men frequently slept with their heads propped on a wooden headrest. Older men often shaved their hair off completely, a common ritual of Muslim men to mark the end of the Hajj, the once-in-a-lifetime pilgrimage to Mecca. Maintaining a shaved head communicates a special status since not everyone is able to undertake the Hajj.

By the Second World War, some nomads were leaving the desert and settling in towns. In many cases, men were starting to wear Western clothing on a regular basis. In the 1960s

Figure 2.3 Young women braiding their hair in a style that signaled their availability for marriage.

after Somalia became an independent nation, male delegates to the United Nations wore three-piece suits. Female flight attendants for the national airline wore jackets and pillbox hats as part of their uniform. Even women who served in auxiliary units of the military and police force wore miniskirts, jackets, and neckties. Although the miniskirt was always controversial and few Somali women today dress in Western garments, they are accepted by and are very common among men.

Since the 1970s, Somalia has been struggling with political turmoil. In 1991, the nation collapsed into civil war, forcing hundreds of thousands to flee the country as refugees. Along the way Somalis have made many changes in their behavior and dress. For example, many pieces of precious jewelry were lost, stolen, or even sold to pay for essentials like food and transportation out of Somalia. Many people literally fled the country with just the clothes on their backs. Even so, some of the old practices of modifying the body are still common; a source of comfort and pride in Somali culture.

During my dissertation research I spoke with many Somali refugees in Minnesota, home to the largest Somali community in the United States with an estimated 40,000 to 60,000 people. Although a few, most notably two university professors, settled in the area before the civil war, most came to the United States as refugees beginning in the mid 1990s. For women, the most common styles of clothing are the *jilbab* (a solid-color ensemble that covers the entire body and fits closely around the face), the *dirac* and *garbasaar* (a loose, colorful dress and shawl), and modified versions of Western dress that fulfill the requirements of Islam. The first two might look "traditional" but they originated in the 1970s when Somalia was beginning to experience severe turmoil.

A costume history would probably only deal with clothing, but Somali dress as a whole is much more subtle and complicated. In the Twin Cities, for example, young men keep their hair neatly shaved, never in braids as many African American men currently do. Older men still use henna to dye their beards, and women use henna to dye their hair and fingertips. Only younger women use nail polish, but many prefer dark colors that look like well-dyed henna, not fashion colors like red and pink.

In the United States, the continued use of scents to enhance the body is of particular interest. When I spoke with Somali women who owned clothing shops in the "Somali malls," they excitedly showed me objects like tins of frankincense and electric incense burners. Just as in the Horn of Africa, many refugees use smoldering frankincense fumes to change the scent of their bodies and clothing. In Minnesota, since most live in urban apartment buildings and are forced to keep windows closed throughout the winter, whole buildings can end up smelling like frankincense. At a public lecture I attended, one American-born building manager explained that non-Somali tenants often say it "stinks." He did not understand or even really sympathize with the Somali point of view that this fragrance is a pleasant reminder of home. A cashier at a department store in St. Paul confessed to me that although her store allowed Somalis to make returns like any other customers, the garments always came back with an undesirable smell. For Somalis who might not realize that their sensibilities clash with typical American notions of what "smells good," this practice is simply a way to try on clothes at home where modesty of the body, a key aspect of Islam, is guaranteed, rather than trying them on in the store's fitting room.

Although fashionable young women have found a place in their dress for platform shoes and cell phones, Western scents have not won the same kind of acceptance. Instead, women of all ages use "Secret Man" perfume. One merchant gave me a vial of this musky, alcohol-free scent and it immediately brings up memories of the Somali malls whenever I open it.

Joanne Eicher's comprehensive definition of dress (2000) brings us to a much more rich and subtle understanding of Somali dress than a typical "costume history." Could this be the case among other non-Western cultures? Somali dress might be an extreme and in many ways unique case, but obviously there is "more than meets the eye" to Somali dress.

NOTE

1. As part of my dissertation on the social history of Somali dress and aesthetics (Akou 2005), I had the opportunity to do archival research at the Smithsonian's National Museum of African Art and the National Museum of Natural History. I was excited to pore over photographs and books written by explorers, academics, and colonists in the nineteenth and early twentieth centuries, but for me the real treasure was at the Natural History Museum's Department of Ethnology. When I first got in touch with the museum, my expectations were minimal; the archivist who arranged my visit was not sure there was much to see. Her

search of the museum's database for Somali objects made of "textiles" turned up only a few items: some pieces of cloth, a cushion made from a basket case covered with leather and shells, a few baskets for carrying food and milk, and a nomadic tent that was on display at the museum's African Voices exhibit. Even so, I made the decision that however little there might be, I still wanted to see it. The archivist, Susan Crawford, also kindly opened the twenty or so cabinets with Somali objects regardless of what they contained. While few objects were made of textiles, dozens of items related to dress such as pieces made to be worn or carried on the body or used to modify it: beads, wooden combs, headrests, handmade sandals, shields, daggers, and incense burners. Had I been studying "costume history," I might have ignored these objects. I wish I had taken more photographs, but at the time I simply did not appreciate how relevant they were. In conducting the literature review for my dissertation, I was surprised to find that I would be writing the first comprehensive history of Somali dress.

REFERENCES

Akou, H. M. (2005), "Macrocultures, Migration, and Somali Malls: A Social History of Somali Dress and Aesthetics," Doctoral dissertation, University of Minnesota.

Drake-Brockman, R. (1912), *British Somaliland*, London: Hurst & Blackett.

Eicher, J. B. (2000), "Dress," in C. Kramarae and D. Spender (eds), *Routledge International Encyclopedia of Women: Global Women's Issues and Knowledge*, pp. 422–3, New York: Routledge.

The Standard Library of Natural History, Embracing Living Animals and Living Races of Mankind. (1911), Vol. 5, New York: The University Society.

3 DRESS, HUNGARIAN SOCIALISM, AND RESISTANCE

Katalin Medvedev

INTRODUCTION

My father passed away at the age of seventy-five but in my mind's eye he will always be younger, good-looking, and well-dressed, a distortion of my subjective memory. My dreams of him are all in color, another distortion of my memory. After all, we lived in socialist Hungary where colors in the 1950s and 1960s were bleak, dull, or faded. Gray was the dominating shade both of houses and people's dress and there were no color photographs until well into the 1970s. In my dreams my father wears crisp, light-blue shirts, his trademark.

My mother also shares my fascination with my father's blue shirts. To this day, the shirts hang meticulously in a big wardrobe, starched and ironed, as if my father exists inside them. Under socialism, owning such a vast number of material goods was suspicious, so I marvel at the rows and rows of blue shirts, many of them from the socialist era. I also wonder at my father's appreciation for dress, which I believe I have inherited. Through my father I learned that clothes are significant because they reveal important social details about the wearer and allow a view into the wearer's consciousness (Eicher *et al.* 1995, 2000). I realize clothes make up a significant portion of one's cultural capital (Bourdieu 1984), and my father's sartorial predilections ultimately contributed greatly to my own aesthetic, academic, and professional interests.

In the socialist uniformity of my childhood, it gave me great satisfaction to know that my father was different from my peers' fathers, a majority of whom, unlike many women of the time, preferred conformity. Most of my father's clothes were of good quality fabric and tailor-made. My father also had a yen for elegant shoes, which were hard to come by in a climate of scarcity and want, but which he somehow managed to acquire. When he could not afford to eschew totally the mass-produced, ready-made, somber apparel of the era, he gave it a twist. He would wear a colorful tie or a cravat, printed shirts, or sweaters like an Oxford don. All these accoutrements considerably strained the family budget and remained often the subject of heated arguments between my parents.

My father's appearance created a different mood as well. He brightened the gloominess of everyday socialist life, which people around him seemed to appreciate. His fashionable outfits were clearly more suitable for lounging on the terrace of a Paris café than for his engineering job at the Hungarian Railways. And the way he carried himself conveyed a hedonistic attitude, in direct contrast to production- and ideology-oriented socialism. I believe that my father's sartorial cosmopolitanism was a (sub)conscious act of self-distinction and an attempt to escape social determination. His dressing against socialist standards covertly tested the confining limits of the authority of the Hungarian totalitarian regime.

DESIGN FOR DISASTER

Totalitarian ideology and fashion make an ill-fitting pair (Lipovetsky 1994). Totalitarian regimes, rigid and disciplinary, aim to control human nature fully (Aron 1965). They seek to erase individualism as well as to overhaul one's environment completely. They disregard, suppress, or bend a person's interests and desires, and level out social, cultural, economic and, at times, even gender differences, all in the name of a common good. Totalitarian ideologues overlook everyday realities and, instead, focus on the future and are ready to sacrifice their subjects for distant, abstract goals. Hence, under totalitarianism, the daily dress choices of citizens are regarded as a public affair. They need to be monitored, made uniform, and underscore one's political allegiance as well as demonstrate one's ideological conversion.

In contrast, fashion is fluid, capricious, and driven by change. Dress, a manifestation of fashion, is a tool of self-expression and individuality. It is a visible marker of social, cultural, and economic status, and a source of communicating one's convictions, aspirations, personal sentiments, and sexuality (Eicher *et al.* 2000). Dress is also driven by the moment, by the ephemeral, and is linked to the user's needs and feelings in the present. No wonder then that fashion has been viewed as dangerous in restrictive communities. Karl Marx, in *Das Capital,* for example, discusses the "murderous, meaningless caprices of fashion" (1974: vol. 1, 450). Because his tenets were followed to the letter in socialist countries, the desire to be fashionable was regarded as a sign of an empty mind and low moral standards.

Following the Marxist concept of unity of form and content, socialist fashion and socialist ontology needed to overlap, expressing the harmony of a collective mind and body. Socialist fashion had to be visibly different from bourgeois fashion because it was driven by a different consciousness and different socioeconomic goals. The most important requirement was to negate pre-socialist economic, social, and cultural backgrounds and differences and create a homogeneous society. It had to be democratic in the sense that it defied all class connotations. Socialist dress was not supposed to emphasize one's individuality or attract attention; instead, it had to encourage collective thinking and foster a team spirit. It was expected to extol the virtues of simplicity over ornamentation and had to be economical in its use of materials. The emphasis was on pragmatism and functionalism, helping to facilitate people's work. Because it had to be accessible to all, it was mass-produced, and rarely was aesthetically pleasing. While the role of capitalist fashion is to accelerate consumption and maintain stylistic diversity by initiating rapid style changes, the role of socialist fashion was to cut back consumption and create sartorial stability and uniformity. As far as the inclusion of "fashion" in socialist dress was concerned, only one thing mattered: all citizens had to be adequately dressed.[1] How dress influenced human well-being, psyche, or fancy did not matter – at least not under the first phase of totalitarian socialism.

By the 1960s, however, ideological regulation and authoritarian control of socialist fashion became somewhat problematic. A tension between the antimaterialistic rhetoric and the promises of the Marxian utopia of communist abundance surfaced. Within communism, socialist subjects were told, everybody's material needs would be met and fulfilled. But that conviction begged the question: Why, then, would people have to keep their material needs under check? After all, fashion consumption would indicate a sense of material fulfillment and would extend the political allegiance of the population. Thus, a thriving fashion scene would not contradict the ideals of socialism. But because the totalitarian regime in Hungary, until the second half of the 1960s, visibly failed its citizenry on material fulfillment and political freedom, dress became a highly politicized locus of social commentary. Because most forms of public representations were under constant surveillance or literal censorship, people veered toward nonverbal means of self-expression either in a bid for individuality or to show resistance, both politically inscribed statements in 1950s Hungary.

My father was the exception to the male rule when he sartorially distinguished himself from his peers because dress as an instrument for politicizing was essentially a subversive female practice at the time. Despite the official, equalizing ideology, women in socialist Hungary remained the second gender (Funk and Mueller 1993). Their traditional affinity for clothes and their inability to reject the pull of material objects were regarded as signs of bourgeois contamination and political backwardness in a masculinist and patriarchal totalitarian culture. Persistent material desires indicated that women's ideological conversion was not fully successful or complete, according to the totalitarian creed.

While the West turned toward visual and material pleasures after the Second World War, socialist-bloc countries focused on inward, ideological values. The official dismissal of women's interest in traditional femininity and materiality, however, had an adverse effect. The Hungarian regime's refusal to recognize dress as being more than a simple need of life turned it into a potentially radical, while also subtle and safe, medium of self-expression. Clothes themselves and one's attitude to personal appearance became tools of dissent and critique and an outlet for "talking back" to an oppressive state.

Most Hungarian women were loyal to socialist ideals and principles of equality. They appreciated many of the socialist provisions as well, such as low-cost childcare, free health benefits, and educational and professional advantages (Funk and Mueller 1993). They balked, however, at embracing ideological abstractions; instead, they became more determined to seek corporeal gratification. They truly appropriated the Marxist tenet that material reality determines human consciousness. Therefore, they began to contest the chasm that existed between their concrete material needs, personal desires, and public opportunities.

The Hungarian regime's insistence on ideology only fueled women's desire for objects, especially feminized objects such as stylish apparel and cosmetics; women even committed offenses to acquire such items. The shortages of necessities, the permanence of poverty, and the expectations of frugality as a result of forced industrialization and militarization triggered by the Cold War marred women's psyche and self-confidence for decades. Even the most basic dress items, such as brassieres, stockings, or winter coats, were seen as luxuries. At the same time, the coarse fabrics and industrial-grade shoes were not only uncomfortable, but also humiliating to wear. If a woman managed to get her hands on a presentable outfit, she would invariably be faced with a lack of appropriate accessories.

All this blew out of proportion the importance of dress in socialist women's everyday reality. In a culture of deprivation, Western dress articles became fetishes and Westerners who donned these articles were seen as beautiful as well as possessing a superior intelligence (Emoke Tomsics, personal communication, March 24, 2004). Women's sartorial misery demonstrated not only the political failures and economic inadequacy of the regime, but also turned dress into a deeply emotional, personal issue.

OUT OF THE CLOSET

In 2004, as part of my scholarship in dress, socialism, and gender, I interviewed twelve Hungarian women, ages sixty to eighty, on their recollections of socialist fashion in the 1950s and 1960s and their relationship to clothes for my thesis that clothes had a "special" role in the formation of the Hungarian female socialist psyche and consciousness. Despite their diverse social backgrounds and personal histories, none of them regarded the topic as insignificant or trivial.

My informants were intensely clothes-conscious and remembered well their apparel of 50–60 years ago. Some of them have held on to their clothes long past their shelf life of trendiness, in the same way my father saved his shirts. Their sentiments about dress were deeply connected to how they saw themselves: as people who overcame totalitarianism, but were forever marked by it. Even the women who did not care much about fashion were able to give me a detailed description of their wardrobes, which suggests that because they possessed so few clothes at the time, every item was regarded as precious. Another reason was that obtaining any dress item took tremendous effort (domestic thriftiness, pooling of family resources, and skillful manipulation of the dire economic and social conditions), making it a major achievement and a valued object. Since one could not own a house or a car in the 1950s and 1960s, clothes became the items that best reflected one's social standing.

My interviewees mostly had positive associations with dress. The women preferred to talk about outfits that made them feel adventurous and desirable, or earned them praise. Their stories about dress in their childhood through their adult years evoked recollections of youthful beauty, strong relationships with family and friends, and political awakenings.

Under communism, questioning the totalitarian regime's dictates was potentially danger-ous; therefore, getting information about another person's political leanings through the nuances of her or his appearance was a general practice. Socialist citizens developed a keen sense of being able to read between the lines. They discerned and interpreted sartorial signs of dissent or conformity with ease. The state, which claimed to be "above fashion" even while demanding absolute adherence to its antimaterialist ideology, had not expected to face much resistance in the way of people's dress choices. Literal sanctioning or open politicization of dress practices would have revealed the fragility of the regime, that it could be unnerved by such a "lightweight" medium as fashion. So the state was lulled into a false sense of security and citizens steadily built up their subversive strategies.

Each of my interviewees used dress in a different way to create and assert her selfhood under socialism. The narratives of two women provide an example of the development of Hungarian socialist women's politically linked sartorial consciousness. While Anni benefited from the communist takeover, Eva suffered from it. The juxtaposition of their stories helps reveal that dress was a widely recognized form of political discourse under socialism.

FROM THE OUTSIDE IN: ANNI

Anni portrays working-class Hungarian women who gained advantages from socialism, which made upward mobility possible for the working class. Anni's fascination with dress was rooted in her childhood. She was born in 1945, a war child, to a homemaker mother and a policeman father. In the aftermath of the Second World War, Hungary was devastated. With an infrastructure almost completely destroyed and factories looted of machinery, first by the retreating German military and then by the Soviet army. Food was scarce; dress was viewed as a luxury. Focused on survival, most Hungarians clothed themselves in what remained from before the war, and not much survived the bomb attacks. Daily wages quickly disappeared since the rate of inflation kept mounting steadily. Salaries were spent almost as soon as received because no one could predict what could be found in the few available shops.

In the postwar years, children's clothes did not exist, so Anni's clothes as a newborn came from re-creations of her mother's well-worn outfits or from used items whose fabrics would suit the delicate skin of a baby. For years, Anni was either dressed in such outfits or hand-me-downs. Sharing dress items and circulating them was typical in socialist Hungary. Because Anni was her parents' first-born her clothes usually had some extra decoration. Her mother, an expert seamstress, embroidered little motifs on Anni's outfits and unraveled old sweaters and re-knit them for her daughter.

Most dress items or textiles after the war were available through rationing cards. The scarcities in the shops, however, ensured these cards would mostly go unused. Anni recalled that her mother did not buy any dress items for an entire year. Then, one day, her family heard about the arrival of good quality fabric at the local shop. Anni's mother rushed there and spent her entire annual ration on yards of pink voile with little white dots. Anni recalled her mother's elation as a response to material deprivation, like a drowning person clutching at straws. She remembers that for years everything – the family's linen, nightwear, slips – was made of the pink voile. It apparently took more than a decade to use up all the fabric.

Shoes were also difficult to come by, the lack lasting almost the entire first phase of socialism. Anni was fortunate in this respect, too, because her father, a state employee, was supplied with uniforms, thus bolstering the family budget. Anni's father was given a pair of boots yearly as part of his uniform; policemen were also supplied with extra leather soles. Since her father was very good at caring for his shoes, he always had extra soles left, which then would be given to the local shoemaker who would, in turn, make shoes for Anni. In the summer, most Hungarian socialist children went barefoot. For special occasions, Anni's mother made her rope-soled sandals, which were rather unattractive. Still, she stood out wearing them because the children in the neighborhood did not have any. In other words, however rudimentary her attire was, Anni was *always* different from her peers.

She vividly remembers getting her first leather sandals in 1954 for Easter. In general, apparel was considered the most important gift choice and the holidays were when the children could expect such treasures. Dress, thus, was linked to major celebrations in Anni's mind. She also learned early on that she had to be careful with her outfits because they were meant to last for a long time and serve several generations. Socialist subjects had to recycle, but instead of fostering antimaterialist sentiments, it only taught them to respect material goods highly. For instance, Anni said her mother wore a coat for ten years before it was turned into a dress for Anni. So, dress items had many lives in socialist Hungary. Anni and her two sisters were taught to appreciate dress from early on. They were instructed to never sit on the floor in their outfits nor be involved in rough-and-tumble play, to climb trees, or jump over fences. They were also socialized into being "feminine" and never dressed in pants.[2]

The most important thing was to have a "cultured appearance." As Anni's mother put it, no matter how simple one's dress, if one is clean and the dress is displayed with care, one will always be greatly valued. Caring for outfits was time-consuming and physically challenging. Anni's mother spent one day a week on washing, and another day on starching, ironing, or mending the family wardrobe. On festive occasions, Anni and her sisters mostly wore white shoes (Figure 3.1). They used chalk, dissolved in water, to make them look whiter. In retrospect, Anni thinks her mother's deep interest in making her children wear white shoes to emulate the look of bourgeois children came from her envy of these children in her own working-class youth. The other reason she chose to dress her children above her means was that she regarded their clothes as investments in a better future and class position.

As a little girl, Anni usually had three outfits each season; the fanciest was taken out only for special occasions. Anni alternated her two regular outfits weekly. The same was true for her underwear. When her mother washed the dress and underwear, Annie would wear the other fresh set. When she returned from school, she would immediately take off her dress and wear a housedress or a worn garment.

In the 1950s when people began to run out of prewar dress items, children were ordered to wear school uniforms. According to Anni, this move was not intended to eliminate class differences, but rather to cover them up, indicative of the duplicitous nature of the

Figure 3.1 Anni's siblings and her mother wearing white shoes
(1960). Photograph courtesy H. Anni.

socialist regime: people's sacrifices had to be hidden. As was expected of a good socialist citizen, Anni was well groomed and more presentable than many of her classmates. Judging others by their dress was so deeply ingrained in Anni that she would not make friends with unkempt children. The best-dressed student in Anni's class was the teacher's daughter. Anni still remembers the deep envy she felt on seeing a brilliant-green dress the teacher's daughter wore one day that stood out in the mostly washed-out colors of the other children's clothes.

Dress very much influenced Anni's social relations. The family lived in a small community where everybody knew everybody and people's outfits were often the talk of the town. Only the doctor or the pharmacist could get away with flaunting bourgeois tastes because their services were very much needed by the state. For example, residents knew that the doctor could afford to sport a white suit in the summer because the doctor also used his nurse as his cleaning lady and washerwoman. Using the services of another individual was tacitly allowed for certain citizens. Anni yearned to belong to this group, despite the fact that in the contemporary political climate nothing could be worse than being labeled "petit bourgeois." People were chastised for wearing wasteful and elaborate apparel, jewelry, hats, or even nail polish.

Because creating a satisfying outfit entailed so much work, as it most likely involved forgoing other needs, and because when almost nothing was available, women's transforming skills were equated with virtue, socialist Hungarians' dress received enormous appreciation from their peers. An early realization of this fact turned Anni not only into a clotheshorse, but also into somebody who used dress as a primary means to make a public statement about her personal achievements and successes throughout her life.

After 1956, Anni's family's financial situation began to improve.[3] They had access to more commodities and their living standard gradually rose. By 1959, Anni's wardrobe went beyond functional clothes; for example, she forced her mother to buy her a red rock 'n' roll skirt for her from a classmate who had relatives in the West and received parcels of clothing from them. Her aunt, who worked in a hospital, also supplied Anni and her sisters with high-fashion smuggled goods, which Anni loved to flaunt. Despite the fact that Hungarians like Anni were loyal socialist subjects who benefited from socialism, they saw nothing paradoxical in buying Western goods made by the "enemy." For Anni, the visibility of these status symbols was important because they helped her gain entry and acceptance into the local "in-crowd."

In the 1960s, as a teenager, Anni dressed to emphasize her shapely figure. Her outfits at the time show she thought of herself as a sexual being. Even her Communist Youth Organization uniform was not worn as expected of a regular cadre (Figure 3.2). She wore it tight fitting, and often complemented it with high heels and left her long, blond hair falling loose. She still cultivates a hyperfeminine appearance today. As a young woman, Anni was liked by men and she was popular among women, too. Much of the recognition derived from her fashion-forward attitude and the creative clothes sewn by her mother. As the years went by, Anni received a university education, got a good job, had her own family, and prospered. But, instead of opting for the understated styles of the middle class of her childhood, she continued to favor colorful prints and fabrics, fake fur, and costume jewelry, conveying a curious mixture of proletarian and bourgeois taste. She represented the classes in the later phase of socialism: the former proletariat who became the new bourgeoisie, enshrining its own taste in fashion standards.

Anni fit well into the expectations of the way of life of Hungarian leader Janos Kadar's "goulash communism," the result of the social compromise between the state and its citizens that followed the 1956 uprising. This compromise in exchange for political loyalty

Figure 3.2   Dyed blond hair and heels. Anni wearing the Communist Youth Organization uniform, with a twist, in the 1960s. Photograph courtesy H. Anni.

gave people access to more consumer products and, within limits, more freedom of self-expression (Botos *et al.* 1988).

The social opportunities offered to the working class benefited Anni, who, while adhering to the regime's ideology through her actions and her words, actively participated in the political process of renegotiating the boundaries of state intervention and the rights and freedoms of the individual. Of importance, she did this with her insistence on rejecting sartorial modesty.

THE REVERSE GAZE: EVA

Eva was born in 1941, into a middle-class family in eastern Hungary. Her father, a social democrat opposed to communism, worked as an agronomist managing a big estate. There-fore, Eva was viewed as a class enemy in the Hungarian socialist regime after the Second World War. This perception continues to affect Eva's life because socialist existence was an uphill struggle for Eva's family. Eva, the only child in her community not allowed to join

Figure 3.3   On the estate. Eva's mother elegantly dressed in 1938.
Photograph courtesy B. Eva.

the Communist Youth Organization, received a university education only later in life, never married, and to this day lives in a tiny apartment.

The traditional upbringing of middle-class women in Hungary before the war included learning embroidery, crocheting, and sewing. When Eva's father went into hiding after the war to avoid being sent to a labor camp, Eva's usually elegantly dressed mother had to forgo her style sensibilities and focus on fending for herself and her daughter and son (Figure 3.3). Whereas Eva's first dresses as a child were bought in city stores or made by the local dressmaker, later ones were made by her mother.

Even the occasional "silver lining," in the form of gifts from relatives who had left Hungary for the West much earlier, ended up being tarnished. The gifts rarely arrived intact. The relatives would list the contents on the side of the containers to discourage corrupt officials from helping themselves to the contents. It often happened, however, that important items were either missing or switched with lower quality substitutes. Sometimes Eva's family would get a coat different from the one listed, at other times only one shoe. The items were problematic for another reason as well. Most 1950s apparel in the United States (the fabric, colors, and designs) did not suit the lifestyles or environment of a Hungarian village. To compound the problem, the hats, cocktail dresses, fine gloves, and frilly children's clothes oozed prosperity and created a longing in people like Eva for another life, somewhere behind the ominous Iron Curtain. These sartorial desires prompted Eva to nurture antiregime sentiments, putting her in a treacherous position, not only as contradicting the regime's demands, but also as waging a battle within herself.

Eva's mother refashioned many of these gifted apparel items or traded them with local residents for simpler styles, other items, or even textiles, but Eva's dress standards of her earliest years were ultimately somewhat maintained. By the time she entered high school, she also could sew, darn, crochet, and knit. From then on she designed and executed her dresses by herself. When the first fashion publications reappeared in Hungary in the late 1950s, she bought them all. Eva described how the magazines themselves stimulated a sense of awe and excitement, as if the stylish images somehow transformed into the real thing. For her, sewing soon became not only a survival skill but also a favorite pastime.

Her abilities, her innovation, and her aesthetics gave her satisfaction and helped her construct a self-affirming identity with which she could conduct herself with dignity (Figure 3.4). Most people around her were as poor as she was; however, she used her skills to

Figure 3.4   Socialist elegance. Eva in an outfit made from a male "parcel" suit in 1963. Photograph courtesy B. Eva.

her advantage to fulfill her aspirations of carrying on her mother's stylish heritage. Dress, as Eva put it, was also a psychological shield to protect her inner self. It was the only aspect of life she could control fully. On a conscious level, her attitude to dressing with individuality and with a Western flair could be interpreted as a mundane female desire for fashion. On a subconscious level, however, through dress, she projected a defiance of the socialist discourse of corporeal uniformity and contested the negative treatment she received from the bureaucrats of the regime. She knew her sartorial sense affected the sentiments of those who saw her and understood that she was projecting an alternative standpoint. Like Anni, Eva became one of thousands of disparate Hungarian women who, through dress, were instrumental in stirring up a consciousness and setting in motion winds of political change.

DRESSING-UP BLUES

When we had to go through my father's belongings in Hungary after his death, my mother and I vowed not to become sentimental. But my mother found it hard to discard his blue shirts. She even refused to give them away to my brother ("Not on a slob like your brother!" she said) although she was perfectly comfortable offering him my father's car, his favorite Swiss-made watch, his power tools, even his electric razor.

When I visit Hungary I have a recurring ritual as soon as I arrive at my parents' home that helps me settle in and adjust to the Hungarian way of life faster. I open drawers and cupboards and examine their contents. I spend quite a bit of time looking through my father's possessions, which are still the same and still as blue. When I stroke them or inhale their scent, I sense his presence: his smile, his slight stoop, his delicate hands. When I shut the wardrobe, his presence vanishes.

When I talked about this disappointing realization with my mother, she claimed it happens because clothes were so much a part of my father's image and identity. They expressed best who he was: handsome, vain, and relaxed. My father was the son of déclassé Russian aristocrats who saw great advantages in maintaining a stylish appearance. Further, as an émigré from the Balkans, where men's appearances were considered to be more important than those of women, he was more ingrained in the art of apparel and accessories. Under totalitarianism's heavy hand, my father was rare in being a man who took risks by breaking out of the mold. Usually the women of his generation used their sense and sentiments to act subversively through the medium of dress.

Totalitarianism is not only an oppression: it is also a culture. As Jules Prown (1993) argues, because key aspects of a culture are embodied in its objects and in the relationships to the objects, by following my memories of my father's dress choices and Anni's and Eva's sartorial recollections we are able to perceive aspects of socialist daily existence and consciousness that have been hidden from traditional social histories wherein these macro-level analyses portray communist women as a gray, homogeneous, and politically passive mass. Anni's and Eva's relationship to their clothes defy socialist women's uniform representation.

Their sartorial choices in an era of scarcities mirror their personal and social aspirations. Their stories demonstrate how, through dress, many Hungarian women were able to make a clear but safe public statement about dissatisfaction with the material and ideological aspects of the regime. Their small everyday acts of dressing in an alternative fashion transformed them physically, psychologically, and politically. In refusing to denounce material goods, and in insisting on the right to fashion, women, like Anni and Eva, played a significant role in creating a shift in communism's momentum. By their relentless demand not only to produce, but also to consume, they helped steer the regime out of totalitarianism. They ended up not only refashioning themselves, but socialism as well.

NOTES

1. It was a serious political goal because, before the Second World War, Hungary was referred to as the country of three million beggars (Botos *et al*.1988).
2. It has been widely argued that socialism disregarded gender differences and turned women almost into asexual beings. One of the pertinent examples of defying this homogeneous representation of socialist subjects is that women almost always chose to dress in a feminine fashion outside the workplace. Since gender was not regarded as an important category of social analysis, femininity itself became a radical notion.
3. The goal of the 1956 bloody revolt in Hungary was the restoration of a multiparty democracy. The Soviets crushed the uprising, but, after the tragic events, Hungary never returned to virulent totalitarianism.

REFERENCES

Aron, R. (1965), *Democratie et totalitarianisme*, Paris: Editions Gallimard.
Botos, J., Gyarmati, G., Korom, M. and Zinner, T. (1988), *Magyar Hetkoznapok: Rakosi Matyas ket emigracioja kozott, 1945–1956*, Budapest: Minerva.
Bourdieu, P. (1984), *Distinction*, Cambridge, MA: Harvard University Press.
Eicher, J., Roach-Higgins, M. E. and Johnson, K. K. P. (eds). (1995), *Dress and Identity*, New York: Fairchild Publications.
Eicher, J., Evenson, S. L. and Lutz, H. (eds). (2000), *The Visible Self*, New York: Fairchild Publications.
Funk, N. and Mueller, M. (eds). (1993), *Gender Politics and Post-Communism: Reflections from Eastern Europe and the Former Soviet Union*, New York: Routledge.
Lipovetsky, G. (1994), *The Empire of Fashion: Dressing Modern Democracy*, Princeton: Princeton University Press.
Marx, K. (1974), *Das Capital*, London: Laurence & Wishart.
Prown, J. D. (1993), "The Truth of Material Culture: History or Fiction?" in S. Lunbar and W. D. Kingery (eds.), *History from Things: Essays on Material Culture*, London: Smithsonian Institution Press.

4 CLOTHES MAKE THE EMPIRE: BRITISH DRESS IN INDIA

Donald Clay Johnson

Imagine to yourself the lovely object of your affections ready to expire with heat, every limb trembling and every feature distorted with fatigue, and her partner with a muslin handkerchief in each hand employed in the delightful office of wiping down her face, while the big drops stand impearled upon her forehead.

> S. C. Ghosh, *The Social Condition of the British Community in Bengal, 1757–1800*

Fancy, then a white horse, which had been bathed in sweat, and then gradually covered over with a coating of dust. On slackening its paces this had dried into large dirty patches. Down its face rolled two muddy tears. Out of the vehicle it had been dragging jumped a short, stout man, dressed in a loose flannel suit, with a pith hat, the brim of which was so broad, the crown so high, and the shape so suggestive of Bedlam.

> C. P. A. Oman, *Eastwards, or, Realities of Indian Life*

This essay examines the clothing worn by the British, people of a nation located in the temperate zone of the world, when they lived in the Indian subcontinent, an area primarily in the tropics. The sense of touch from wearing Western fabrics such as flannel and the sense of smell produced from profuse sweating reflect their strong sentimental need to remember and to maintain their British way of life within the vast British Empire.

PREPARING TO GO TO INDIA

Learning one would be going to India to live for several years, if not a lifetime, immediately raised the question of what to do about clothing. Throughout British rule those going to India either made up all their clothing in England before leaving or waited until arrival in India and then had a tailor make clothing for them. Considering British fashion held sway among the British in India, the London-made perspective seemed most logical since one would have the latest styles. The amount of clothing recommended to be taken to India by those so inclined was amazingly large. Among other things, an 1847 guide recommended:

72 pairs socks (48 cotton, 12 silk, 12 woolen)
72 shirts
32 waistcoats (24 fine flannel, 6 holland, 2 dress)
72 handkerchiefs (48 pocket, 24 fine cambric)

36 pairs gloves (24 kid, 12 cotton)

34 pairs trowsers (12 white dress, 12 duck for riding, 6 holland, 1 cachmere, 2 coloured, 1 dress)

15 coats (6 holland, 6 white linen, 1 frock, 1 shooting, 1 dress). (Old Resident 1847: 88)

Almost a century later, in 1923, Kate Platt, former Principal Lady of Hardinge Medical College and Hospital for Women, in her guide detailed what should be purchased in England and what should be made in India. A downside of this England-purchase option, however, was that what clothiers deemed appropriate dress for India often was not and the newcomer could not use the clothing.

Nevertheless, another factor favored the England-made decision: having the parents or relatives pay for the clothing made up for the teenage boy. *Real Life in India, Embracing a View of the Requirements of Individuals Appointed to Any Branch of the Indian Public Service* … told parents what would happen if their son did not get his basic provisions in London.

> Setting aside the undoubted fact, that everything in the shape of wearing apparel and other objects of personal use and comfort, are of superior materials, better made, and cost less than similar articles in India, it is positively cruel to leave a young soldier entirely on his own resources the moment he arrives in the country.
>
> In procuring clothes and camp equipage, therefore, he is obliged to run into debt, or suffer himself to be victimized by the wily sharks, in the form of dubashes, sircars, banians, and box wallahs, who swarm about the cadet's barracks. These are calamities from which a providential parent will hold it a duty to protect his son; and this can only be done by giving him such an outfit as shall render him entirely independent of every article of supply but those which he cannot be certain he will require until he has arrived in India. (1847: 62–3)

A tailor in India, however, could make up clothing at a fraction of the London cost. Another consideration favoring having clothing made in India was the potential of getting colors that matched with a man's military unit. "In the traditional army manner, the kits you were issued with at home were never suitable for the regiment you were joining. The khaki was a different shade, your hose wasn't the right colour, the puttees [cloth leg coverings] weren't the right shape or size and everything had to be bought afresh, out of your own money" (Allen 1975: 40). One did need to take some articles of clothing from England to serve as samples: for Indian "tailors work expeditiously, but cannot get on without a pattern. They imitate very well … as the story goes, if they see a patch in an old coat or other garment, given them as a pattern, they will be sure to put one in that part of the new one" (Sherwood 1910: 254). One of the challenges in India was availability of fabrics and accessories for British needs. The damp months of the monsoon, for instance, made shopping impossible as "[n]o milliner will sell silks or satins during these damp months, because they cannot expose them to the air" (Shrimpton 1992: 59).

Every official event in Calcutta at Government House precipitated floods of European women picking the shelves of dry goods merchants absolutely bare to get materials for making new outfits. Some in India relied on family and friends in England periodically to send clothing to them. Emily Eden's letters, for instance, contain many thankful expressions to relatives and friends for shipping dresses and other articles of clothing to her (Eden 1872: vol. I, 306, vol. II, 96).

Helpful guides for preparing to live in India constantly appeared. During the eighteenth and first half of the nineteenth centuries there undoubtedly was a marked difference between the clothing made in England and that made in India since everything was hand stitched in both countries. After the adoption of the Singer sewing machine in the decade of the 1850s, there were fewer differences.

CLOTHING FOR TRAVEL TO OR FROM INDIA

Having decided what to do about clothing while in India, one had to determine what to take on the ship to India. In the early days the sea voyage could take as long as six months and ships until the late nineteenth century did not have laundry facilities. Some guides simply suggested passengers take old clothing for the voyage and discard it when very soiled and it could no longer be worn. One did, however, need to have some formal clothing as the tradition continued of dressing for dinner while at sea.

How different, though, the return trips to England were. Spending time in India affected the British in many ways, one of which was frequent changes of clothing each day. Mrs. Mary Sherwood returned to England in the first half of the nineteenth century with several of her children. She set up an elaborate routine to ensure the availability of fresh clothing on the sea journey for her family, and she described it in her memoirs:

> I ... spread as many sheets as I meant to make up bundles. On each sheet I laid a week's linen for every individual, according to the smallest Indian allowance – a change a day, including frocks for the children. To these I added napery sufficient for the week. The tailor was then called in and each bundle tightly rolled and sewed up, and committed to a camel trunk; there were half-a-dozen trunks. One trunk at a time was brought up from the hold, when we were at sea, and put into the cabin; each week we took out a bundle, and when we closely and neatly packed up the linen which had been used, it was put in the place of the clean bundle, till the whole in one box had been thus exchanged; after which that box was restored to the hold, and another brought up. (Sherwood 1910: 415)

Once on board Mrs. Sherwood, however, observed, "I had so far forgotten Europe and its habits as to think we could not do with less" (ibid.: 411).

The opening of the Suez Canal in 1869 and the establishment of shipping lines such as the Peninsular and Oriental (commonly known as the P and O) made the sea trip more a cruise in contrast to the earlier long and sometimes dangerous passage. Clothing for a P&O

cruise by the end of the nineteenth century changed remarkably from that of the age of sail and stressed the social life on board ship. From the female point of view:

> Blue serge is always useful and appropriate, and nothing is nattier or more practical than a well-made skirt and coat of this. As large a number as possible of shirts or blouses should be taken, and a striped flannel one is advisable for the first few days of the voyage. Any sensible and tailor-made gown is useful but after Port Said is passed lighter things become a necessity. Smart cottons or washing silks are wanted then, but loose lace or flying ribbon ends do not add to comfort, and should be avoided. One wants a couple of evening gowns for the voyage, and a dainty tea-gown is useful, but a black silk, with bodice not markedly *decollete*, is never amiss, and with a couple of pretty silk blouses can be made to furnish desirable variations. While petticoats should be worn with discretion, as tar and pitch are not unknown if one moves off the holy-stoned snowiness of the upper deck. Light-coloured cottons, and made rather short are less extravagant wear. A comfortable cape, a waterproof and a close-fitting cap are all useful if the weather is not perfectly calm. (Billington 1895: 328)

The status, protocol, and bonding of those from various parts of India or within the social structure even manifested itself in what they wore returning to India after a home visit. From the male point of view:

> As the voyage progressed it was also observed that evening dress was not now just plain black. Some were wearing black trousers and white dinner jackets, some were wearing the opposite. Enquiries soon revealed that the more important clubs in India had their own ideas of what should be worn. For instance, it seemed that the Punjab Club members must wear white jackets and black trousers, and Calcutta Club members black coats and white trousers, and so on... (Allen 1975: 44)

CLOTHING WORN IN INDIA

Arrival in India meant adapting to life in the tropics. The heat during the summer months was unbearable to someone from a temperate zone. Wearing anything became a challenge; even bathing did not provide much relief as

> [t]he water for your bath is actually tepid, but bathe you must, and then to dress, an operation of no small trouble and vexation, for no sooner are you out of your bath than the perspiration pours in streams over you, and although the punkah [fan] is taking the most vigorous bounds through the air, you cannot keep cool. (Oman 1864: 197)

The monsoon followed the hot Indian summer and brought its own particular challenges. Bombay, for instance, gets eighty inches of rain in a three-month period. The resulting humidity meant fungus and bumper crops of insects which invaded and ravenously devoured clothing. Trying to cope with this meant having "to burn fires to dry mattresses, books, and pillows, which begin to smell horribly fusty. Gloves are all shut up in glass stoppered bottles" (King 1884: vol. I, 262). Others put their woolens and silks in airtight, soldered boxes during the monsoon. But it was not always effective and the dreaded funguses and mildews appeared. Emily Eden declared it all to be a conspiratorial plot.

> The degree of destructiveness of this climate it is impossible to calculate, but there is something ingenious in the manner in which the climate and the insects contrive to divide the work. One cracks the bindings of the books, the other eats up the inside; the damp turns the satin gown itself yellow, and the cockroaches eat up the net that trims it; the heat splits the ivory of a miniature, and the white maggots eat the paint; and so they go on helping each other and never missing anything. (Eden 1872: vol. II, 101–2)

The British in India tended to live more extravagantly than they could in England; and, whenever possible, attempted to replicate the life of the English aristocracy. In eighteenth-century Calcutta, "ladies dressed their hair into pyramids of gauze, powder, feathers and pomatum according to all the astounding fashions of London. These structures were then topped with head-dresses of white muslins, and with fancy bandeaux, coloured, gilded or embroidered to match their sashes and stomachers" (Ghosh 1970: 115). B. V. Roy described typical male eighteenth-century attire in India as

> a large busy wig tied at the ends, a long coat reaching below the knees, with large sleeves and cuffs, a finely embroidered vest, breeches, buckled tight at the knees, long stockings, and shoes decorated with buckles. The men at this period were very partial to bright colours as well as a profusion of laces and embroideries in their dress. For example, vests or waistcoats were made of gold brocade, or blue satin embroidered with silver, or were sprigged and flowered, costing two or three hundred rupees each. (1946: 34)

Not only were there challenges from the climate to wearing such attire, but also from animals as William Hickey learned:

> I was awakened by something as I imagined, running over the bed, which alarmed me a good deal from an apprehension of tigers, jackals, snakes, and other noxious and ferocious animals and reptiles. After remaining more than an hour under considerable anxiety, I dropped asleep, from which I was again disturbed by I knew not what. Instantly starting up I felt happy at finding light appearing. Having completely opened the windows, I saw not less than a dozen prodigious Bandecoot rats performing their antics about the room. Upon taking off a silk net I always wore over my hair when in bed, I found several holes gnawed by these animals, attracted by the powder and pomatum, of which according to the then fashion, I wore a large quantity. Upon mentioning the circumstance at breakfast, I was told I had escaped marvellously in not losing the whole of my hair. (1919–25: vol. II, 197–8)

The British in India certainly did not forget their heritage and they faithfully celebrated British holidays and notable events as a sentimental attachment to their faraway homeland. But celebrations and festivals which occur during pleasant times of the year in England did not necessarily always happen during times of the year in India when it was comfortable to dress formally. The outstanding example of this was the sovereign's birthday. Hickey describes dressing for the event in Calcutta in "a coat of pea green, lined with white silk and richly ornamented with spangled and foiled lace, waistcoat and breeches decorated to like manner being also of white silk" (ibid.: 173). Others wore such things as "a full-trimmed suit of rich velvet" (ibid.: 176). The birthday of George III, June 4, however, fell at one of the most challenging climatic times in India. April and May are noted for their dry and intense heat, which begins to moderate slightly in June; but as the monsoon clouds appear, the humidity climbs, and eventually the rains begin. Wearing silk or velvet in such weather induced profuse sweating resulting in tactile and malodorous sensations from the itchy, wet, and smelly clothing.

Although George III died in 1820, George IV's birthday was August 12, and William IV's was August 21. Both August birthdays fell near the end of the monsoon, a time of heavy rain and high humidity. Although Victoria was born on November 21, Parliament decreed her birthday to be May 24, a better time of the year in England to celebrate; but in India it unfortunately fell at the peak of the hot weather. Thus from 1760 to Victoria's death in 1901, the celebration of the monarch's birthday occurred in India during climatically challenging times. One account of the event simply stated a "ball is given in the hottest month on the Queen's birthday, and on that evening the quantity of red dye which comes off the officers' coats on to the ladies' white dresses is most laughable" (Oman 1864: 79).

What one wore at official events at Government House in Calcutta reflected the wishes of the Governor-General or, after 1857, the Viceroy. Lord Cornwallis in the late eighteenth century dispensed with much protocol and was fondly remembered when guests sat to dinner for his command "off coats" and gentlemen quickly removed them. Lord Lytton, however, after the Imperial Assembly of 1878, when Queen Victoria became Empress of India, decreed ladies must wear gowns with trains to all state occasions (Fowler 1987: 207).

British officials rigidly followed London formal dress protocols for official events that included Indian or local dignitaries. Two accounts of the resulting sweltering effects come from Emily Eden and Mary Curzon. Eden describes an 1836 formal reception given by her brother, Lord Auckland, the Governor-General. "It was a burning hot day and George and his whole household had to put themselves into full-dress immediately after breakfast, which is no joke with the thermometer at 94 [degrees]" (Eden 1872: vol. I, 162). Curzon, almost seventy years later at the start of the twentieth century, described a comparable formal setting while on an official tour in the Persian Gulf.

> The heat was so great [in Muscat] that I did not go to the *Argonaut*, but watched the Sheikhs and the British arriving in full dress. All the staff had to wear full dress, and their sufferings in their tunics were pitiful. George wore his fullest dress, and fairly suffocated at the prospect of investing the Sultan with the GCIE [Grand Commander Order of the Indian Empire] and robing himself as Grand Master to conduct the ceremony. (Curzon 1985: 147)

The elaborate clothing needs for formal occasions in India reached their zenith with the Imperial Durbar of January 1903, in Delhi. The official delegation from London which represented King Edward VII brought forty-seven tons of dresses and uniforms for the Durbar events (Fowler 1987: 283).

For those Europeans who could afford it, there were numerous changes of dress during the course of a day. Mrs. Sherwood noted a child typically had four changes of clothing, and more if there was an accident or spill which damaged what the child had on (Sherwood 1910: 366–7). Maria Graham found ladies in Madras often had three changes of clothing during the late afternoon and evening hours.

> About five o'clock the master of the family returns from his office; the lady dresses herself for the Mount Road [daily drive to take the air]; returns, dresses, dines, and goes from table to bed, unless there be a ball, when she dresses again, and dances all night; and this, I assure you, is a fair, very fair, account of the usual life of a Madras lady. (1812: 131)

One of the notable characteristics of the British was dressing for dinner, which they sentimentally felt defined taste, morals, and, indeed, being British. Among a few British groups, ways evolved of following the tradition but also of being modestly comfortable. David Burton observed in

> the early nineteenth century [a male guest] was expected to arrive for dinner in a formal black coat. Then a faintly ridiculous ritual would be enacted, where the host or hostess would invite him to swap his heavy black coat for a lighter one. This he would politely accept, and he would then go out to the verandah where his bearer would be waiting with the lighter jacket, having been instructed to bring it along in anticipation of this very invitation. (1993: 28)

No matter where they were at dinnertime – whether at Government House, Calcutta, or on tour and in a tent – most British dressed formally for dinner. From the perspective of present-day attitudes toward clothing such dressing for dinner seems strange. Philip Mason felt

> there were three good reasons for keeping up in India a custom which was obsolescent in Esher or Weybridge. For a great part of the year, it was a matter of elementary comfort and cleanliness to change clothes in the evening and, since the bearer, who put them out for you, had nothing like enough to do, it was no more trouble to put on one kind of clothes than another. But there was also the more complex feeling that it was necessary to "keep up standards". This of course did influence us a good deal and it is easy to make fun of it. But there was a good reason. Aldous Huxley, on a tourist's visit, noticed that many of the inhabitants of India might have sat as models for the old man of Thermopylae who never did anything properly. And in a sense it was by doing things properly – more often at least than most Indians – that the British had established themselves in India and that so few ruled so many with so slight a use of overt force. There was a subconscious awareness of this that involved us in continual effort and

expressed itself in all kinds of ways – from insisting on absolute precision in military drill to the punctilious observance of outdated etiquette, or a meticulous insistence on a knife-edge crease to khaki shorts. (Allen 1975: 18)

The British did wear lighter weight fabrics, even if they retained British fashion. Emily Eden recorded "[e]veryone was ill at church, and there are no punkahs [fans] up, and we are still in our silk gowns from dread of the eight months of white muslin that are coming on" (Eden 1872: vol. I, 317). Thus, between the eighteenth century with its use of brocades, velvets, and heavy materials, the British in nineteenth-century India modified wearing fabrics to such local Indian ones as muslin to help cope with the hot climate. Incorporating Indian textiles into their clothing was hardly universal. Mrs. Fenton, however, observed the strong pull of emotional attachment to Britain, particularly for women:

> [p]erhaps there is no place with less to mark a foreign land than a ball-room, where all the company are European and all the dresses English or French; for it is, I must tell you, the extremity of bad taste to appear in anything of Indian manufacture – neither muslin, silk, flowers, or even ornaments, however beautiful. This at first amazed me; when I wanted to purchase one of these fine-wrought Dacca muslins I was assured I must not be seen in it as none but half castes ever wore them. (1901: 82)

How ironic that although most British women in India steadfastly refused to consider incorporating anything from India's rich textile traditions into their dress, women in England constantly asked their friends and relatives in India to acquire such distinctive textiles for them. Mrs. Fenton commented that Dacca muslin "dresses sell in London as high as £7 and £10. I do remember thinking myself as fine as the Queen of Sheba in one given me by dear Aunt Angel" (ibid.: 82). At the highest levels of society in Calcutta there was not always this avoidance of Asian textiles: Emily Eden used Singapore and Chinese silks for some of her dresses. Mary Curzon similarly incorporated distinctive Indian fabrics in the clothing she wore and could claim to be the vicereine with the finest taste in clothing. After a six-month visit to England and wearing many of these notable dresses made from Indian fabrics, she returned to India with a request of Queen Alexandra to have her coronation gown and several other outfits for other events made there (Fowler 1987: 277).

BRITISH SPECIAL CLOTHING IN INDIA

Death among the British community was common and often happened extremely quickly and unexpectedly. Since the British came from the most technologically advanced society of its day, they applied their scientific acumen to devise ways to remain healthy. Writings on health and clothing reflect an entirely different approach to medicine.

> Attention to clothing is also of very great importance to European residents in India, and in order to be secure from the ill effects of sudden changes in the atmosphere, it is advisable to wear flannel next the skin. This in the hot season may be rendered easily supportable by being lined with mull muslin, and as it absorbs the perspiration, the

wearer will feel more comfortable and even some degrees cooler than those who profess not to be able to bear any thing but the lightest and thinnest apparel. (Roberts 1845: 39)

Dysentery, fevers, rheumatism, sunstroke, and lung and liver disease are sometimes clearly traceable to errors in clothing – the last two no doubt, in consequence of the sympathy between the organs implicated and the skin, the action of which, as a regulator of heat, is not sufficiently borne in mind. The best kind of under-clothing would seem to be a material which, while it is a poor conductor of heat, at the same time readily absorbs perspiration, and is light and unirritating. Fine gauze flannel, or woollen textures interwoven with cotton, present the safest fabrics for shirts in hot climates; for as wool condenses the vapour, the skin remains warm while evaporation from its surface is going on, and therefore the too rapid loss of caloric, by which chills are caused, does not ensue. (Hunter 1873: 41–2)

Two parts of the body require more particularly to be protected in India – the brain and the liver. For the former nothing answers so well as the pith hat, broad-brimmed, and well ventilated. To protect the liver natives have the girdle and they bind their clothes in thick folds about the loins; but a piece of flannel next to the body serves the double purpose of protecting the liver from the sun and the abdomen from the cold when it is damp weather. (Robbins 1883: 196)

Quite the coolest dress that I took with me was a grey alpaca, lined with a decisive yellow silk and made with a yellow silk blouse. This was in accordance with a suggestion by Sir George Birdwood, who had a sound scientific theory for his recommendation. No one, he argues, ever got sunstroke or heat fever from exposure to a dark source of warmth, or even to the most powerful furnace. It is the chemical rays of the sun that work the mischief, and it is the photographer who gives us the hint for their exclusion. He glazes his windows, and uses lamps shaded with red or yellow, and thus manipulates his plates with safety. It is quite immaterial for wear whether the yellow is inside or out, and as fashion does not usually favour our appearance in such brilliant colouring, I allied, or rather, Messrs. Howell and James did for me, mine with light grey alpaca, and brought for once artistic effect and hygiene into excellent accord. The natives, it may be mentioned, have used yellow linings for their tents for countless generations. (Billington 1895: 335–6)

The results of such investigations blended science with myth and folklore and brought into use two things, the pith helmet and wearing flannel around the midriff. Designs for the pith helmet, or *sola topi*, varied greatly, and ranged from the Meerut version with its covering of pelican skin and feathers to something resembling an inverted soup bowl (MacMillan 1988: 137). Julius Jeffreys, a doctor whose work in the middle of the nineteenth century promoted the adoption of the *sola topi*, further advocated covering one's spine with cork to absorb perspiration (Renbourn 1957: 208). Bernard Cohn declared that by 1870 the British had "generally adopted a 'uniform,' the distinctive components of which were sola topi with pugri, spinal pad, and cholera belt or flannel cummerbund" (1996: 159).

Use of the *sola topi* and flannel begs the question as to why the British did not simply adopt Indian dress to deal with the climate? During the eighteenth century many Europeans indeed did wear Indian clothing. Most writers on the subject link the transition to wearing only British dress to the increasing number of European women coming to India starting in the early nineteenth century. While the increasing presence of European women in India may have been a factor in the use of European dress, there are several other things which merit consideration.

First, if the British were to adopt Indian dress, what, specifically should they wear? Given the large size of the Indian subcontinent and its numerous cultural groups, there was no standard dress used across this vast area. Dress varied greatly, often within particular areas.

Second, writers who lament the failure of the British to adopt Indian dress overlook the fact that the sun never set on the British Empire, a worldwide empire that had within it hundreds of types of dress. Although India was the crown jewel of the British Empire, it was but one of many tropical areas within the colonial system. What could be the norm that would be used not just in India but throughout the British tropical world?

Third, the British thought themselves successors of the Mughals as rulers of India. The Mughals retained the use of their cut and stitched Central Asian clothing throughout their rule. Such stitched dress contrasted greatly with the unstitched cloths typically worn by Indians. The visual identity established by such distinct dress helped to set apart the Mughals and, subsequently, the British as groups separate from the Indian populace. The number of British in India was extremely small, especially when compared to the total population of the subcontinent. Given the small number of Europeans in India, having a distinctive dress that was not part of Indic traditions helped both to identify and to unify them. A Frenchman, Victor Jacquemont, who came to India in 1829, knew the importance of clothing in establishing identity and how this needed to be maintained, and he observed: "[i]t goes without saying that in states under the domination or protection of England, or simply in alliance with her, I continue to wear European clothes, which are enough to turn any fairly white man into a *sahib*, that is, a gentleman" (1936: 38).

Not only did the British retain their sartorial traditions throughout their empire, the Danes, Dutch, French, and Germans also kept their European clothing in their colonial empires. Although Americans did not have a colonial possession until 1898, missionaries from New England went to Hawaii earlier in the nineteenth century. James Michener in his historical novel, *Hawaii*, records that these missionaries put on long woolen underwear on October 1 every year and continued to wear such underwear until April 1, just as they did back home in New England (Michener 1959: 257).

Clothing sentimentally bound the British living in the tropics to Britain. While a few changes had to be made to adapt to the tropical climate of India to preserve their health, there never was any doubt which clothing they preferred. The Suez Canal marked the transition from India to Europe, which those leaving India needed to acknowledge. The final ritual farewell was made, as always, where the East ended and the West began: "As we left Port Said and sailed into the open waters everyone was paraded with their topees [hats] on deck and at a given signal we all flung our topees into the sea and that was the last of India" (Allen 1975: 219).

REFERENCES

Allen, C. (1975), *Plain Tales from the Raj: Images of British India in the Twentieth Century*, London: André Deutsch.

Billington, M. F. (1895), *Woman in India*, London: Chapman & Hall.

Burton, D. (1993), *The Raj at Table: a Culinary History of the British in India*, London: Faber and Faber.

Cohn, B. S. (1996), *Colonialism and its Forms of Knowledge: The British in India*, Princeton: Princeton University Press.

Curzon, M. (1985), *Lady Curzon's India: Letters of a Vicereine*, New York: Beaufort Books.

Eden, E. (1872), *Letters from India*, London: R. Bentley, 2 vols.

Fenton, Mrs. (1901), *Journal of Mrs. Fenton: A Narrative of Her Life in India, the Isle of France (Mauritius), and Tasmania During the Years 1826–1830*, London: Arnold.

Fowler, M. (1987), *Below the Peacock Fan: First Ladies of the Raj*, New York: Viking.

Ghosh, S. C. (1970), *The Social Condition of the British Community in Bengal, 1757–1800*, Leiden: Brill.

Graham, M. (1812), *Journal of a Residence in India*, Edinburgh: Archibald Constable.

Hickey, W. (1919–25), *Memoirs of William Hickey*, London: Hurst & Blackett, 4 vols.

Hunter, G. Y. (1873), *Health in India, Medical Hints as to Who Should Go There, and How to Retain Health Whilst There and on Returning Home*, Calcutta: Thacker.

Jacquemont, V. (1936), *Letters from India 1829–1832, being a Selection from the Correspondence of Victor Jacquemont*, London: Macmillan.

King, Mrs. R. M. (1884), *The Diary of a Civilian's Wife in India, 1877–1882*, London: Richard Bentley & Son, 2 vols.

MacMillan, M. (1988), *Women of the Raj*, London: Thames & Hudson.

Michener, J. (1959), *Hawaii*, New York: Random House.

Old Resident. (1847), *Real Life in India, Embracing a View of the Requirements of Individuals Appointed to Any Branch of the Indian Public Service, the Methods of Proceeding to India and the Course of Life in Different Parts of the Country*, London: Houston and Stoneman.

Oman, C. P. A. (1864), *Eastwards, or, Realities of Indian Life*, London: Simpkin, Marshall & Co.

Renbourn, E. T. (1957), "The History of the Flannel Binder and Cholera Belt," *Medical History* 1: 211–25.

Robbins, W. E. (1883), *A Hand-book of India and British Burma*, Cincinnati: Walden & Stowe.

Roberts, E. (1845), *The East India Voyager, or, The Outward Bound*, London: J. Madden and Co.

Roy, B. V. (1946), *Old Calcutta Cameos*, Calcutta: Ashoka Library.

Sherwood, Mrs. [Mary] (1910), *The Life and Times of Mrs. Sherwood (1775–1851) from the Diaries of Captain and Mrs. Sherwood*, F. J. Harvey Darton (ed.), London: Wells Gardner, Darton & Co.

Shrimpton, J. (1992), "Dressing for a Tropical Climate: The Role of Native Fabrics in Fashionable Dress in Early Colonial India," *Textile History* 23: 55–70.

5 AFRICAN AMERICAN ENSLAVEMENT AND ESCAPING IN DISGUISE

Helen Bradley Foster

Enslaved African Americans escaped from their conditions by ingenious disguise. An estimated 6,000 people narrated their life experiences, including stories of flight from confinement, between 1703 and 1944 (Gates 1987: ix). More than 100 of these memoirs were published before the end of the American Civil War. In the 1930s, the United States government's Works Progress Administration collected approximately 2,500 narratives in seventeen states, the largest autobiographical collection ever recorded from a single cultural group. In all slave memoirs, dress figures in descriptions of day-to-day activities, special events, sacred rituals, humiliating punishments, and acts of resistance (Foster 1997). The narratives analyzed here recount the horrifying disciplinary actions and the ultimate form of resistance: the escapes of enslaved Americans.

PUNISHMENT

Instances wherein dress or its absence became the type of degrading torture inflicted by white "masters" included: additions to the body, such as brands, iron chains, mangles, and headgear; the forced wearing of clothes of the opposite sex; and the subtraction of clothing, particularly stripping the body before flogging. Of topical interest, the memories of punishments delivered during the period of enslavement form a basis which demonstrates that the more recent, early twenty-first-century instances of the torture of other bodies and minds by modern Americans is but another contemporary example on a long, historical continuum of cruelty.

The memories of witnesses and victims of the period before emancipation attest to humiliation as the paramount sentiment caused by the barbaric acts. European Americans, because of their own cultural regard for covering the body, well understood the mortification that branding, manacles, forced cross-dressing and undressing would cause those of West African ancestry, whose own cultures, and the European dress customs they later adopted in the Americas, promoted fully clothing the body. An important observation by Olaudah Equiano (or Gustavus Vassa, b. 1745, in Guinea), while at church in Falmouth, England, shows the concern of African men with adequate clothing as he contrasts the dress of English women with that of African women: "I thought them not so modest and shamefaced as the African women" (1987 [1841]: 43).

BRANDING AND BELLING

Once an African became enslaved, marks of ownership began. John Phillips' journal records the purchase of slaves from the king of Whidaw:

> Our surgeon is forced to examine the privaties [*sic*] of both men and women… Then we mark'd the slaves we had bought in the breast, or shoulder, with a hot iron having the letter of the ship's name on it, the place before being anointed with a little palm oil, which caused little pain, the mark being usually well in four or five days, appearing very plain and white after. (Palmer 1990: 59)

In his autobiography, Equiano later notes in the West Indies: "It was very common in several of the islands, particularly in St. Kitt's, for the slaves to be branded with the initial letters of their master's name…" (1841: 76).

Since antiquity, chains and manacles have symbolized slavery. These additional burdens of enslaved African Americans are ubiquitous in both the literature and visuals of the period. Another gruesome shackle added cacophony and a humiliating crown to some enslaved people's lives. Charlotte Brooks, enslaved in Virginia and Louisiana, recounts a tale told by Jane Lee about a runaway woman: "She said they put deer-horns on her head to punish her, with bells on them" (Albert 1988 [ca. 1890]: 20). A similar, but more disturbing, documented punishment involved locking an iron band around a person's neck and then attaching a bell to another band over the person's head. A slave so punished endured the constant noise of the bell in addition to the weight and discomfort of the iron bands; and because the bell rang with any movement, the impossibility of escape was ensured.

STRIPPING AND WHIPPING

The narratives contain myriad examples showing that beatings with whips usually first entailed stripping the enslaved of clothes. In yet another setting, Equiano, after witnessing the abuse against a free black in Savannah, Georgia, writes:

> I was therefore much embarrassed, and very apprehensive of a flogging at least. I dreaded, of all things, the thought of being stripped, as I never in my life had the marks of any violence of that kind. At that instance a rage seized my soul, and for a little I determined to resist the first man that should attempt to lay violent hands on me, or basely use me without trial; for I would sooner die like a free man, than suffer myself to be scourged, by the hands of ruffians, and my blood drawn like a slave. (1841: 103)

Frederick Douglass (b. 1818, Maryland; Figure 5.1), describes the whipping of an elderly man: "Colonel Lloyd ma[d]e old Barney, a man between fifty and sixty years of age, uncover his bald head … and receive upon his naked and toil-worn shoulders more than thirty lashes at a time" (1968 [1845]: 34).

Mary Prince, enslaved in the West Indies, voices the disgrace of being stripped in public:

Figure 5.1   Frederick Douglass.

Is it happiness for a driver in the field to take down his wife or sister or child, and strip them, and whip them in such a disgraceful manner? – women that have had children exposed in the open field in shame! There is no modesty or decency shown by the owner to his slaves; men, women, and children are exposed alike. (1987 [1831]: 83)

Most often, the narrators notably recall their memories of women bearing this pain and humiliation. The following testimonies concentrating on women's beatings exemplify that men, as well as women, suffered the shame of the female body's public exposure.

Solomon Northrup, born free but sold into slavery for twelve years, remembered with guilt an episode that began when four stakes were driven into the ground in preparation for the master's punishment of Patsey. The master then

ordered her to be stripped of every article of dress. Ropes were then brought, and the naked girl was laid upon her face, her wrists and feet each tied firmly to a stake. Stepping to the piazza, he took down a heavy whip, and placing it in my hands, commanded me to lash her. Unpleasant as it was, I was compelled to obey him.

The mistress and her children watched as did slaves huddled nearby. After about thirty lashings, Northrup finally refused to continue. The master then seized the whip himself. Northrup describes the continued beating: "She was terribly lacerated – I may say, without exaggeration, literally flayed." When the beating ceased, "her dress was replaced, but it clung to her back, and was soon stiff with blood" (1968 [1853]: 197–9).

Julia A. J. Foote (b. 1823) recalls a particularly horrifying whipping:

> My mother was born a slave in the State of New York. She had one very cruel master and mistress. This man, whom she was obliged to call master, tied her up and whipped her because she refused to submit herself to him, and reported his conduct to her mistress. After the whipping, he himself washed her quivering back with strong salt water. At the expiration of a week she was sent to change her clothing, which stuck fast to her back. Her mistress, seeing that she could not remove it, took hold of the rough tow-linen garment and pulled it off over her head with a jerk, which took skin with it, leaving her back all raw and sore. (1988 [1886]: 9–10)

Another horrendous example comes from Mary Prince, as she remembers Hetty, a fellow slave, who was pregnant when a

> cow had dragged the rope away from the stake to which Hetty had fastened it. My master flew into a terrible passion, and ordered the poor creature to be stripped quite naked, notwithstanding her pregnancy, and to be tied up to a tree in the yard. He then flogged her as hard as he could lick, both with the whip and the cow-skin, til she was all streaming with blood... After severe labor, she delivered a dead baby. Hetty never regained her strength, but continued to be whipped by both master and mistress, and before long she too died. (1987 [1831]: 57)

On an even more personal level, Mary Prince remembered another master who "has often stripped me naked, hung me up by my wrists, and beat me with a cow-skin, with his own hand, until my body was raw with gashes" (ibid.: 62–3).

Victoria Perry reports of her "master": "When he got mad at any slave he whipped them all... He tied them to post or tree, stripped their clothes to the waist, and whipped them until he grew tired. She said she had seen her mother whipped in such a manner until she bled" (Joyner 1991: 90).

Benjamin Drew remembered when his mother was whipped and stripped completely naked: "Dey didn't care nothing 'bout it. Let everybody look on at it" (Winks 1969: 48–9).

CROSS-DRESSING

Accounts let us examine still another form of humiliation when men and women were forced to wear clothes of the opposite sex. As Charlotte Brooks recounts Jane Lee's story, she says:

> Nellie Johnson was sold to a mighty bad man. She tried to run away to her old Virginia home, but the white man brought her back... When they got her back they made her wear men's pants for one year. They made her work in the field that way... Aunt Jane

said once while she was passing on the levee she saw Nellie working with the men on the Mississippi River, and she had men's clothes on then. (Albert 1988 [ca. 1890]: 20)

Men were also forced to wear clothes of the other sex. Louisiana planter, Bennet H. Barrow, for example, made a troublemaking enslaved male "ware womens cloths [*sic*] for running away & without the least cause" (Scarborough 1984: 93).

Another form of desexualization was to shave or cut off a person's hair. In the United States, only women had this inflicted on them. James Brittian (b. 1852) states:

> My grandma ... said she was a Molly Gasca [Madagascar] negro... She sure did look different from any of the rest of us. Her hair it was fine as silk and hung down below her waist. The folks said Old Miss was jealous of her and Old Master... One day she whipped my grandma and then had her hair cut off. From that [time?] on my grandma had to wear her hair shaved to the scalp. (Rawick 1972, vol. 6.1: 217–18)

Harriet Jacobs, who escaped from North Carolina in the 1830s, also had "a fine head of hair." Her jealous master gave the following punishment when she became pregnant by a black lover:

> When Dr. Flint learned that I was again to be a mother, he was exasperated beyond measure. He rushed from the house and returned with a pair of shears. I had a fine head of hair; and he often railed about my pride in arranging it nicely. He cut every hair close to my head, storming and swearing all the time. (1987 [1861]: 77)

ESCAPE

Few enslaved people took such punishments as described above without some form of rebellion. In terms of revolt, the most fundamental impulse was to seek freedom by escaping bondage. Scholars estimate that at least 100,000 people attained their freedom in this way. In spite of success being extremely uncertain, and the threat of severe punishment if apprehended, the run for freedom continued until the enforcement of legal emancipation. The narrators' numerous discussions about attempts and successful escapes include making note of the clothes worn at the time and emphasizing the need for adequate and appropriate clothing.[1]

But escape proved perilously difficult and in many instances a runaway's dress and even physical aroma were to the advantage of the chaser. Bodily scent, for example, assisted those hunting the runaways. This occurred when hound dogs were put on the trail. Arthur Shaffer retold this story related by his grandfather, Hilley Chavious (freeborn in 1833). Chavious described what occurred when a person attempted escape in Virginia:

> In most instances the master would rally his overseer and his bloodhounds and give a determined chase to save his property. On missing the slave or slaves, the first thing to be done was to procure a garment or a shoe that bore the body scent, call up the dogs and allow them to familiarize themselves with the smell. This was a dog's identification of the person he was to trail. (Rawick 1971, vol. 1.5: 19)

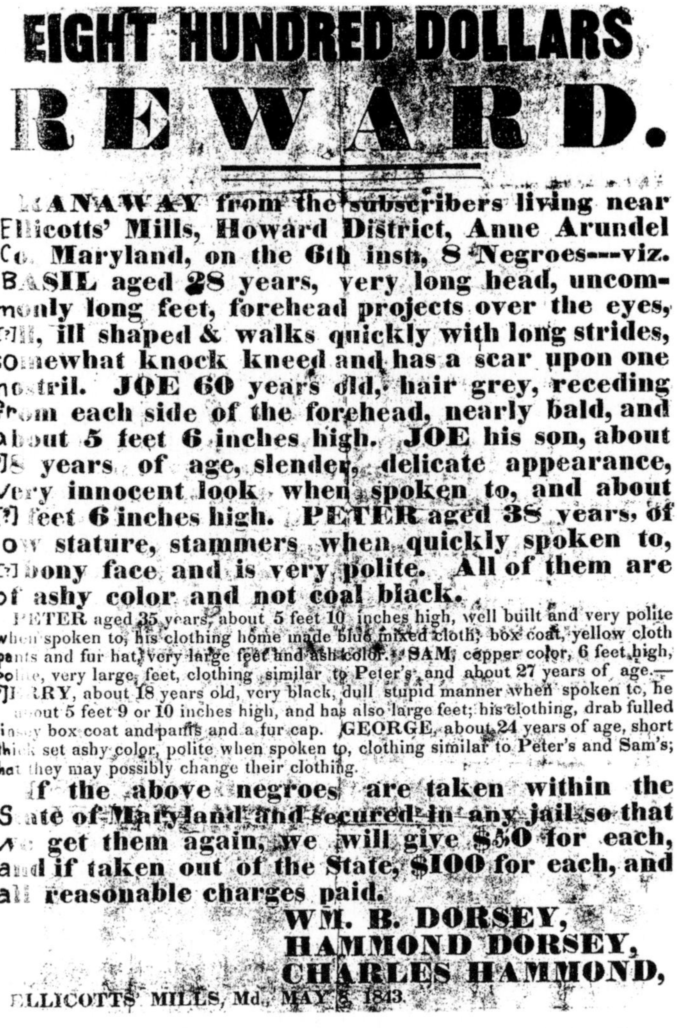

EIGHT HUNDRED DOLLARS REWARD.

RANAWAY from the subscribers living near Ellicotts' Mills, Howard District, Anne Arundel Co. Maryland, on the 6th inst, 8 Negroes---viz. BASIL aged 28 years, very long head, uncommonly long feet, forehead projects over the eyes, [?], ill shaped & walks quickly with long strides, somewhat knock kneed and has a scar upon one nostril. JOE 60 years old, hair grey, receding from each side of the forehead, nearly bald, and about 5 feet 6 inches high. JOE his son, about [?]8 years of age, slender, delicate appearance, very innocent look when spoken to, and about [?] feet 6 inches high. PETER aged 38 years, of low stature, stammers when quickly spoken to, [?]bony face, and is very polite. All of them are of ashy color and not coal black.

PETER aged 35 years, about 5 feet 10 inches high, well built and very polite when spoken to, his clothing home made blue mixed cloth, box coat, yellow cloth pants and fur hat, very large feet and ash color. SAM, copper color, 6 feet high, polite, very large feet, clothing similar to Peter's, and about 27 years of age.—[?] RRY, about 18 years old, very black, dull stupid manner when spoken to, he about 5 feet 9 or 10 inches high, and has also large feet; his clothing, drab fulled linsey box coat and pants and a fur cap. GEORGE, about 24 years of age, short thick set ashy color, polite when spoken to, clothing similar to Peter's and Sam's; that they may possibly change their clothing.

If the above negroes are taken within the State of Maryland and secured in any jail so that we get them again, we will give $50 for each, and if taken out of the State, $100 for each, and all reasonable charges paid.

WM. B. DORSEY,
HAMMOND DORSEY,
CHARLES HAMMOND,

ELLICOTTS' MILLS, Md., MAY 8 1843.

Figure 5.2   Runaway advertisement for Harriet Jacobs, Virginia, 1835. Historical Society of Carroll County, Maryland.

As a means of apprehension, runaway ads posted by slave "owners" carefully described the fugitive, including the clothes he or she most likely wore at the time of escape (Figure 5.2). In the narratives of people who had achieved freedom by dressing in disguise, they rarely give specifics on how this was accomplished. Omission of the particularities thwarted recapture of others attempting escape by similar means. Or, as Frederick Douglass wrote: "The practice of publishing every new invention by which a slave is known to have escaped from slavery has neither wisdom nor necessity to sustain it" (1855: 328; also see, Douglass 1845: 105–6, 111).

Nevertheless, documents do exist that explain how altering appearance became a means to freedom. Three main categories of disguise are evident: dressing in a costume rather than typical slave clothing, cross-dressing as the opposite sex, and passing for white because of lighter skin color. These descriptions of concealment bring to mind the trickster, a character prevalent in West African and African American folklore. In the United States, this character most often comes forth in tales from the period of enslavement and most often concerns "John the slave" cleverly deceiving the "master." Br'er Rabbit becomes a metaphor for the human trickster, as the wiley, smaller animal outsmarts the mean-spirited, larger Br'er Fox and Br'er Bear.[2] Based on the oppressed's one-upmanship over the oppressor without the latter being aware that he has been made a dupe, the trickster tales brought occasional psychological relief to the enslaved, but only ingenious contrivances for successful escape brought actual physical relief.

COSTUMING

Runaways were usually between the ages of fifteen and thirty-five, the years of childbearing and child rearing, thus accounting for the fact that far fewer women made the attempt than did men (Joyner 1991: 95). Nonetheless, women became prime examples of escaping enslavement by dressing so as to be unrecognizable. In fact, no other figure in the history of runaways deserves the title "Trickster" more than the brave, formerly enslaved woman, Harriet Tubman (Figure 5.3), who was expert at disguising herself in costume when helping others escape. A Union officer wrote of her: "as a spy and a scout ... Dressed as a freed-woman, with a bandana on her head, this short plain woman could travel anywhere in Rebel territory without arousing suspicion" (quoted in Sterling 1984: 259). Tubman became the most legendary of the tricksters of the Civil War period. For example, in 1858, Charles Nalle escaped from slavery in Virginia. Slavecatchers caught up with him two years later in Troy, NY. Tubman was there and joined a gathering of abolitionists who were not allowed into the building to witness the proceedings concerning returning Nalle into slavery. In order to get inside, Tubman "wrapped herself in a shawl and sought admission to the proceedings carrying a food basket. Her props helped her appear elderly and innocuous (she was only thirty-four at the time)" (Clinton 2004: 137). After the federal commissioner sentenced Halle back into slavery, Halle was manacled, at which point Tubman dramatically dropped her shawl, grabbed Halle, and whisked him into the large antislavery crowd who made sure of his escape (ibid.: 138–9).

Others using costume as disguise included William Hayden who fled enslavement by dressing as a beggar in an "old ragged suit" with "patched and repatched pantaloons" and an old hat shaped into "a three cornered cock" (1846: 132–3). Andrew Jackson, born 1814, and enslaved in Kentucky, revealed his cleverness in making his clothes ragged toward a different purpose:

> I gathered my clothes together, ... I started off in the direction of a piece of woods, and
> there tore up those I desired least, and threw them down, besmeared with blood which

Figure 5.3   First published image of Harriet
Tubman, 1869.

I obtained to give them the appearance of having been torn from me by a wild beast, in
order that I might prevent any one from pursuing me until I could escape beyond their
reach. (1847: 9)

CROSS-DRESSING

Being forced to wear clothes of the opposite sex proved one of the most humiliating
punishments dealt by whites. Therefore, of much interest is the fact that both men and
women recounted cross-dressing as a means of running away in disguise. Edinbur Randell,
born in Alabama, enslaved in Florida, and interviewed in 1854, escaped and stowed away
on a ship in Jacksonville headed for Maine. When Randell was discovered, the captain put
into harbor at Martha's Vineyard where, at night, Randell stole a boat and found refuge
among nearby Indians. Randell relates that his means of getaway from the island occurred
when Beulah Vanderhoof, a Native American, "put a gown, shawl, and bonnet upon me,
took me … to the house of her grandmother, Mrs. Peters, hid me in the garret, and then
went to engage a boat to take me from the island" (Blassingame 1977: 323).

Harriet Jacobs escaped from a man who attempted to make her his concubine. By dressing in "a suit of sailor's clothes – jacket, trousers, and tarpaulin hat" and wearing these on the very streets of her hometown and not being recognized, she made her successful getaway (1987 [1861]: 111). But even after Jacobs made it to Philadelphia, she continued, until emancipation, to don two heavy black veils and to cover her hands with gloves in public for fear of being recaptured by her former "master" (ibid.: 159).

During one of her trips back to Maryland to bring out family and even strangers, Harriet Tubman brought her brother's sweetheart to Canada. To facilitate this woman's escape, Tubman's brother "bought her a suit of men's clothing… She found the male attire at their secret hiding place and dressed like a man to make her getaway from the neighborhood" (Clinton 2004: 84). Tubman, herself, dressed to alter her appearance in two ways during her exploits back to the South during the Civil War. On the one hand, she wore certain articles of men's attire (Figure 5.3) and "[s]he was proud of the fact that she had worn 'pants' ["bloomers"] and carried a musket, canteen and haversack, accoutrements which she retained after the war" (quoted in Sterling 1984: 260). On the other hand, "Once when she had to pass through a town near her former Maryland home during daylight, she walked the streets incognito, equipped with a large sunbonnet pulled down over her face and, as an extra measure of precaution, two live fowl" (Clinton 2004: 89). According to Tubman's autobiographer, Catherine Clinton, "Harriet was nearly always prepared with a change of costume or some other diversion" (ibid.: 89).

PASSING

The most obvious way to differentiate between African and European ancestry is skin color. But the rape of African American women by white men during the period of enslavement often meant their children had lighter skin than that of their forebears. Because of this, lighter enslaved people could use their very skin color as disguise.

One of the most fascinating and oft-repeated cases of this type of disguise concerns the enslaved couple, Ellen and William Craft. In 1848, Ellen Craft, nearly white in skin color, dressed and posed as a sickly white gentleman accompanied by his servant, in reality her darker-skinned husband, William Craft (Figure 5.4). So as not to be given away by Ellen's feminine voice, William explained to others that his "master" had a sore throat and could not talk. In this pretense, they escaped from Georgia to Philadelphia to England (Robinson 1999: 528; Toppin 1973: 126).

Moses Roper, another fair-skinned runaway, escaped from North Carolina to Boston in the 1830s. But still not considering himself safe in the North, Roper continued to pose as white. He writes: "I shaved my head and bought a wig… Some of the family discovered I wore a wig, and said that I was a runaway slave, but the neighbors all round thought that I was a white…" (1838: 81).

The social mores of the United States have always meant that a person with any ancestry of African origin was considered only of that descent no matter if most of his or her ancestry

Figure 5.4   William and Ellen Craft.

was European. In the South, this relegated even the most light-skinned person to African American communities. The long-term psychological effects of leaving those communities to live as a white American could often be horrendous because those who passed for white had to forsake what "they underst[ood] themselves to be" (Kroeger 2003: 7). Lighter-skinned African Americans who fled by pretending to be European Americans, and who continued the pretense once they were free, unlike their darker-skinned brothers and sisters who established socially cohesive communities in the North, forsook forever the cultural communities of their birth.[3]

AFTERMATH

Costumes, dress of the opposite sex, even posing as a European American proved advantageous to a number of runaways. These escapes to freedom provoked indignation, even frustration and outrage, on the part of the master class and certainly provided a sense of triumph for the formerly enslaved. Yet, African Americans who had freed themselves by various methods of tricking the "master" demonstrate in their testimonies that throughout their lives there remained bittersweet ambiguities about what they had achieved.

For those who had made it to the North, this often meant forever leaving family behind. A poignant example of this concerns Harriet Tubman's experience. After escaping to her own freedom, Tubman returned to Maryland several times to successfully rescue three brothers and their families, her elderly parents, and nieces and nephews. History regards her feats as exceptional. But although she rescued so many of her family members, her attempt to free her husband, John Tubman, and take him North was to no avail: he had taken up with another woman and refused to leave. "Her friends reported that Harriet took this turn of events very hard" (Clinton 2004: 82–3).

Escapees often had to abandon not only relatives, but also friends forever. Frederick Douglass writes of his "pain of separation" on leaving Baltimore in two of his autobiographies (e.g., 1845: 110). In 1855, he says:

> I had the painful sensation of being about to separate from a circle of honest and warm hearted friends, in Baltimore. The thought of such a separation, where the hope of ever meeting again is excluded, and where there can be no correspondence, is very painful. It is my opinion that thousands would escape from slavery who now remain there, but for the strong cords of affection that bind them to their families, relatives and friends. (1969 [1855]: 333)

No longer enslaved, some lighter-skinned African Americans gained freedom by disguising their very ancestral identities and passing as European Americans in the white culture. Darker-skinned fugitive African Americans and their descendents in the North found themselves still segregated from the larger public services and institutions. Yet, while isolated from mainstream society because of skin color, they nonetheless bonded together and continued to retain older traditions while forging new customs within their own communities, no longer needing to play the trickster in disguise.

If found, the escaping person faced horrific, humiliating punishment or death for the attempted act: the try for freedom always involved high stakes. To European Americans who legally held fellow humans as captives in perpetuity, the attempt, successful or not, was seen as an immoral deception. For the escapee, life itself depended on deception, adding multiple layers of moral reversals to the history of American racist slavery and its existential paradox of "freeing oneself."

NOTES

1. As examined elsewhere, escapees acquired these items of dress in various ways (see Foster 1997: 201–2). The references used in the current discussion, however, offer no evidence of where and how people procured the dress used for their disguises. James W. C. Pennington (b. ca. 1826) describing his escape from Maryland, for instance, simply says: "I had but four pieces of clothing about my person, having left all the rest in the hands of my captors" (1849: 41).
2. Joel Chandler Harris retells these animal tales in *Uncle Remus* (1921 [1880]); John W. Roberts devotes a chapter to a thorough comparison between Br'er Rabbit tales and those about John the slave (1990: 17–64).
3. See for example, Kwame Anthony Appiah and Henry Louis Gates, Jr. (1995) and Nella Larsen (1929).

REFERENCES

Albert, O. V. R. (1988 [ca. 1890]), *The House of Bondage or Charlotte Brooks and Other Slaves*, reprint with Introduction by F. S. Foster, New York: Oxford University Press.

Appiah, K. A. and Gates, Jr., H. L. (eds). (1995), *Identities*, Chicago: University of Chicago Press.

Blassingame, J. W. (ed.). (1977), *Slave Testimony: Two Centuries of Letters, Speeches, Interviews, and Autobiographies*, Baton Rouge: Louisiana State University Press.

Clinton, C. (2004), *Harriet Tubman: The Road to Freedom*, New York: Little, Brown and Co.

Douglass, F. (1968 [1845]), *Narrative of the Life of Frederick Douglass, An American Slave*, New York: Signet.

Douglass, F. (1969 [1855]), *My Bondage and My Freedom*, New York: Dover.

Drew, B. (1969), *The Fugitive: A North-side View of Slavery*, in R. W. Winks (ed.), *Four Fugitive Slave Narratives*, Reading, MA: Addison-Wesley.

Equiano, O. (1987 [1841]), "The Interesting Narrative of the Life of Olaudah Equiano or Gustavus Vassa, the African," in H. L. Gates, Jr. (ed.), *The Classic Slave Narratives*, New York: New American Library.

Foote, J. A. J. (1988 [1886]), "Plucked From the Fire," in S. Houchins, "Introduction," *Spiritual Narratives*, New York: Oxford University Press.

Foster, H. B. (1997), *"New Raiments of Self": African American Clothing in the Antebellum South*, Oxford: Berg.

Gates, H. L., Jr. (ed.). (1987), *The Classic Slave Narratives*, New York: New American Library.

Harris, J. C. (1921 [1880]), *Uncle Remus: His Songs and His Sayings*, New York: Grosset and Dunlap.

Hayden, W. (1846), *Narrative of William Hayden: Containing a Faithful Account of His Travels for a Number of Years, Whilst a Slave in the South*, Cincinnati, OH.

Jackson, A. (1847), *Narrative and Writings of Andrew Jackson of Kentucky*, Syracuse, NY: Daily and Weekly Star Office.

Jacobs, H. A. (1987 [1861]), *Incidents in the Life of a Slave Girl: Written By Herself*, J. F. Yellin (ed.), Cambridge, MA: Harvard University Press.

Joyner, C. (1991), "The World of the Plantation Slave," in *Before Freedom Came: African-American Life in the Antebellum South*, Richmond: The Museum of the Confederacy, pp. 50–99.

Kroeger, B. (2003), *Passing: When People Can't Be Who They Are*, New York: Public Affairs.

Larsen, N. (1997 [1929]), *Passing*, New York: Penguin.

Northrup, S. (1968 [1853]), *Twelve Years a Slave*, S. Eakin and J. Logsdon (eds), Baton Rouge: Louisiana State University Press.

Palmer, C. A. (1990), "The Middle Passage," in *Captive Passage: The Transatlantic Slave Trade and the Making of the Americas*, Washington, DC: The Smithsonian Institution Press, pp. 53–75.

Pennington, J. W. C. (1849), *The Fugitive Blacksmith or Events in the History of James W. C. Pennington*, London: Charles Gilpin.

Prince, M. (1987 [1831]), *The History of Mary Prince: A West Indian Slave*, M. Ferguson (ed.), Ann Arbor: University of Michigan Press.

Rawick, G. P. (general ed.). (1971 and 1972), *The American Slave: A Composite Autobiography*, Westport, CT: Greenwood Publishing.

Roberts, J. W. (1990), "Br'er Rabbit and John: Trickster Heroes in Slavery," in *From Trickster to Badman: The Black Folk Hero in Slavery and Freedom*, Philadelphia: University of Pennsylvania Press, pp. 17–64.

Robinson, L. C. (1999), "Craft, Ellen and William," in K. A. Appiah and H. L. Gates, Jr. (eds), *Africana: The Encyclopedia of the African and African American Experience*, New York: Basic Civitas Books, p. 528.

Roper, M. (1838), *A Narrative of the Adventures and Escape of Moses Roper from American Slavery*, Philadelphia: Merrihew and Gunn.

Scarborough, W. K. (1984), *The Overseer: Plantation Management in the Old South*, Athens, GA: University of Georgia Press.

Sterling, D. (ed.). (1984), *We Are Your Sisters: Black Women in the Nineteenth Century*, New York: W. W. Norton.

Toppin, E. A. (1973), *The Black American in the United States*, Boston: Allyn and Bacon.

Winks, R. W. (ed.), (1969), *Four Slave Narratives*, Reading, MA: Addison-Wesley Pub. Co.

6 THE ROLE OF SCENTS AND THE BODY IN TURKEY

Marlene R. Breu

The body emits natural scents and smells from clothing such as leather and textiles, from odors that permeate those supplements, from fragrances that we add in products applied to the hair, skin, or inside the mouth, and from products placed on the body for the very purpose of masking or preventing body odors. Members of the academic textile and apparel profession have largely concentrated on visual stimuli and given little attention to the sense of smell as it relates to the various categories of dress Joanne B. Eicher and Mary E. Roach-Higgins outlined (1992). Yet Constance Classen, David Howes, and Anthony Synnott suggest "smelling an article of clothing belonging to a person will often give a much stronger impression of that person's presence than seeing the piece of clothing would" (1994: 116).

Of the five human senses, smell is the only one with a direct link to the brain, immediately passing olfactory stimuli into our emotional and memory centers (Jacob 2005). While the physiology of smell is the same for all people, there are distinct cross-cultural differences in mentifacts and sociofacts (ways of thinking and behaving) related to natural or artificial smells emitted from the human body and body supplements. Western culture, unlike some, minimizes the study and discussion of smell outside the pleasant aspects derived from culinary and floral stimuli, and the pleasant artificial scents in our environments. Classen, Howes, and Synnott suggest certain aspects of our late twentieth-century culture are "inodorate" with neither body scents nor added fragrances being a part of the majority of our group interactions (1994: 175, 185).

In 1986 *National Geographic* published an article titled "The Intimate Sense of Smell," with an accompanying photograph of female judges, hired by a research agency to study the efficacy of deodorants by smelling the underarms of male subjects (Gibbons 1986). The article contained a statement about a woman who rolled over to her husband's side of the bed when he left in the morning just to enjoy his scent. This article prompted my interest in the topic of smell and the desire to understand it in the context of textiles, dress, and personal relationships. Ten years later, while undertaking research in rural areas of Turkey, I observed a grandfather put his little granddaughter on his lap and inhale, with obvious delight, the aroma of the natural body scent of her sweaty head. This poignant example alerted me to cross-cultural differences in sociofacts people exhibit with regard to odors emitted from the body. Over a period of sixteen years, I conducted fieldwork in Turkey, involving numerous visits to villages and urban areas in the western third of the country for the purpose of data collection on Turkish traditional dress and its various components.[1] The topics of body scents, body odors, and fragrances in relation to dress are rich with possibilities for study in dress-related topics. With concern for offensiveness through discussion of a sometimes highly personal topic, Boyd Gibbons said, "What we lack is not a profound sense of smell but encouragement to talk about intimate odors" (1986: 328).

This essay explores the physiology of the human sense of smell and then discusses natural and applied scents in human relations within the contexts of personal identification, group assimilation, and sexual behavior. A selection of personal interpretations of the cross-cultural differences in the way natural and applied body scents mediate social behaviors follows. I use the term *body scent* to mean the scent emitted from the body, including those from supplements carried on the body. *Body odor* is the scent emitted from the body that is considered malodorous, resulting from the action of bacteria on the compounds secreted primarily in the regions of underarm and pubic hair or from body supplements that absorb unpleasant body and environmental odors. A *fragrance* is a scent added to the body that is intended to be pleasant. I use *scent*, *odor*, and *smell* interchangeably.

PHYSIOLOGY OF SMELL

The chemical response of smell, and the closely related sense of taste, allows us to experience our environment. Like other animals, our sense of smell provides a warning system of impending danger or alerts us to such things as the approach of a storm, overripe foods, the presence of poor quality air, or the onslaught of an illness. According to Gibbons, this practice was used prior to modern sophisticated methods of health care (1986). Evidence exists from antiquity of the use of scents for magic, protection, seduction, or generally for odorizing or deodorizing (Classen *et al.* 1994; Le Guérer 1994).[2] Our sense of smell arouses or repels us in sexual encounters. It may also help us recognize people such as our babies or our mates. Helen Keller reported that, with her acute sense of smell, she could tell when a man was in her presence. More than one of us has sniffed a textile to help determine its attributes. In Turkey, as an indicator of content and quality, a vendor encouraged my companion to smell the fabric she was considering.

The sense of smell involves intricate, complicated physiology involving reception of smell molecules passed through a system of detection to the limbic system in the brain, which allows us to perceive them. Odor molecules, if small enough, will vaporize. They reach the detection system via the nose or from food passing at the back of the mouth. They flow over specialized bones and nerve endings, which, if the odors were irritating, would cause us to react with a sneeze. The molecules are picked up by some of the approximately 10 million olfactory receptor neurons of the olfactory epithelium, located in a region 5 cm square, which, unlike other nerves of the body, send the sense directly into the brain. On their way, the molecules bind to hair like olfactory cilia containing small receptors, and neurons send the messages to olfactory bulbs. Within structures called glomeruli, the odors are reduced in complexity and move into the limbic system, a region devoted to motivation, emotion, and memory (Gibbons 1986; Jacob 2005). Once there, smells can stimulate "production of hormones controlling sex, appetite, body temperature and other functions. The limbic system also reaches into the neocortex, site of the brain's higher processes, to stimulate conscious thoughts and reactions" (Gibbons 1986: 337). Olfactory memories and emotions prompted by smell last long and fade less quickly than other senses (Jacob 2005). Scents may evoke positive or negative memories and emotions, including those from leather, textiles, or other body supplements. Research shows women have a more acute sense of smell than men and variation occurs with respect to age, ethnicity, and other factors. Olfactory functioning may be diminished by aging, and certain diseases and drugs (Gibbons 1986; Jacob 2005).

SCENTS IN HUMAN RELATIONS

Humans are leaky chemical units, emitting their characteristic scents into body supplements and the atmosphere. Research documents that smell plays an important role in interpersonal relationships and social transactions. It also shows a person's body scent provides information about state of health, occupation, and disposition. Karen Wright suggests our sense of smell is linked to our physical and mental selves (1994). Annick Le Guérer says, "It can be argued that because of the physiology of the olfactory apparatus, the most direct and profound impression we can have of another person is his (or her) smell" (1994: 23). Georg Simmel, one of the few early sociologists who studied body scent, would certainly agree. He writes the "atmosphere of somebody is the most intimate perception of him" (1908, quoted in Largey and Watson 1995: 317). Gale Largey and David Watson recognize the role of body scent in their discussion of impression management: "[t]o establish and maintain a socially accepted olfactory identity actors engage in two basic practices: deodorizing and odorizing" (1995: 319). Continuing scientific studies regarding the body's responses to scent and individual responses to body scents are important to the study of dress with the proliferation of scents available for bodily enhancement and the ability of textile supplements to absorb odors. Three rubrics discuss how scents emitted by the body and body supplements play a role in interpersonal relationships.

PERSONAL IDENTIFICATION

Individuals vary in the amount of acidity on the skin, thus contributing to individual differences in body scent and body odor. One's scent reflects diet, physical and mental health, age, sex, occupation, and ethnicity (Le Guérer 1994). Condition or cleanliness of body supplements and other factors create further variations within a single individual. Preventing secretions with antiperspirants, changing the smell of secretions with deodorants, perfumes, and incense, choosing a regime of hygiene for the outer body and inside the mouth, are ways to alter scents. The degree to which individuals utilize these factors depends on their proximity to other people, financial resources, availability of water supplies for bathing, and their cultural environment or milieu. Added scents, those that come from body additions such as leather or textiles and from perfumes or perfumed body products, may confer an identity onto a person. Perfume companies suggest identities through advertising by implying a fragrance leads to such traits as being sexy, bold, or daring. The ads suggest such identities may be perceived by the individual using the product and/or those who experience the scent.[3]

Body scents or odors also act as markers of moral or occupational identity. Cultural constructs for acceptable presentation of the body, including what is an appropriate or inappropriate smell, fall into categories of morality often associated with religious beliefs. Excluding people in social encounters based on intolerance of odors emitted from the body and placing a stigma of moral inferiority on them is well documented (Classen *et al.* 1994; Largey and Watson 1995; Le Guérer 1994: 30).

Cross-cultural differences in the perception of individual scents are well illustrated by Classen *et al.* in their discussions of the Middle East and other parts of the world (1994). Jack Weatherford, in his engaging account of the life of Genghis Khan, writes that in the steppes culture in which Genghis Khan lived, a person's scent, along with the breath and blood, historically has held deep meaning and is considered part of a person's soul. His account of Genghis Khan establishing a strong friendship bond says it was accomplished ceremonially by the two men exchanging their sashes full of their body scents and thus accepting the essence of each other's souls (2004: 36).[4]

Carol Delaney observed in her extensive fieldwork in a Turkish village that foul odors, especially from human excrement, are carefully dealt with. "But personal odors in general are an intimate part of the self, and like glances appear to be an aspect of the person that extends beyond his or her bodily boundaries: an invisible but personal substance that moves and can permeate others" (1991: 79). Personal scents, Delaney observed, should be perceived only by members of families, and the act of smelling another person, as in the case of the grandfather whom I observed, should be done only by family members.

Rural Turkish women, and in some cases urban women, continue to have dowry boxes filled with textiles, including those given by mothers and grandmothers and those produced by women in anticipation of their marriages (Figure 6.1). One young woman at the time of marriage refused to open her dowry chest, given by her grandmother, because she did not want to disturb her grandmother's scent in the textiles.

These examples suggest in Turkey, and elsewhere, natural body scent may be an acceptable personal identifier whereas, in the United States, only scents added to the body in the form of fragrances may be acknowledged as acceptable for this purpose. While it is not generally encouraged in Turkey that an individual smell unpleasant as a result of body odors, natural body scents from excretions through the skin are not as negatively perceived as they are in the United States and a greater variation of what is considered unpleasant or unacceptable exists. Our modern textile industry has even engineered fibers that reduce natural body scents carried in fabrics by creating permanent antimicrobial protection.[5] Among the mentifacts regarding personal scent, in American culture we find the tendency to associate

Figure 6.1   Dowry chest. Among the items in such chests are heirloom pieces from mother and grandmother, clothing that carries olfactory remembrances of relatives.

natural body scent with notions of the primitive and uncultured and added scents with the cultured (Cohen 1992).

GROUP ASSIMILATION

In interactions within social groups, body scents, including added fragrances and malodors deemed inappropriate, can act as a mechanism for inclusion or exclusion. Somerset Maugham said the daily morning bath still divided people more effectively than did birth, wealth, or education (Classen *et al.* 1994: 166; Le Guérer 1994: 30). Members of a group may consciously or unconsciously achieve a similar level of olfactory presentation through the use of similar commercial perfumes, scented oils, or other added fragrances, by acceptance of a level of body odor, or by having no detectable smell at all. Classen *et al.* write that "odors are essential cues in social bonding" (1994: 2).

Residents of some villages in Turkey where I conducted research make their livelihood from livestock. In these villages animals often occupy the ground level of a home, with the resulting infusion of animal odors into living spaces and body supplements. This has implications of a social and political nature for relationships between rural residents and those in urban areas. Most urban Turks function in modern, Westernized work and living situations and embrace the teachings of Kemal Atatürk, founder of the new Republic, who espoused modernization and adoption of European manners of behavior. The socioeconomic differences between the rural and urban are heightened by such olfactory divisions.

One aspect of smell, however, crosses the lines of rural and urban Turkey. Lemon cologne is a pervasive fragrance in rural and urban homes, in buses, at restaurants, and many other places where people congregate (Figure 6.2). The cologne is offered as a refresher at the end of a meal or as a gesture of hospitality – splashed on the hands of an individual who then rubs the hands, arms, face, and neck with the scent. With a high alcoholic content, it serves not only to feel cool and refreshing, but also to sanitize the skin, and leaves a faint but pleasant essence of lemon. This ritual may be interpreted as a means to remove or to cover natural body scents and body odors and thus symbolize the guest's entrance into the group. Delaney says in the ideal Turkish culture, "Smells in social space should be

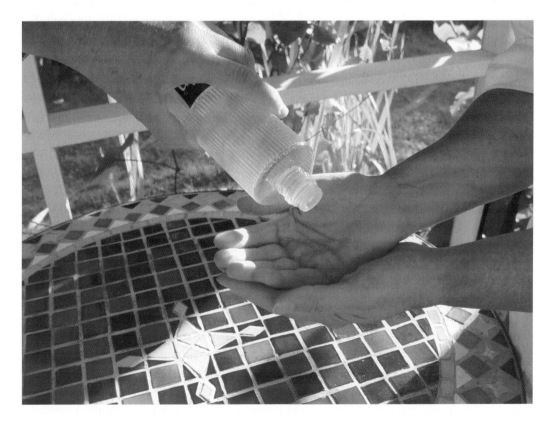

Figure 6.2   Lemon cologne, a ubiquitous scent in Turkish culture.

fresh, pleasing, and impersonal" (1991: 79–80). Bodily smells even extend to burials when rose water is sprinkled on the hands of those at the service, and later on the floor, which Delaney interprets as the importance of scent "not only in disguising the sensuality of body odors, but also in drawing a perfumed boundary between sacred and profane activity and in establishing a communion of believers" (ibid.: 317–18).

In the ancient world, according to Classen *et al.*, "collective perfuming was an important means of entertaining and impressing the masses and of establishing group solidarity" (1994: 27). People used fragrant smoke or incense in addition to liquid scents. Similarities in body scents resulted as the all-enveloping incense infused those in its environs with the same smell. Clothes in the ancient world and even today in some parts of the Middle East are infused with fragrance by placing them over a source of incense (ibid.). The use of incense in religious ceremonies, begun by the sixth century, is tied closely to the notion of creating a connection to God through the ascending smoke, but incense is also particularly valuable as a medium for establishing the community of worshipers because of its transitory nature and ability to obscure individual human scents and replace them with a shared fragrance. The practice continues today in religious traditions such as in the Armenian Orthodox Churches of Istanbul, which have a formalized ritual of censing during the Divine Liturgy and a collection in church treasuries of metal objects of great spiritual and historical significance devoted to censing (Marchese and M. R. Breu, forthcoming).

In contrast, modern US culture favors the lack of scent within groups. An outstanding example is businesses that formally or informally control the olfactory presentation of their workers. Deodorizing or odorizing for the office may follow formal or informal dictates to satisfy the needs of people working in close proximity. Murray Wax suggests it may also serve as a method of minimizing the individual and maximizing group conformity as "[t]his minimizing of human odors may be interpreted as part of the attempt to minimize the physical being and to emphasize the social role and office" (1965: 39). Thus, the lack of scents also brings people together in a common cause.

SEXUAL BEHAVIOR

Emily Secaur writes: "[The nose] is the organ of perception of odors and surely odors have enormous sexual significance, whether emanating from a perfume bottle at $50 an ounce, or from the bodies of healthy men and women" (1995: 49). Obvious effects of body scents and odors on sexual relationships exist where intimacy affords opportunities to experience the total olfactory package of the other individual. As research continues to help explain the physiology behind our sense of smell, we eventually may have a more sophisticated explanation for sexual attraction itself and physiological explanations of the differences in the way one individual perceives the body scent of another. Examples of the role of body scent in relationships do appear in literary works. Examples in poetry and prose include tales of individuals carrying objects of their lovers' wardrobes filled with the essence of the body and of women dropping their perfume-scented handkerchiefs on the ground to make this essence available to their lovers. George Henry Lewes reports from Goethe's unpublished papers that the German author writes he regretted not having taken a slipper or other object belonging to his lover on a trip in order to partake of her body scent (1965: 321). Weatherford described the kidnapping of Genghis Khan's mother and permanent separation from her husband as a highly emotional moment when she "thrust her blouse into his face as a parting gesture and said 'Take this with you so that you may have the smell of me with you as you go'." Her husband reportedly clutched her blouse to his face as he disappeared from her life forever, taking a part of her soul with him as a reminder of her love (2004: 12).

Accounts of men collecting the scent-infused undergarments of their lovers, or inhaling the essence of a lover by sniffing her undergarments during sexual activity, may be deemed fetishes by some; but, by others, as logical behaviors of members of the animal kingdom possessing a sophisticated sense of smell. The wife who recalled pleasant memories of her deceased husband by standing in the closet surrounded by his clothing used her sense of smell as an expression of human sexuality through memory associations carried in the scent-infused textiles. Folk dances of the Mediterranean region include movements allowing a male to wave his handkerchief filled with his underarm sweat under his female partner's nose (Le Guérer 1994: 10). In these situations, body supplements act as the key transmitters of the essence whether natural or artificial.

Cultures vary in terms of the roles and their controls of body scent in sexual activities. While this information is obviously difficult to collect systematically, recommendations or prescriptions may appear in oral or written data and through observation. For example, it is important in Islam that participants wash after intercourse but no prescription is given in the Qu'ran for washing the body before, except in the case of a woman who is at the end of her menstrual cycle. Both men and women are obligated to perform a complete ritual bath after intercourse in order to be eligible to engage in a specific list of activities that includes worship. Alex Comfort, in his popular book, *The Joy of Sex*, encouraged the reader to enter sexual activities with a clean, but not immediately washed, body, and no added fragrances, so one's natural body scent could be enjoyed. He also recommended women should transfer the essence of their vaginal scent to the backs of their ears as an effective pheromone in place of perfume (2002: 92).

CROSS-CULTURAL DIFFERENCES IN THE USE AND APPRECIATION OF SCENTS

Classen *et al.* provide numerous examples of cultural variations in mentifacts regarding scents. They write, "Odors are invested with cultural values and employed by societies as a means of and model for defining and interacting with the world" (1994: 3). Le Guérer observed "Life-style, diet, exercise, occupation, and hygiene, varying as they do from one culture or group to another, all have an effect on the body and its emissions and provide individuals with guides and points of reference" (1994: 25–6). Soldiers have claimed to have sensed the presence of the enemy through smell. For instance, a United States marine in the

Vietnam War said, "But you can't camouflage smell. I could smell the North Vietnamese before hearing or seeing them. Their smell was not like yours or mine, not Filipino, or South Vietnamese either. If I smelled that smell again, I would know it" (Gibbons 1986: 348–9).

Individuals learn through acculturation what is and what is not appropriate in regard to the presentation of the body, particularly appropriate mentifacts and sociofacts associated with body scents, odors, and added fragrances. Cross-cultural variations occur relative to what is designated as a desirable or pleasant body scent, and what is malodorous. How much personal space is generally allowed for individuals may have bearing on these variations, such as in crowded spaces found in the large cities of Turkey and the Middle East. In Turkey, individuals are in close proximity to one another, a result of crowded conditions in cities and cultural acceptance of bodily closeness with one another. Making accidental contact with people on the crowded streets of cities such as Istanbul needs no acknowledgment or apology. In hot weather, when skin is sweaty, the practice of greeting others by kissing or touching on both cheeks continues. Village homes are small, and, continuing practices from a nomadic lifestyle and the settled Ottoman period, often have few rooms. A single room may function as a living, dining, and sleeping room and area to greet guests. Family members are in frequent casual bodily contact with one another.

Edward T. Hall reported the easily observable emphasis on fragrances in Turkey also appeared in the Arab world (1966). Stores devoted to the sale of fragrant oils for both men and women and a tradition of ornately decorated small glass perfume bottles exist in Turkey and the Middle East.[6] Sabiha Tansuğ, Charlotte A. Jirousek, and Serim Denel report that in Turkey foul smells from the mouth or body historically were considered a sin or shameful, especially on Friday, the day one went to the mosque. Flowers or herbs were used to cover the smell of sweaty feet and shoes (2005: 252). D. See Ko, in her discussion of foot binding in China, stated the bound foot was not provocative without the adornment of the appropriate coverings and lavish use of perfume and fragrant powder (1996).

Flowers and herbs hold a primary place in the traditional culture of Turkey for olfactory and visual pleasure. I recorded numerous examples of potted herbs in both rural and urban interior and exterior environments, such as on dining tables at home or in restaurants. Common practice is to remove and rub the leaves to enjoy the fragrance. The use of real or artificial flowers and flower motifs on traditional dress is evident. In many areas, items of traditional dress incorporate fragrant flowers and seeds, such as strands of cloves used as necklaces and decoration for headdresses, to "make the woman smell good" (Tansuğ *et al.* 2005: 260) (Figure 6.3). One of the most pervasive items of traditional dress that has continued into modern village life is a headscarf (*yazma*) decorated with needlelace (*oya*). The majority of the *oya* patterns are clearly floral, and some traditional headdresses, including those of men, are resplendent with flowers. Tansuğ, Jirousek, and Denel say: "Flowers were an essential beauty and luxury in life that was integral to daily experience" (ibid.: 252). Because of the connection between smell and memory, the sight of flowers may suggest the pleasant scents they hold in nature and thus create the idea that the wearer smells pleasant.

Figure 6.3 Traditional headdress from the village of Kocakovacik, Turkey, showing the use of cloves incorporated into the decoration.

Greater appreciation of scents continues in Turkey and Asia as compared to the West in general and the United States in particular. Of interest, the western Romans adopted scents and mentifacts regarding personal and added scents from the East, and continued using those scents through successive centuries. A variety of social and political events and scientific advances occurring in the West in the eighteenth and nineteenth centuries, particularly the discovery of germs, resulted in the devaluation of body scents and changes in ideas and uses of added scents (Classen *et al.* 1994). Classen *et al.* suggest the denigration of smell in today's Western culture is partly a result of the fluid, less contained nature of scents that is counter to our impersonal, rational, and less emotional orientations (ibid.).

CONCLUSION

The Roach-Higgins/Eicher classification system recognizes more than a visual response to dress. This essay shows our olfactory response may be far more salient than previously understood. Body supplements in the form of odors or fragrances, not part of the natural body scent, and the natural or absorbed smells of supplements, may play an important role along with natural body scent in structuring our relationships, socially and culturally. Further research in the natural and social sciences may be difficult to establish because of the sensitive and personal nature of the topic, but many opportunities exist to observe behaviors related to the way we use scent as dress or along with dress in mediating our sociocultural environments.

NOTES

1. I used the ethnohistorical research method involving open-ended interviews, semistructured and non-structured questions, examination of extant artifacts, participant observation in villages, market towns, urban areas, and other venues, and examination and interpretation of literature. The original intent of the data collection in the early years did not involve the component of scent. It evolved in time as responses regarding scent were offered and practices observed.
2. Fragrances are also mentioned in the Bible. See 2 Chronicles 16:14, Psalms 45:8, Song of Songs 4:10, Daniel 2:46, John 12:3, and Revelations 5:8. Luke 7:36–50 describes the encounter between Jesus and a woman who anoints His feet with perfumed oil, considered very precious at the time.
3. An estimated twenty-four billion dollars are spent yearly on scented products in the United States, among them: perfumes, toothpastes, shaving lotions.
4. Weatherford's history of Genghis Khan is based on *The Secret History of the Mongols*, an original Mongolian document discovered in the nineteenth century and deciphered in the twentieth century, describing the details of Genghis Khan's life.
5. For an example, see, www.polartec.com/fabrics/odor.php for information on a product that provides protection from body odors (retrieved June 21, 2007).
6. The important private Sadberk Hanım Museum in Istanbul exhibited a private collection of perfume bottles in 1993 and published an exhibition catalog entitled "The Heritage of Scents" (Sadberk Hanım Müzesi, Piyasa Cad. 27–29, Büyükdere, 80890 Istanbul, Turkey).

REFERENCES

Classen, C., Howes, D., and Synnott, A. (1994), *Aroma: The Cultural History of Smell*, New York: Routledge.

Cohen, C. B. (1992), "Olfactory Constitution of the Postmodern Body: Nature Challenged, Nature Adorned," in F. E. Mascia-Lees and P. Sharpe (eds), *Tattoo, Torture, Mutilation, and Adornment: The Denaturalization of the Body in Culture and Text*, Albany, NY: State University of New York Press, pp. 48–78.

Comfort, A. (2002), *The Joy of Sex*, New York: Crown Publishers.

Delaney, C. (1991), *The Seed and the Soil: Gender and Cosmology in Turkish Village Society*, Berkeley: University of California Press.

Eicher, J. B. and Roach-Higgins, M. E. (1992), "Definition and Classification of Dress: Implications for Analysis of Gender Roles," in R. Barnes and J. B. Eicher (eds), *Dress and Gender: Making and Meaning in Cultural Contexts*, Oxford: Berg, pp. 8–28.

Gibbons, B. (1986), "The Intimate Sense of Smell," *National Geographic* 170 (3) (September): 324–61.

Hall, E. T. (1966), *The Hidden Dimension*, New York: Anchor Books and Doubleday.

Jacob, Tim. (2005), *Olfaction: A Tutorial on the Sense of Smell*, retrieved January 2005, http://www.cf.ac.uk/biosi/staff/jacob/teaching/sensory/olfact1.html.

Largey, G. P. and Watson, D. R. (1995), "The Sociology of Odors," in M. E. Roach-Higgins, J. B. Eicher, and K. K. P. Johnson (eds), *Dress and Identity*, New York: Fairchild, pp. 313–24.

Le Guérer, A. (1994), *Scent: The Essential and Mysterious Powers of Smell*, New York: Kodansha International.

Lewes, G. H. (1965), *The Life of Goethe*, New York: Frederick Ungar Publishing Co.

Marchese, R. T. and Breu, M. R. (Forthcoming), *Treasures of Faith: Sacred Relics and Artifacts from the Armenian Orthodox Churches of Istanbul*.

Secaur, E. (1995), "Body Image and Plastic Surgery," in M. E. Roach-Higgins, J. B. Eicher, and K. K. P. Johnson (eds), *Dress and Identity*, New York: Fairchild Publications, pp. 44–50.

See Ko, D. (1996), "The Body as Attire: The Shifting Meanings of Foot Binding in Seventeenth Century China," *Journal of Women's History* 8 (4): 1–18.

Simmel, G. (1908), *Sociologie*, Leipzig: Duncker and Humblot.

Tansuğ, S., Jirousek, C. A., and Denel, S. (2005), "The Turkish Culture of Flowers," in R. Marchese (ed.), *The Fabric of Life: Cultural Transformations in Turkish Society*, Binghamton, NY: Global Academic Publishing, pp. 249–74.

Wax, M. (1965), "Themes in Cosmetics and Grooming," in M. E. Roach and J. B. Eicher (eds), *Dress, Adornment, and the Social Order*, New York: John Wiley and Sons, pp. 36–45.

Weatherford, J. (2004), *Genghis Khan*, New York: Three Rivers Press.

Wright, K. (1994), "The Sniff of Legend," *Discover* (April): 61–7.

7 AWAKENING THE SENSES: THE AESTHETICS OF MOROCCAN BERBER DRESS

Cynthia Becker

Styles of dress in Morocco during life-cycle transitions, such as childbirth, circumcision, first menstruation, and marriage, can be described as multisensory. For example, before a young boy is circumcised, women apply cool wet henna to his hands and feet. Adolescent Berber girls marking their first menstruation and their transition from girlhood to womanhood once commonly underwent the painful process of tattooing their faces, hands, and ankles with greenish-blue lines joined to form geometric designs. During a marriage celebration, wedding guests engage all their senses: women chew on bitter morsels of walnut root to brighten their gums and dye them a bright orange color; women sprinkle fragrant rose water on wedding guests to welcome them; young girls rejoice in the festive occasion, drumming, dancing, and singing popular songs; married women sit calmly and majestically, bearing the weight of their best multilayered dresses and their numerous silver and gold necklaces, bracelets, and earrings worn especially for the occasion; all the guests inhale the fragrance of sweet-smelling herbs burning in a nearby charcoal brazier.

This essay, based on my ongoing study of Berber dress in Morocco, considers the multisensory aesthetics of Berber dress during rites of passage ceremonies, concentrating on southern Morocco.[1] It builds upon Joanne Eicher's research concerning dress and her contention that the mobile nature of the human body, its three-dimensional form, and its organs of perception contribute to the body's aesthetic display (Roach and Eicher 1973: 75–6). Eicher recognized that dress, including body painting, tattooing, jewelry, hairstyles, and headgear, is dependent on the visual as well as the senses of taste, smell, sound, and touch to communicate values concerning ethnicity, gender roles, and social status (1995). This essay considers the connection between sensory experiences and life-cycle transitions. The use of dress to activate the different senses congruently during rites of passage ceremonies instigates the event, heightens the experience of the observers, and completes the transformation of an individual from one stage in the life cycle to the next.

One of the most ubiquitous substances used throughout Morocco during rites of passage ceremonies is henna. Henna, a small shrub with whitish-colored flowers, grows in many parts of Morocco. People dry its leaves and pound them with a mortar and pestle to create a powder that is then mixed with water to create a thick, green paste. Although henna changes color when it dries, the green color of wet henna reflects its beneficial powers, since green is associated with vegetation and fertility. People also told me that the color green was the Prophet Mohammed's favorite color, and in his old age, he dyed his graying beard with henna. Even today people who claim ancestry from the Prophet Mohammed's lineage often dress in green to assert their familial connection to the Prophet.

Women see henna as beautiful and use it to create intricate geometric and lace-like designs on the soles and sides of their feet and the palms and backs of their hands. After a couple of hours, the dried henna flakes off the skin, temporarily dyeing those areas covered with the henna paste. The final color depends on the quality of the henna, how long the henna is left on the hands, and the texture of the skin. Good henna will stain the skin a deep orange color which gradually fades over the next two or three weeks. Rougher skin will absorb the henna more readily than soft skin, and its color will be richer and more vibrant. In Morocco, women sometimes mix different artificial substances with the henna to stain the skin a dark, black color.

Other senses associated with henna also emerge. Women typically mix sweet-smelling herbs with henna to mask its strong odor. People also appreciate the tactile quality of henna. Wet henna is cool to the touch, and, in the hot desert oases of southern Morocco, Berber women enjoy brushing it through their hair on a weekly basis, covering their henna-colored hair with a headscarf. In fact, the use of henna brings so much pleasure to women that its use during Ramadan is discouraged.

These women continue a practice where, until the 1970s, Berber women in southern Morocco used henna and aged butter to create their large elaborate hairstyles covered with layers of tassels, scarves, and silver pendants (Figure 7.1). In these desert regions rainfall was infrequent and water supplies scarce. Since women rarely had the opportunity to wash their hair with water, they regularly applied wet henna and aged butter to their hair because henna thickened the hair and also activated a sensation of coolness and kept them feeling fresh. The butter also conditioned their hair and scalp and structurally reinforced their elaborate hairstyles and increased sheen. After a week or so, the women simply brushed the mixture out of their hair to keep it clean, reapplied a new layer of butter and henna, and restyled their hair.

Women wearing the hairstyle seen in Figure 7.1 often applied bright-yellow and orange dabs of pounded pomegranate skins and saffron to the outer surface of the buns fashioned on the sides of their heads. Sweet-smelling herbs added to powdered pomegranate and saffron, as well as the herbs added to henna, scented their hair with a pleasant fragrance.[2]

Although it is rare to see these hairstyles in contemporary Morocco, a woman's thick and shiny hair continues to be associated with health and fertility. The association of thick, long hair with womanhood is further demonstrated by an examination of the hairstyles of young girls. Until the 1970s, young girls commonly wore the hairstyle seen in Figure 7.1.[3] A woman shaved her daughter's hair so that a thin, vertical band of hair ran from the front

Figure 7.1   This colonial-era photograph shows a Berber woman from southern Morocco wearing the indigo-dyed clothing, amber necklace, large silver bracelets, and elaborate headdress once commonly worn by Berber women on a daily basis. Photo by Mireille Morin-Barde, 1950–1952, copyright Édisud.

or middle of her head to the nape of her neck. Girls also grew a single lock of hair on the right side of their heads. In Figure 7.1, both the small girl and her mother have very short bangs. Bangs are connected to fertility, as illustrated in a Tamazight song praising the bride during Berber weddings in southern Morocco that says, "The line of rams arrived at the water before the ewes and looked like bangs."[4] This song, comparing bangs to plentiful sheep lining up near a stream and drinking, serves as a wish that the bride will have many children. When a girl reached puberty, she stopped shaving her head and allowed her hair to grow long.

During the wedding ceremony, the bride places her long hair on display. A woman from her family slowly and deliberately brushes her hair in public for everyone to see. Berbers believe the thickness of a bride's hair and braids correlates with her ability to have children: the thicker her hair, the more children she potentially will have. A bride who does not want to become pregnant immediately after her marriage will ask her mother to hide the brush used to style her hair during the wedding ceremony. Once she decides to have children, she asks her mother to show her the brush again.

Women and men not only value henna for its use in styling hair but also for its physical and metaphysical healing properties. Women, for example, believe henna absorbed through the skin strengthens bones, teeth, and hair; they also apply henna to sprained ankles and wrists. After working in the fields, men soothe their weathered hands by applying a layer of henna. During rites of passage ceremonies, the deep orange color of skin dyed with henna provides spiritual protection and evokes the blood that will be spilled during occasions such as childbirth, circumcision, and first-marriage celebrations in which a bride is expected to be a virgin. Henna protects the body during these rites of passage ceremonies due to its association with "divine blessing" (*baraka*), purifying the body by allowing its *baraka* to be absorbed through the skin (Kapchan 1993: 8).

The use of henna to provide metaphysical protection occurs during male circumcision ceremonies. Prior to the circumcision, women smear henna on the hands and feet of their young sons, staining them a deep orange color with henna. Circumcision marks the end of their status as small boys protected by their mothers and marks their entrance into the *umma* (community) of Muslims. Henna's *baraka* passes through the surface of the body to infuse it with the positive healing energy necessary after the circumcision process. Most important, the pleasant smell of henna mixed with herbs protects the child from the harm of spiritual beings called *jnoun* (singular *jinn*), who prey on people passing through life-cycle phases. The consequences of angering the *jnoun* are strokes, illness, and even death. The *jnoun*, who love fragrant smells, are pacified into inaction by the herbs.

When a boy is circumcised, a mother warns her neighbors of this upcoming event. Women explained that foul smells can compromise the health of small children, and children can fall ill after smelling the scent of the blood shed by a circumcised boy. Therefore, women tie bags of sweet-smelling herbs and cloves around their children's necks to protect them.

People passing through rites of passage must also be protected against the evil eye. The evil eye, a belief associated with a negative look or gaze, can be interpreted as another way of seeing.[5] People believe feelings of jealousy can motivate an intense gaze or stare. The negative energy that lurks behind the evil eye activates it and gives it harmful energy. This powerfully active and potentially destructive look can be negated by purposely wearing something to attract attention. Since the first gaze is believed to be the most harmful, the act of diverting the evil eye by wearing something strange and hideous distracts the looker and negates the evil eye's detrimental effects. Women sometimes dress boys undergoing circumcision in necklaces and anklets with pendants that feature beaded lizards, cowrie shells, silver coins, small knife pendants, small packets of protective herbs, and the tails of goats, all of which attract the first harmful gaze of the evil eye. Leather pendants decorated with five cowrie shells also protect against the evil eye, the number five symbolizing the five fingers of the human hand. Hands block the negative gaze of the evil eye.

The act of hiding something completely from sight also protects against the potentially harmful and intense stare associated with the evil eye (Westermarck 1968 [1926]: vol. 1, 423). The loom symbolizes the creative powers of women, and, as a woman weaves, her textile passes through youth, maturity, and eventually death when it is cut from the loom.[6] Just as particular forms of dress protect people passing through the life cycle, women who work wool are believed to be particularly susceptible to attacks of the evil eye and the *jnoun*, and women take precautions to protect themselves. Women weave protective motifs in their textiles that burst and blind the harmful malignant evil eye and deflect the harmful *jnoun*. For example, weavers refer to the zigzag pattern commonly found on Berber textiles as a sickle, scissors, saw, or eyebrow while they commonly refer to the diamond and triangle as representing a mirror, eye, or hand. The sickle, scissors, or saw protect because these sharp objects can pop and burst the evil eye. In addition, a mirror can deflect the negative gaze of the evil eye and the hand can block it, rendering it null and void. The *jnoun* also dislike sharp, metal pointed objects, such as knives and needles, and people may sleep with these objects under their pillows for protection.

Rural Berber women weave men's hooded gowns, first worn by young men during an important moment of the life cycle: the arrival of puberty. In the past, women commonly wove and presented their sons with their first hand-woven gown when they were around thirteen or fourteen years old, publicly marking their transition in status from boyhood to manhood and the assumption of male responsibilities. The act of wearing this heavy wool garment activates the sense of touch and demonstrates how dress involves the embodiment of gender roles. Boys had to be both literally and metaphorically strong enough to wear the heavy wool gown. Boys of this age began accompanying their fathers to market and often spent nights traveling in the open desert with the herds, where the wool gown protected them from the harsh environment. The weight of the heavy wool reminds a boy of his age and status as a young man with increased responsibilities.

For adolescent Berber girls, the act of tattooing their faces, necks, wrists, and ankles publicly marked their change in social status from girlhood to womanhood. Tattoos were associated with the flow of blood, not only because the physical process itself involved bloodshed but also because adolescent girls were tattooed sometime between the ages of eleven and fourteen, a time that generally coincided with their first menstrual cycle. Unlike the male circumcision ceremony, no ceremonies were held in conjunction with the tattoo process. Rather, women casually tattooed their nieces, cousins, and daughters. They traced the design on the skin using soot from the bottom of a cooking pot. A pointed object, sometimes a palm tree spike, knife, or needle pricked the design outlined in soot. Women placed alfalfa on the wound to give the design its desired green color. As well as publicly marking their transition from girlhood to womanhood, tattoos served as a permanent and ever-present symbol of their potential fertility. These tattooed women would soon become wives and mothers and their status increased if they gave birth to and raised numerous children.

Tattoo motifs generally varied from group to group in Morocco, allowing women to publicly and permanently express group identity through their tattoos. Women frequently stated that they replicated the tattoos of their mothers and grandmothers, evoking the Tamazight proverb *Sker mayd skern imezwura*, or "Do what the first ones did." Therefore, tattoos permanently etched into the skin communicative marks that allowed women to relay visually certain aspects of their identity without speaking a word. However, individual design variation did exist within a particular group and often designs varied from generation to generation. For example, some women's facial tattoos only included designs on their foreheads while others also tattooed their chins and noses. Also if a woman married into a group with tattoo styles different from her own, she may have inspired the younger generation to copy her, having introduced new tattoo styles into the group.

Tattoo designs consist of a series of short straight lines used to create geometric compositions. Specific names for individual tattoo motifs may have existed in the past, but Berber women I talked with typically did not have specific names for the patterns they used. Rather they compared their tattoo designs to things found in their natural environment. For example, the design in the center of the woman's chin in Figure 7.2 was called "palm tree," "snake vertebrae," and "shaft of wheat" by different women. Women notice that a particular tattoo design shares stylistic features with an object present in their contemporary surroundings, naming the motif after the object. Hence the names given to tattoo designs often vary from group to group and person to person.

More important than the meaning of individual tattoo designs was the tattoo process itself. Tattoos conveyed group membership but since individual variation did exist between tattoo styles, tattoos are more accurately viewed as gendered symbols of women's creative powers. Furthermore, the act of humanizing textiles with motifs similar to those tattooed on their own bodies equates women's physical reproductive powers with their roles as propagators of artistic tradition. Women are believed to give birth metaphorically to their artistic creations and the fact that adolescent girls are tattooed at the time of their first menstruation equates tattoos with the status given to women based on their ability to have children. Therefore, tattooing inscribed gender in a memorable fashion, transforming a natural body to a body permanently inscribed with cultural meanings.

The process of tattooing, like most forms of dress manifested during life-cycle transitions, typically stimulated more than just the sense of sight. Unlike impermanent forms of body modification, such as henna, tattoos brought physical discomfort, activating the senses in an unpleasant manner. Berber women had their foreheads, noses, chins, backs of ankles, and tops of hands tattooed. Many women told me how painful the tattooing process was, especially when their faces were tattooed. In rural areas of Morocco, tattooing did not decline until the 1970s and this decline was met with dramatic changes in Berber women's daily dress. Prior to the 1970s, Berber women living in southern Morocco performed heavy manual labor on a daily basis. The society admired physically strong women who could endure long walks in the intense sun carrying on their backs loads of wood or ceramic

Figure 7.2   Amazigh women from the Anti-Atlas region, such as the woman shown here, wore indigo-dyed wrap around their garments held at the shoulders with silver fibulae and they tattooed their chins. Photo courtesy of the National Anthropological Archives, 1930–1959. Smithsonian Institution/04066400.

jars filled with water. Berber women wore heavy silver jewelry on a daily basis while the wealthy additionally wore expensive necklaces made from large amber beads (Figure 7.1). This jewelry was worn on a daily basis as women collected heavy loads of firewood and water, ground grain by hand to make bread, and tended goats and sheep. The painful tattoo process and the heavy silver jewelry worn by married women emphasized and gave visual expression to the ideal physical qualities of vigor and stamina.

In contemporary Morocco, tattooed women are sometimes ashamed of the tattooed markings on their bodies. Most women perceive their tattoos as unfashionable, provincial, and unsophisticated. Some women swore that they never wanted tattoos and blamed their tattoo marks on aggressive childhood friends, whom they claim held them down and forcibly tattooed them. It is difficult to tell whether these women actually were tattooed against their will or whether the current stigma attached to tattoos causes them to use this story to save face. Some women actually use various chemicals to burn unwanted tattoo marks from their skin. The changing roles and increased opportunities available to women in contemporary Morocco mean a woman's status is determined increasingly by her individual achievements based on education, rather than on her ability to bear children and perform manual labor. This contributes to the decline of tattooing.

More recent understandings of Islam have also led to few women younger than thirty years old having tattoos. From the 1970s, the practice of tattooing began to decline in rural Morocco as it was deemed contrary to Islam. Tattooing is believed to be in violation of Islamic beliefs, because Islamic tradition prohibits anything that permanently changes God's perfect creation. According to the Hadith, the Prophet prohibited tattooing, cursing women who tattoo and those who get themselves tattooed.[7] Furthermore, people told me that because tattoos stop water from penetrating into the skin, they render ineffective the ritual ablutions prescribed before daily prayers.[8]

The types of dress that accompany rites of passage ceremonies not only actively engage the senses, as does tattooing, but they may also disengage or dull the senses in order to maintain a feeling of control over and protection of the body during precarious liminal phases of the life cycle. For example, during Berber wedding ceremonies in rural southern Morocco, a woman covers the bride's head and face with a red cloth, sewing the sides of the cloth shut to create a type of mask that limits the bride's sensorial contact with the outside world (Figure 7.3). The cloth severely reduces the bride's vision, although she can see faintly through the loose weave of the fabric. This covering also protects her against harmful spiritual forces, such as the evil eye and the *jnoun*.

Wedding guests also protect themselves from the wrath of the *jnoun* during the wedding. Since body orifices are also considered vulnerable points of entry for the *jnoun*, as noted by Edward Westermarck, female wedding guests chew bitter walnut root to stain their lips and gums a red color and to protect themselves from harm (1968 [1926]: vol. 2, 345). During the ceremony, a brazier filled with live embers and perfumed incense, made of musk, frankincense, and aromatic resins and plants, is passed from guest to guest. Guests purify their bodies with the thick fragrant smoke that arises after incense is dropped on live embers. Fragrant substances are protective but they are also pleasant and welcoming. For example, as seen above, women sprinkle rose water from decorative flasks on wedding guests as a gesture of hospitality.

Additional protection against the *jnoun* is provided when a charcoal brazier is placed in front of the bride. Women drop morsels of fragrant incense into the burning embers, placating the *jnoun*. The bride sits motionless and the red headdress minimizes her vision. Furthermore, she does not partake in the elaborate feast of tea, cookies, couscous, and vegetable and meat stew served to the wedding guests. However, she can smell, the thick, perfumed smoke of burning incense and hear women chanting wedding songs in her honor.

Figure 7.3   A procession of women accompanied this Berber bride (seen on a mule) to her husband's home. (Several women shown here requested anonymity, so this photograph was altered using photo retouching software, extending their head coverings to conceal their lower faces. The fashion of covering the lower face is typical of southern Morocco.) Photo by the author, 2001.

The slow, methodical wedding songs chanted by elderly women remind the bride of the seriousness of this rite of passage. Many unmarried Berber women told me that when they hear wedding songs, they immediately become uncomfortable, envisioning their own weddings with nervous anticipation. Young unmarried women, today, typically engage in their own festivities at a wedding. They gather in an area away from the elderly women who chant wedding songs in honor of the bride. Young women prefer to sing lighthearted songs, to drum quick rhythms, and to perform the latest dance moves.

The bride wears many layers of clothing, and such a cumbersome dress also stresses the importance of this rite. Women wrap a thick wool belt with long tassels around the bride's waist. The belt and its tassels slowly swing as the bride walks or participates in a wedding dance, accentuating the horizontal, rounded aspects of her body. This visually suggests the ample figures associated with women who give birth to many children. Married women are typically proud if their bodies become fleshy and stout as they age, thereby demonstrating their reproductive abilities and increasing their status in a society that honors the generative powers of the female body.

The aesthetic of movement is also important to the Berber bride and it accentuates female fertility. A married woman's individual status within her family and her community largely depends on her ability to give birth. Hence, Berber women's dress incorporates forms, symbols, and colors referring to female fertility. The bride wears silver fibulae or brooches (tise*ynas*), fastened to her white, draped garment at her shoulders. The brooches, once commonly worn by Berber women on a daily basis, have a kinetic quality and also reflect an aesthetic of movement (Figure 7.3). A large silver chain is typically attached to the bottom of each pendant, draped between the two pendants. To the chain, Berber women sometimes attach two small, round conical boxes with bulging carved lids called shiny box (*lamriat)* from which five smaller pendants dangle. When a bride walks and dances during the wedding celebration, the chain moves to the rhythm of her body and the *lamriat* swings back and forth, suggesting an analogy to women's breasts that is furthered by their shapes and placement over the chest. The five small pendants intensify the *lamriat's* kinetic energy. Movement, therefore, contributes to the aesthetic of wedding dress and also accentuates female fertility and the bride's future role as a mother.

The aesthetic of movement is also crucial to the embroidered head coverings (*tahruyt)* worn by Berber women in southern Morocco as a modesty garment outside their homes. Berber women embroider the colorful floral and geometric designs on a large panel of indigo-dyed cloth. Women appreciate the visual beauty of indigo cloth, but also enjoy its smell. Of more importance, indigo cloth temporarily stains the skin and, when it eventually washes off, women claim their skin is brighter and healthier.

After a woman embroiders elaborate motifs onto the cloth, she attaches small metallic sequins to its entire surface with short wool threads. Because the sequins are not flush with the textile, they move when a woman walks, causing the head covering to shimmer in the bright North African sunlight. By enveloping the head and body, the covering fulfills Islamic modesty requirements, but its brightly embroidered motifs and metallic sequins, paradoxically, also attract much attention.

Women embroider bright green, red, orange, yellow, blue, and purple curvilinear and zigzag lines onto the surface of the deep-blue indigo cloth to create vibrant patterns. The names given to the patterns by women include pigeon tracks, trees, flowers, blades of wheat, and coins of money: clear references to fecundity, plenty, and bounty. They carefully organize these embroidered patterns around a central band. This central band, worn horizontally across the back, forms a ground line for the embroidered designs, which appear to rise up or grow out of it. The central band divides the cloth of the head covering (*tahruyt*) into two equal halves, and women embroider the same pattern on either side of the central band using complementary colors.

Women's use of balance and symmetry in the visual composition of the *tahruyt* may also be interpreted as adding a third dimension to the motifs. One side of an embroidered image represents the front of the object and its mirror reflection the reverse side, creating a flattened representation of a three-dimensional entity. In sum, the embroidered motifs appear to create a large fertile landscape covered with vegetation, transforming women's bodies into canvases resembling the natural world and its bounty and associating the female body with fertility and reproduction. This connection between women and fertility is a conscious one supported by the fact that when a woman ages and becomes an elder in the society, her own perceived loss of sexuality and fertility is marked by wearing head coverings decorated with only minimal amounts of embroidered decoration and sequins.

Multisensory describes the aesthetics of Berber dress during rites of passage ceremonies. The sweet smell of incense and rose water, the bitter taste of walnut root, the heaviness of a woven wool gown and thick silver bracelets, the feel of cool wet henna, and the pain of receiving a tattoo all contribute to Berber dress. A multisensory analysis of dress relies on my own real-life experiences, such as the opportunity to sit in a crowd of women who have recently incensed their bodies, the chance to listen to their call-and-response songs, and the opportunity to see the slow, swinging movement of heavy silver fibulae. I experienced exhaustion and giddiness after staying up for four nights to celebrate a Berber wedding, and my understanding of the multisensory nature of Berber dress comes from having seen, heard, tasted, touched, and smelled the rich variety of Berber dress arts.

NOTES

1. My study of Berber art began in 1995 with the support of a Fulbright grant and grants from the American Institute of Maghreb Studies. In this essay I use the term Berber to refer to the indigenous peoples of North Africa, since it is the term more familiar to readers in Europe and the United States. The word Berber was given to them by outsiders and derives from the ancient Greek word *barbaros* or "barbarian." Instead Berbers refer to themselves using the name of their particular group or they use the Tamazight term Imazighen, defined as "the free people."

2. See Aida Kanafani for a similar discussion of fragrant hair oil used to style women's hair in the United Arab Emirates (1983: 44).

3. These hairstyles are rarely seen in Morocco today. For an overview of hairstyles in different regions of Morocco, see Emile Laoust (1920: 142–5), Jean Jarrot (1935: 267), A. M. M. Langel and P. Marcais (1954: 8), Mireille Morin-Barde (1990), and Edward Westermarck (1968 [1926]: vol. 2, 409).

4. Tamazight is the indigenous language of Berbers in Morocco. Addi Ouadderrou assisted in the translation from Tamazight to English.

5. Edward Westermarck includes a thorough description of the evil eye ([1926] 1968: vol. 1: 414–78). In addition, James Bynon (1984) and Clarence Maloney (1976) write about the evil eye.
6. See Irmtraud Reswick (1981: 60) for similar beliefs in Tunisia.
7. The following, from Sahih al-Bukhari, condemn tattooing: 3:242; 7:533; 7:535; 7:536 (Khan 1983).
8. Joseph Herber (1921) provides a thorough review of tattoos and their prohibition in Islam.

REFERENCES

Barnes, R. and Eicher, J. B. (eds). (1992), *Dress and Gender: Making and Meaning in Cultural Contexts*, New York: Berg.
Becker, C. (2006), *Amazigh Arts in Morocco: Women Shaping Berber Identity*, Austin: University of Texas Press.
Bynon, J. (1984), "Berber Women's Pottery: Is the Decoration Motivated?" in J. Picton (ed.), *Colloquies on Art and Archaeology in Asia No. 12*, London: University of London, pp. 136–61.
Eicher, J. (ed.). (1995), *Dress and Ethnicity: Change Across Space and Time*, Oxford: Berg.
Herber, J. (1921), "Tatouages Marocains-Tatouage et Religion," *Revue de l'Histoire des Religions* 83: 69–83.
Jarrot, J. (1935), "Coiffures d'Enfants," *Rèalisations* 1 (10): 265–8.
Kanafani, A. (1983), *Aesthetics and Ritual in the United Arab Emirates: The Anthropology of Food and Personal Adornment Among Arabian Women*, Beirut: American University of Beirut.
Kapchan, D. (1993), "Moroccan Women's Body Signs," in K. Young (ed.), *Bodylore*, Knoxville: University of Tennessee, pp. 3–34.
Khan, M. M. (1983), *The Translation of the Meanings of Sahih al-Bukhari: Arabic English*, Lahore: Kazi.
Langel, A. M. M. and Marcais, P. (1954), "Les coiffure à Tindouf," *Travaux de l'Institut de Recherches Sahariennes* 12 (2): 113–21.
Laoust, E. (1920), *Mots et Choses Berbères: Notes de Linguistique et d'Ethnographie: Dialectes du Maroc*, Paris: A. Challamel.
Légey, F. (1926), *Contes et Légendes Populaires du Maroc: Recueillis à Marrakech*, Paris: E. Leroux.
Maloney, C. (1976), *The Evil Eye*, New York: Columbia University Press.
Morin-Barde, M. (1990), *Coiffures Feminines du Maroc: au Sud du Haut Atlas*, Aix-en-Provence: Édisud.
Reswick, I. (1981), "Traditional Textiles of Tunisia," *African Arts* 14 (3): 56–65.
Roach, M. E. and Eicher, J. B. (1973), *The Visible Self: Perspectives on Dress*. Englewood Cliffs: Prentice-Hall.
Westermarck, E. (1968 [1926]), *Ritual and Belief in Morocco*, New York: University Books, 2 vols.

8 THE POWER OF TOUCH: WOMEN'S WAIST BEADS IN GHANA

Suzanne Gott

For the Asante, a matrilineal people of southern Ghana, the most fundamental form of female dress consists of the strands of beads women use to adorn that area known as *asen*, an Asante term referring to the hips and pelvic area (Christaller 1933: 441). The one to six strands of beads rest loosely upon women's hips. Called *tomoma*, an Asante word whose English equivalent "waist beads," is a euphemistically imprecise way of referring to this adornment for the most sexually charged, private part of the female body (ibid.: 526). Conventionally concealed from view, waist beads hide beneath the layers of cloth worn for women's customary clothing styles. In the past, if a man other than a husband touched this part of a woman's body or the bead strands hidden there he could be charged with adultery (McLeod 1981: 144).

In present-day Asante, younger and more formally educated women generally refrain from wearing waist beads on a regular basis in large part because they consider waist beads inappropriate for the dresses they now wear for much of their daily routine. While *tomoma* will remain modestly concealed beneath women's customary two-piece wrapped ensemble or *kaba* (syncretic ensemble combining the two-piece wrapped style with a European-inspired sewn blouse), waist beads become clearly visible when worn with Western-style clothing. In addition to the immodesty of such visibility, to wear waist beads with a dress shows a lack of fashion sense.

Yet, despite such concerns of propriety and stylishness, the wearing of waist beads with dresses did become a popular fashion in the Asante capital city of Kumasi during the late 1980s. One Kumasi friend reported that it became popular at this time for women to wear large, oversized waist beads in order to make the bead strands more clearly visible beneath their dresses. During this period, women wearing waist beads under a dress often affected a gait that caused their waist beads to click together, producing a distinctive sound audible to those nearby. Within Asante culture, such auditory as well as visual suggestions of a woman's waist beads are considered especially enticing to men.

By virtue of such associations, *tomoma* are a mode of female dress and ornamentation specifically directed toward sensuality and the sensation arousal. Today, white-collar professionals and college students who no longer wear these beads on a daily basis still buy waist beads to wear when going to bed with husbands or boyfriends. During a lively discussion among women friends, one woman proclaimed the benefits of wearing waist beads by stating, with characteristic Ghanaian wit, "when I put them on, my husband counts them like a rosary!" In a similar vein, "high-tension wire" became a popular name for waist beads in the late 1990s.

Yet, over and above such explicitly sexual associations, the sensual and affective qualities the Asante associate with women's waist beads find expression in a more profound and spiritual manner. According to customary beliefs of the Asante and other Akan peoples of southern Ghana, there are certain "precious" beads of supernatural origin that have the capacity to enhance female fertility through the power of touch, especially when worn as waist beads. And, to a certain extent, this belief in waist beads' fertility-enhancing powers extends to include those waist beads of imported or locally manufactured glass and plastic beads that most Asante and Akan women wear, on either a regular or periodic basis, throughout the course of their lives (Figure 8.1).

WOMEN'S WAIST BEADS AND THE MIRACULOUS POWER OF TOUCH

Within the Ashanti region, it has been a long-established practice for mothers to adorn infant daughters with strands of beads tied loosely around their hips, wrists, ankles, and above their calves and forearms in the belief that this will aid in the development of a

Figure 8.1 Waist beads, women's cloth, toiletries, and cosmetics displayed in an open-air stall at Kumasi's Central Market. Kumasi, Ghana, June 1990, photo by the author.

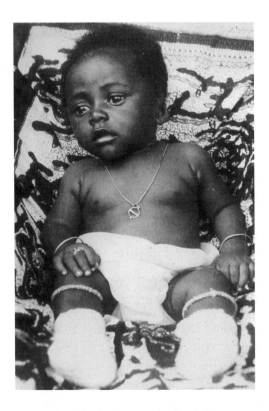

Figure 8.2 Album photograph of an infant adorned with bead strands above the calves. Kumasi, Ghana, 1970s, photographer unknown.

full, beautifully shaped body (Figure 8.2).[1] Following the initial months of infancy, this adornment is generally reduced to one or more strands of waist beads, miniature versions of those worn by the mothers. One older Asante woman explained the reasoning behind this practice: "If you put on beads, they will make you 'heavy' so that your buttocks are made beautiful" (interview, Kumasi, September 1990) – referring to waist beads' capacity to "grow curves" through physical contact, or the power of touch, in order to enhance female fertility, sexuality, and childbearing.

Asante scholar, Bishop Peter Sarpong, documented and analyzed the significance of the presentation, wearing, and display of waist beads during the coming-of-age "nubility" rites once held for virtually all Asante girls after reaching puberty and a marriageable age. On this occasion, the initiate's family or future husband presented her with special gifts of *tomoma* and the silky women's loincloth customarily held in place by the waist beads, as a means of marking her entrance into female maturity and sexual life (1977: 18–19). During the public procession marking the conclusion of these nubility rites, the beautifully attired initiate would be preceded by a little girl wearing only a loincloth and several strands of precious waist beads considered to possess supernatural, fertility-enhancing powers. Sarpong observes that the "preciousness," or extraordinary value, of these special beads: "lies not so much in their beauty – many are hideous to look at – as in their antiquity and their supposed potency for self-reproduction, under certain conditions. Only a few women possess them and they guard them as they would no other possession" (ibid.: 46).

The precious waist beads worn by the little girl serve to display, by proxy, the waist beads worn by the initiate underneath her clothing (ibid.: 45–6). By their proximity, these special waist beads might also exercise their reproductive powers to ensure the initiate's fertility as she enters into Asante womanhood. This ritual display of precious waist beads also symbolically expresses the linkage between human reproductive powers and the fertile subterranean realm of maternal earth deity Asase Yaa, which is the source for precious beads with their fertility-enhancing powers. This linkage, Sarpong notes is not simply based on Asase Yaa as a "symbol of fecundity," for the Asante earth goddess "is the fertile woman *par excellence*" (1974: 18).

THE POWERS OF PRECIOUS BEADS FROM THE EARTH'S FERTILE REALM

According to Asante and Akan customary beliefs, precious beads such as those displayed during Asante girls' nubility rites originate within earth deity Asase Yaa's fertile realm. These precious "ground beads" dwell deep beneath the forest floor, often in close association with the nugget gold that may be found throughout the gold-rich Akan regions. The Asante and Akan consider the special ground beads, along with native gold, to be living supernatural forces that possess powers which may be employed in various dimensions of customary belief and religious practice.[2]

Early European accounts of life on West Africa's lower Guinea Coast, or Gold Coast (modern Ghana), observed the significance of beads and gold to local peoples not merely as objects of adornment, but as spiritual entities that might be worn upon the body. Writing in 1602, Dutch trader Pieter de Marees documented the manner in which local peoples adorned themselves with special beads and golden ornaments, a practice he astutely observed had much deeper significance than simple ornamentation. Such adornment also provided individuals with an important, widely used means of personal protection.

Gold Coast men, de Marees found, generally wore "a string of polished Venetian Beads mixed with golden beads and other gold ornaments around their knees, in nearly the same way as young ladies in our Lands wear their Rosaries around their hands" (1987 [1602]: 34). Men preparing for battle would "take their Rosaries, with which they make their *Fetisso* [Portuguese term for such power objects], and hang them around their bodies: they think that if they wear them, their *Fetissos* will protect them and that they will not be slain" (ibid.: 89).[3] Gold Coast women would "hang around their Belts many little straw-wisps on which they string beans and Venetian beads, regarding these also as their *Fetissos* or *Sainctos*" (ibid.: 39). Before an individual would eat or drink, he or she would "first give [their *fetissos*] something to eat and drink" (ibid.: 34).[4]

The wearing of protective beads and gold, a practice begun at birth, also extended into the afterlife. In 1704, Willem Bosman, chief Dutch factor at Elmina, observed that prior to burial the deceased would be dressed as richly as possible with fine cloths, gold *"fetiches,"* highly prized "Corals" (i.e., beads), *Conte di Terra* (a special "native" or, perhaps, even "earth" bead), and "other valuable Things … for his [or her] use in the other Life" (1967 [1704]: 230). He bemoaned the adoption of such "superstitions" by certain European traders who had come to the region: "[W]hat is most deplorable and detestable, is, that here are even some *Europeans*, who not only think favourably of, and believe this Idolatrous Worship effectual, but instigate their Servants to it; and are likewise grown very fond of wearing some Trifles about their Bodies, which are consecrated or conjured by the Priest" (ibid.: 224).

For the European authors and readers of such early travel accounts, an African people's apparent failure "to distinguish between personal religious objects and aesthetic ornaments" was considered to be convincing proof of the superstitious irrationality of the African mind (Pietz 1988: 110). Field research by British anthropologist Robert S. Rattray in the 1920s offered a more sophisticated understanding of Asante and Akan conceptions of the supernatural. Of particular interest are Rattray's investigations into the Asante pairing of adornment and supernatural power in the form of the personal power objects called *asuman* (singular *suman*), which are believed to be "the potential dwelling place of a spirit or spirits of an inferior status" to the supreme creator and other Asante deities (1927: 23).

Malcolm McLeod describes *asuman* as "conglomerations or conjunctions of materials believed to be powerful" that may be worn around arms or legs, hung about the neck, or attached to clothing (1981: 57). The resident powers of *asuman* must initially be activated with offerings and must continue to be ritually fed on subsequent occasions. These personal power objects generally consist of some combination of plant or animal parts, precious beads, and/or native gold, and leather or metal amulets of Muslim origin that contain magical Islamic script (Rattray 1927: 12–22).[5]

The source for these power materials, except for Islamic ones, like much of the knowledge and powers of Akan ritual specialists, is the forest wilderness. For many African peoples, the wilderness (or "bush"), those areas outside the boundaries of human society, is a region of great supernatural power (McLeod 1981: 62; Rattray 1927: 22–3).[6] The wilderness, the source for power materials from plants and animals, is the place of origin for supernaturally viable ground beads and native gold, which may reveal themselves miraculously, making their special powers accessible to those fortunate enough to find them.

In the early nineteenth century, Bowdich recorded Asante accounts of precious beads from the earth that possessed reproductive powers enabling them to "not only grow but breed," which revealed their presence by a spiral vapor issuing from the ground (1966 [1819]: 266–8). Late nineteenth-century accounts from the coastal Akan told of travelers to "the far interior," passing through the wilderness at night, who might see "a tongue of flame rise out of the ground," signaling the presence of one or more spiritually powerful beads (Freeman 1967 [1898]: 403–5).

Twentieth-century accounts by Fante elders, a coastal Akan people, describe how a dog or hen covered with gold dust may emerge from the ground, soon to be followed by gold and precious beads miraculously rising to the earth's surface, an event signaling that one is "in the presence of a god." A courageous person can strike the golden animal with a stick to make some of the gold dust fall to the ground and then entreat the deity for permission to collect the precious beads and gold. After the recipient arrives home with these gifts, the deity must be thanked by sacrificing a sheep and sprinkling its blood over the beads and gold (Fynn 1974: 40, 65). Another account describes how a palm wine brewer who had entered the forest found a hen vomiting gold dust under one of his palm trees. After the hen vanished, a spiral vapor began to issue from the spot, followed by hundreds of precious beads (Sackey 1985: 183–4).[7]

For the Asante, the most precious and reproductively powerful ground beads are those known as *abodom*, or *bodom bodom*. The powers for self-reproduction attributed to *bodom* beads find expression in the proverbial saying that "One *bodom* bead, in time, becomes two." The Asante Ekoona clan traces its matriclan's mythical origins to one particularly powerful *bodom* bead. Nana Akua Pokuaa, retired queen mother of Amoman and an elder of the Ekoona clan, proclaimed this supernatural kinship in her greeting to my research assistant, who introduced himself as a fellow clansman: "Ei, child of the Ekoona clan, child of the Bodommowua Bead. Greetings, Bodom, Bodom, Bodom! Greetings to the Bead!" (Interview, Kumasi, July 1999).

In our conversation, Ekoona clan elder Nana Pokuaa recalled an earlier time when the superior supernatural powers of *bodom* beads were more widely recognized, even within the gold-rich Asante and Akan regions:

> As for us, in the olden days, everyone who knew the importance of beads knew that beads had a greater name than nugget gold. As for beads, we do not joke with them. We do not trivialize them. Ei, as for the Bead, Ahwennee Nana [Great Ancestral Bead], if we speak of Ahwennee Nana, people are startled and fearful. It is because it is a traditional thing, and it comes from the ground.[8]

"*Bodom*," Nana Pokuaa continued, "it is '*komfo*'," a priest or priestess (*okomfo*) whose body becomes possessed by a deity, manifesting that deity's powers. "So as for *bodom*," she concluded, "it is a bead that has a greater name than gold, except to one who does not know" (interview, Kumasi, July 1999).[9]

The generative potency attributed to the precious beads from Asase Yaa's underground realm finds its most powerful and dramatic expression in the Bodommowua Bead as mythical ancestress of the Asante Ekoona clan. Belief in the miraculous life-giving powers of maternal earth deity Asase Yaa and the reproductive potential of those precious beads from this fertile realm finds continued expression in customary practices based on waist beads' fertility-enhancing potential and in the contemporary popularity of waist beads within southern Ghana's predominately Christian population.

WAIST BEADS AND CONCEALED POWER

I contend the *hidden* nature of Asase Yaa's subterranean realm served conceptually to intensify the supernatural potency and reproductive powers associated with precious ground beads in Akan customary beliefs – a concealment and intensification of fertility-enhancing power replicated by the wearing of waist beads beneath the layered cloth of women's customary clothing styles.[10] For the Asante and Akan, as for numerous peoples throughout the world, often supernatural potency is conceptually linked to the dynamic of concealment. Thomas McCaskie, in analyzing those Asante personal power objects known as *asuman*, directs our attention to the related Asante verb *suma*, which Johann Christaller's dictionary of the Akan language defines as meaning "to hide, or be hidden" (1995: 312; Christaller 1933: 483). In further study of Christaller, I found the related term *asuman-sem* ("*asuman* matters"), which refers to sorcery, witchcraft, magic, or enchantment (ibid.: 483) – a semantic association that, in a manner similar to the English "occult" from the Latin *occulere* (to conceal), serves to reveal the negative as well as positive dimensions of concealed power. Akan women's concealed waist beads are similarly considered to have both beneficial and destructive potential.

The supernatural powers of precious beads and native gold, although primarily used for beneficial and protective purposes, may also be employed for malevolent witchcraft. Among the matrilineal Akan, individuals are only vulnerable to the destructive powers of witchcraft practiced by members of their own matrikin. The majority of witches are believed to be women, with elderly women particularly suspect (McLeod 1975: 111–12; Rattray 1927: 28–30). Because of these beliefs, elderly female relatives who spend "too much time" with the family's young children may be regarded with suspicion. The "spirit of witchcraft," it is believed, can be concealed in precious things, with witchcraft being transferred "through beads or any precious thing such as gold" (interview, Legon, June 1999). A stereotypical scenario for the surreptitious transfer of witchcraft from a witch-grandmother to her unsuspecting granddaughter is through gifts of "astral familiars in the form of gold earrings, bracelets, or waist-beads" that, when worn, will transform the child into a witch by the power of their touch (Bannerman-Richter 1982: 36–7).

A recurring theme in Akan witchcraft beliefs associates malevolent witchcraft and women's waist beads. In the early 1920s, Asante priest and witch-finder Bonsam 'Komfo Yao Aduwua told Rattray that witches desiring to kill someone always tried "to obtain some object that belonged to the person, ... such as hair, nail-cuttings, or waist beads" (1927: 30). A witch's own waist beads, he observed, might in fact be "a waist-belt of snakes," a belief echoed by Gabriel Bannerman-Richter's intriguing 1980s narrative in which self-confessed witch Ama Ninsin describes a yellow cobra that she "used to keep for its sheer beauty ... I brought it with me to the physical world coiled around my waist. In the physical world I changed it into waist beads... My snake and I were inseparable" (1984: 34).

The popular attribution of waist beads as repositories for witches' powers conceptually relates to the hidden and sexually charged nature of such adornment. A woman's hips and pelvic area (*asen* or waist) and the beads worn there fundamentally link to female fertility and reproduction. The primary features of malevolent Asante witchcraft, McLeod observes, are the desire for *mogya* ("blood"), the killing of women and children, and attacks on human reproduction by "causing miscarriages, abortions, and both male and female sterility" (1975: 111).

Malevolent witchcraft is an inversion and violation of a society's most fundamental relationships and values. For the matrilineal Asante and Akan, destructive witchcraft directed against members of one's own matrikin, who are bound together by *mogya* (the "blood" of kinship transmitted from woman to child), strikes at the very heart of social relations (ibid.: 111–12). Female witches' attacks upon their own and others' fertility violates the most fundamental ideals of Akan womanhood, and the transformation of waist beads into forces for this destructive power perverts the fertility-enhancing nature of waist beads, which are considered to be imbued with the life-giving powers of earth deity Asase Yaa.

WAIST BEADS AND AKAN IDEALS OF WOMANHOOD

For the Asante and other Akan peoples of southern Ghana, women's waist beads – long associated with supernatural forces of fertility and maternity – remain the most fundamental and symbolically powerful form of female dress. Within present-day Asante, older, less formally educated women are generally most conscious of beads' spiritual dimensions and continue wearing waist beads on a daily basis. One elderly Asante woman, explaining her reasons for continuing to wear waist beads long past her reproductive years, emphasized a linkage between waist beads and womanhood that extended into the afterlife:

> It is our custom. If you die and are about to be bathed, these are the first things they would ask for... So the waist beads are always useful to us... I have plenty of these. When I die, they will add them to those [I am wearing]... For each woman who dies, people will call for her waist beads.

"Waist beads," she continued, "are women's property" – the most fundamental means of distinguishing women from men. "When you find a skeleton," she rhetorically queried, "how do you know which is the man and which is the woman? By the beads!" (Interview, Nkukua-Buoho, October 1990).

For this reason, gifts of *tomoma*, or waist beads, and the silky loincloth once worn with women's waist beads, continue to be presented at funerary rites for an Asante woman as a farewell gift to accompany the deceased on her departure into the afterlife and ancestral realm (Figure 8.3). According to Akan customary beliefs, an ancestress guards the entrance to the ancestral world to ensure that all women who enter are wearing waist beads (Brempong 1986: 54). Yet for Christians, as well as those of indigenous belief, dressing a woman's corpse in waist beads and silky loincloth is a powerful symbolic act signifying that the deceased fulfilled the Asante and Akan ideals of marrying and, even more importantly, of "bringing forth children" to ensure the future of the matrilineage. Women from the husband's

Figure 8.3   A customary farewell gift of *tɔmma* and *amoase*
(waist beads and silky loincloth) at an elderly Asante
women's funeral. Kumasi, Ghana, 1990, photo by the author.

matrilineage present farewell gifts of waist beads and silky loincloth reminiscent of the first marriage gifts from a husband to his new bride. Daughters-in-law of those women who bore sons also present waist beads and silky loincloth for use by the deceased in the afterlife. According to my late friend and teacher, Mrs. Mary Owusu-Ansah:

> When a woman goes to sleep in her husband's house, she has to dress fine with nice beads and nice [silky loincloth] … so for that night, the night she conceived, the beads she was wearing must be replaced by the woman who has married the son. So when she meets the husband there, she can put them on. (personal communication, Kumasi, September 1990)

In the words of Auntie Mary, dressing a woman's corpse in waist beads and silky loincloth signifies the deceased had been a "respectable, responsible woman" – a wife and a mother. Yet, even a woman who remained barren receives funerary gifts of waist beads and silky loincloth to signify that although not a mother in the biological sense, the deceased succeeded in achieving "motherliness," the most highly esteemed quality of Asante womanhood, by assisting in the care and welfare of the children of her matrilineage.

CONCLUSION

The Asante and Akan peoples of southern Ghana invest women's waist beads, or *tomoma*, with evocative dimensions that far transcend conventional understandings of ornamentation. According to customary belief, certain "precious" beads are both living and life-giving forces with a generative potency that can be enlisted in the enhancement of female fertility and sexuality. These precious beads reside underneath the forest floor, often in the company of supernaturally viable native gold, within the home of maternal earth deity Asase Yaa, a sacred, hidden realm of fertility and generative power.

To a certain degree, the reproductive powers attributed to these precious "ground beads" extend to the beads of known local or foreign manufacture that women customarily use to adorn their hips and the bodies of female children. These beads are believed to exercise special powers by means of the sensation of touch in promoting the development of the full, well-shaped buttocks and thighs that the Asante and Akan equate with fertility and sexual attractiveness.

The most illuminating means of understanding such adornment is in terms of power rather than beauty, and by an aesthetic sensibility based in sensory perception and affect. The affective impact of these beads is not based in the formal excellence often associated with works of art; instead their sensory and aesthetic power is generated by the extramortal energies believed to reside within such beads. Women's concealment of waist beads beneath layers of clothing has parallels to the hidden nature of the reproductively empowered beads of Asase Yaa's subterranean realm. Such concealment may thus serve as a means of amplifying the sensual power and generative associations of the beads women use to adorn this most private region of the female body.

NOTES

1. Some women report that beads may be placed on infant boys because they, too, "need shape" to be attractive. But if so, these beads are removed after a few weeks while, until recent years, female children continued wearing waist beads through puberty and for the rest of their adult lives.
2. Neighboring peoples also have customary beliefs in beads possessing special powers. The Ewe peoples of Togo and southeastern Ghana believe such beads appear as excrement deposited by the rainbow-serpent deity Dan Anydohoédo as he rises from under the earth to plunge into sacred waters – a supernatural origin similar to the bead-wealth excrement of Òsùmàrè, primordial rainbow serpent of the Yorùbà peoples of southwestern Nigeria and southern Benin (Euba 1981–2: 112; Nourisson 1992: 31–2). For the Krobo of southeastern Ghana, beads and stone celts with special curative powers are produced by the sky deity's lightning striking the earth (Huber 1963: 104–5).
3. For an in-depth analysis of the European terms, *fetisso* or *fitiso*, in early written accounts, see William Pietz (1988).
4. David Howes' investigation of sensual dimensions of the *kula* exchange of Papua New Guinea's Massim region examines the sentience and sensory powers of objects of exchange, especially *kula* shells, which are considered to possess "the capacity to smell, to hear, and to see" (2003: 112–13).

5. The incorporation of Islamic amulets, following their fifteenth-century introduction into northern Ghana by Mande-Dyula and Hausa traders, no doubt was due in part to the fact that these amulets offered spiritual protection in a manner similar to the Asantes' own *asuman* (see Owusu-Ansah 1991).

6. For an in-depth examination of the powers of wilderness in African systems of thought, see Martha Anderson and Christine Kreamer (1989).

7. In the past, precious beads and locally mined gold were stored in open or lidded vessels cast from brass or other cuprous metals (Rattray 1969 [1923]: 313–15; Silverman 1983: 18–23). The supernatural power associated with copper-based metals in many African regions as well as those spiritual forces associated with the transformative casting process suggest not only a functional but also a spiritual dimension to the vessels that accounts for the frequency of their ritual use (Cole and Ross 1977: 67; Herbert 1984: 258–60, 299–301). The corroded condition of many older vessels attests to a widespread practice of burying these containers, either to accompany a deceased family member into the afterlife or as a means of safeguarding family treasures from theft or loss during times of war (Silverman 1983: 20–22). Legendary accounts of the miraculous recovery of precious beads and gold from beneath the forest floor undoubtedly have some relationship to this practice and the occasional discovery of a long-lost vessel.

8. Translation by Dr. Kofi Agyekum, Department of Linguistics, University of Ghana, Legon.

9. The praise name, "bodommowua," that Nana Pokuaa used in referring to the Ekoona clan's ancestral *bodom* bead is an honorific version of *bodom* enhanced by the apparent addition of the word *wuu*, meaning "copious" or "abundant" (Christaller 1933: 578). This praise name emphasizes this special bead's miraculous, as well as maternal reproductive, powers. The ending of Bodomowua ("abundant" or "copious" *bodom* bead) with the letter *a* reflects the common Asante practice of ending female names with an *a* (Christaller 1933: 19, 578, 598, 602). Another praise name for the Ekoona clan's bead ancestress is "Berewua" (Agyeman-Duah 1976), which appears to combine *aberewa* (old woman) with *wuu* (copious, abundant) – an honorific suggesting a conceptual linkage between the clan's reproductively empowered bead ancestress and Asante earth deity, whose full name, Asase Yaa, Aberewa (Yaa [Friday born], Old Mother Earth), may also be augmented with the praise name, "Asase Bo ne Nsie" (Earth, Creator of the Underworld) (Rattray 1969 [1923]: 215).

10. In contrast, Nicholas Saunders' analysis of brilliance in Amerindian metaphysics reveals the ways in which cosmic energies and shamanic powers are made manifest by the wearing and display of shiny, glittering objects (1998).

REFERENCES

Agyeman-Duah, J. (1976), "Amakom Stool History," IAS acc. no. AS 77, recorded on June 15, 1963, *Ashanti Stool Histories, Volume I (IAS acc. nos. 1–110)*, Institute of African Studies, University of Ghana, Legon, October 1976.

Anderson, M. G. and Kreamer, C. M. (1989), *Wild Spirits, Strong Medicine: African Art and the Wilderness*, New York: Center for African Art.

Bannerman-Richter, G. (1982), *The Practice of Witchcraft in Ghana*, Elk Grove, CA: Gabari Publishing.

Bannerman-Richter, G. (1984), *Don't Cry! My Baby, Don't Cry!: Autobiography of an African Witch*, Elk Grove, CA: Gabari Books.

Bosman, William [Willem]. (1967 [1704]), *A New and Accurate Description of the Coast of Guinea, Divided into the Gold, the Slave, and the Ivory Coasts*, A New Edition, With an Introduction by J. R. Willis and Notes by J. D. Fage and R. E. Bradbury, London: Frank Cass & Co.

Bowdich, T. E. (1966 [1819]), *Mission from Cape Coast Castle to Ashantee*, Third edition, Edited with Notes and an Introduction by W. E. F. Ward, London: Frank Cass & Co.

Brempong, O. (1986), "Akan Highlife in Ghana: Songs of Cultural Transition," Doctoral dissertation, Indiana University, Bloomington.

Christaller, J. G. (1933), *Dictionary of the Asante and Fante Language called Tshi (Twi)*, Second edition, revised and enlarged, Basel: Basel Evangelical Missionary Society.

Cole, H. M. and Ross, D. H. (1977), *The Arts of Ghana*, Los Angeles: Museum of Cultural History, University of California.

Euba, O. (1981–2), "Of Blue Beads and Red: The Role of Ife in the West African Trade in Kori Beads," *Journal of the Historical Society of Nigeria* 11 (1–2): 109–27.

Freeman, R. A. (1967 [1898]), *Travels and Life in Ashanti and Jaman*, London: Frank Cass & Co.

Fynn, J. K. (1974), *Oral Traditions of the Fante States: No. 4 Edina (Elmina)*, Institute of African Studies, Legon: University of Ghana.

Herbert, E. W. (1984), *Red Gold: Copper in Precolonial History and Culture*, Madison: University of Wisconsin Press.

Howes, D. (2003), *Sensual Relations: Engaging the Senses in Culture and Social Theory*, Ann Arbor: University of Michigan Press.

Huber, H. (1963), *The Krobo: Traditional Social, and Religious Life of a West African People*, Studia Inst. Anthropos 16, Bonn: St. Augustin.

Marees, P. de (1987 [1602]), *Description and Historical Account of the Gold Kingdom of Guinea*, translated from the Dutch and edited by A. van Dantzig and A. Jones, The British Academy, London: Oxford University Press.

McCaskie, T. C. (1995), *State and Society in Pre-Colonial Asante*, Cambridge: Cambridge University Press.

McLeod, M. D. (1975), "On the Spread of Anti-Witchcraft Cults in Modern Asante," in J. Goody (ed.), *Changing Social Structure in Ghana: Essays in the Comparative Sociology of a New State and an Old Tradition*, London: International African Institute.

McLeod, M. D. (1981), *The Asante*, London: British Museum Publications.

Nourisson, P. (1992), "Beads in the Lives of the Peoples of Southern Togo, West Africa," *Beads: Journal of the Society of Bead Researchers* 4: 29–38.

Owusu-Ansah, D. (1991), *Islamic Talismanic Tradition in Nineteenth-Century Asante*, Africa Studies, Vol. 21, Lewiston, NY: Edwin Mellen Press.

Pietz, W. (1988), "The Problem of the Fetish, IIIa: Bosman's Guinea and the Enlightenment Theory of Fetishism," *RES: Anthropology and Aesthetics* 16 (Autumn): 105–23.

Rattray, R. S. (1927), *Religion and Art in Ashanti*, London: Oxford University Press.

Rattray, R. S. (1969 [1923]), *Ashanti*, Oxford: Clarendon Press.

Sackey, B. (1985), "The Significance of Beads in the Rites of Passage Among Some Southern Ghanaian Peoples," *Institute of African Studies Research Review (N.S.)* 1 (2): 180–91.

Sarpong, (Rev.) P. (1974), *Ghana in Retrospect: Some Aspects of Ghanaian Culture*, Tema: Ghana Publishing Corporation.

Sarpong, (Rev.) P. (1977), *Girls' Nubility Rites in Ashanti*, Tema: Ghana Publishing Corporation.

Saunders, N. J. (1998), "Stealers of Light, Traders in Brilliance," *RES: Anthropology and Aesthetics* 33 (Spring): 225–52.

Silverman, R. A. (1983), "Akan Kuduo: Form and Function," in D. H. Ross and T. F. Garrard (eds), *Akan Transformations: Problems in Ghanaian Art History*, UCLA Museum of Cultural History Monograph Series 21, pp. 10–29.

9 INDIAN MADRAS PLAIDS AS REAL INDIA

Sandra Lee Evenson

Many people recognize the expression: "If it walks like a duck and quacks like a duck, it is probably a duck." The expression summarizes the logic behind identifying an object based on its characteristics. For the Kalabari, the cloth called *injiri*, or Real India, was just such a duck. By thirteen characteristics, the knowledgeable Kalabari consumer distinguished the authentic from the ersatz.

The term Real India defines a type of Indian madras. It is a yarn-dyed, plain weave, cotton, checked or plaid fabric hand woven in South India, almost all production is exclusively for export. Real India has been known by several other names over the last 400 years, from Guinea Stuffs and Callowaypoose to Real Madras Handkerchief (Evenson 1994). As a term specific to the Kalabari, *injiri* is the most accurate; it may be a reference to the seventeenth-century weaving village of Injerum, located near present-day sites of Real India production. For the purposes of this study, the term Real India best captures the Kalabari measure of authenticity. This study traces the trade history of Real India to determine at what points in its history its characteristic features entered the Kalabari aesthetic.[1]

The Kalabari live and work on the Niger Delta of southern Nigeria. Their location on the Niger Delta historically favored an economy based on fishing and the trade of local produce and textiles (Alagoa 1970). When European trading companies landed in West Africa in the sixteenth century, the Kalabari began to have access to cloth from as far away as England and India. Through trade with the Europeans, the Kalabari accumulated wealth in the forms of cloth, guns, and slaves. All three items secured their position as one of the most powerful trade groups in the Niger Delta. Of all the trade cloths that passed through Kalabari hands, fabric from India came to have the greatest material and social significance, specifically what would be called *injiri* or Real India (Eicher 1988).

The Kalabari love of cloth expresses itself within a critical constraint. The primary Kalabari deity is a goddess known as Owame-kaso. She introduced trade to the first Kalabari and taught the Kalabari trading skills useful with Europeans (Horton 1962). Owame-kaso strictly prohibited the Kalabari from using specific trade cloths that Manuella Petgrave identifies as cloth printed with vines, flowers, or leaves (1992). Thus, the Kalabari had a cultural predisposition for selecting checkered and plaid cloth.

From an economic perspective, the amassing of large quantities of this exotic and unique textile became, in part, the most telling indication of the Kalabari trader's prowess. He demonstrated his success to the community when his family and the members of his compound displayed cloth wealth in the form of daily dress. Kalabari traders who introduced Real India with unique and aesthetically satisfying patterns named the cloth after their family. When worn by members of the same household, Real India visually communicated

Figure 9.1 "Chief Jim Jack with wife and the two daughters" from a Kalabari Historical Album. Note the wrappers, or lower garments, of all four family members are of the same Indian madras pattern. Family power and influence were expressed when all members of a compound wore the same pattern. Photograph courtesy of Joanne B. Eicher.

wealth and community influence. As Kalabari participation in the slave trade expanded, Real India became a local currency and identified the Kalabari as an economic force in the Niger Delta. When Kalabari power waned in the late nineteenth century and the "scramble for Africa" placed most black Africans under white European colonial rule, Real India channeled the might and wisdom of the ancestors and river deities back to the colonized Kalabari. In the late twentieth century, Real India used as dress and as display powerfully expressed Kalabari ethnic identity within the larger independent state of Nigeria. Thus, over time, the cultural authentication of these Indian trade cloths into both ritual and daily life demonstrates "the capacity of cloth to encode kinship and political histories…" (Schneider & Weiner 1986: 179).

TERMINOLOGY

The history of the Indian textile trade is well documented (Chaudhuri 1978; Irwin 1955, 1956; Irwin & Schwartz 1966). Many secondary sources contain glossaries of textile trade terms, which I used to compile a glossary of synonyms for Real India over time. From this Real India glossary, I identified the following terms that could be traced, one to another, through time, to Real India:

"Guinea Stuffs" describes several different cotton fabrics, usually striped or checkered, that capitalized the West African slave trade from the seventeenth to nineteenth centuries as both currency and dress. While early references to Guinea Stuffs describe them as cheap, their quality ranged from coarse to fine. Callowaypoose, Nicanees, and Populees exemplify better quality varieties of Guinea Stuffs.

"*Rumal*," translated from the Persian word for face towel or handkerchief, describes a one-yard-square format with borders and a central field filled with printed, woven, or embroidered motifs. Jasleen Dhamija (1994) reports that a *rumal*, when folded into a triangle, was used by Muslim men to cleanse the hands and face before prayer.

"Madras Handkerchiefs" and "Ventapollam Handkerchiefs" originated as a blend of the checked weave of Guinea Stuffs and the bordered format of *rumals*.

"Real Madras Handkerchief," called RMHK in the export trade, contrasts with imitation Madras Handkerchiefs woven on power looms in Europe.

Many secondary sources assumed Guinea Stuffs were synonymous with Real Madras Handkerchief or Real India. An examination of the primary and secondary sources confirms this hypothesis; but it would be more accurate to state that Guinea Stuffs appear to be the antecedent form of Real India.

CHARACTERISTICS OF REAL INDIA

Between the seventeenth and twentieth centuries, a wide variety of brightly colored cotton fabrics were shipped from India to West Africa. Analysis of findings synthesized from earlier research, including both library research and interviews, reveals thirteen characteristics of Real India that differentiated it from other Indian trade cottons.

1. Colors: primarily indigo blue, madder or Turkish red, and off-white, with some yellows, browns, greens, and violets.
2. Dyes: natural dyes, including indigo, until the 1960s when synthetic dyes replaced most natural dyes in an effort to standardize colors and reduce costs; however, indigo use continued.
3. Fiber content: 100 percent cotton.
4. Fabric width: consistently described as one yard wide.
5. Fabric length: three, eight-yard lengths, or twenty-four yards, dates from the late 1920s; sixteen-yard warps were the norm prior to this time (Amalsad 1926).
6. Unique odor: indigo and natural dyes produced a unique odor and taste, contributing one layer of scent to Real India. In addition, the warp yarn was sized with rice starch to ease its handling during weaving (Brunnschweiler 1957) (Figure 9.2). One source noted that the sweat of the weaver as he bent over his loom in the humidity of South India contributed to the unique odor (Fröhlich 1981). An RMHK exporter in Madras added that household cooking odors contributed to the scent of the cloth, because the pit looms used to weave Real India were located in weaver's homes.
7. Yarn-dyed checkered or plaid motif: primary documents described checkered using two colors (e.g., indigo blue and off-white) or plaid using three or more colors (e.g., indigo blue, off-white, and Turkish red). Authors did not specify the number of colors or how complex the color palette. Most primary sources used the term "check" or "checkered," regardless of the number of colors used. The term "plaid" has changed in meaning since the seventeenth century from its original definition as the large shawl or wrap that predated the kilt as Scottish ethnic dress. Visual images of Kalabari men and women wearing examples of Real India dating from at least the mid-nineteenth century establish the fact that both checkered and plaid motifs were in use (Figure 9.1).
8. 36-inch-square repeat: the pattern was not a simple balanced check like modern gingham. Patterns may have used only two colors, but were complex and visually distinctive, accounting in part for the naming of Kalabari cloths.
9. *Rumal* format: some Real India lengths exhibited only a 36-inch repeat, but most featured yarn-dyed checkered or plaid borders enclosing a central field. Eight *rumals* equaled one piece, three, eight-yard pieces per warp.
10. Yarn count: two-color or three-color Real India is the foundation fabric for *pelete bite. Pelete bite* is a Kalabari textile art in which the light and bright threads are cut and subtracted from the whole cloth (Eicher, Erekosima, & Liedholm 1982). Yarn size and thread count must be sufficient so that threads can be removed without compromising the integrity of the final *pelete bite* fabric.
11. Hand woven: in South India, as contrasted to imitations woven on power looms in Switzerland, France, and England. Tentering holes in the selvages distinguished Real India from power-loomed Imitation Madras.
12. Distinctive fold: most trade cloths in the later nineteenth and early twentieth centuries were folded accordion-style. Real India was folded in halves, then quarters, then thirds to enclose the raw edges. Later, with the introduction of the INTORICA line by a Swiss trading company, the cloth was folded to display the INTORICA name woven into the selvages (Evenson 1991).

Figure 9.2   Sizing of cotton warp with rice starch in Chirala, India. The scent of rice starch was one of several that contributed to the unique odor of authentic Indian madras. Photograph by the author, 1994.

13. Yarn dividers: Norman Fröhlich (1981) and D. B. Fröhlich (1993) specify the presence of white weft yarns floated or woven into the cloth between pieces to mark the cutting line.

Each of these characteristics was incorporated and carefully retained over time so that Real India cloths produced for the Kalabari in the late twentieth century were yarn-for-yarn reproductions of named Kalabari cloths revered for generations (Michelman 1991). Each characteristic speaks to the trade history of Real India and its cultural authentication into Kalabari life.

THE TRADE OF REAL INDIA

Based on patterns of the overseas Portuguese textile trade it is possible that the Portuguese exported Real India from South India and imported it into West Africa as early as the sixteenth century (Vogt 1975). Between 1410 and his death in 1460, Prince Henry the Navigator sponsored a number of voyages down the coast of West Africa, in part to capture a portion of the Arab spice trade. Once Vasco da Gama rounded the Cape of Good Hope (after Bartholomew Diaz) and landed on the western coast of India at Goa in 1498, the eastern sea route between Europe and Asia expanded. For the first time in history, European and Asian trade routes converged into a global trade network.

As Portuguese traders entered the South Asian trade system, they participated in an existing trade pattern in which cotton cloth was the currency of choice in the spice trade. Traders exchanged gold bullion for brightly colored cotton textiles in the ports of South India, and then the textiles were exchanged for spice in the Malay Archipelago and the Moluccas, the fabled Spice Islands. Ships laden with spice returned to the Red Sea and Persian Gulf ports of the Ottoman Empire, where they were converted to bullion for another round of the same journey. Meanwhile, caravans led by Asian and North African Muslim merchants left Hormuz and Aden for ports of the Eastern Mediterranean, such as Alexandria and Beirut. Once in the Mediterranean, the spice changed hands and was carried throughout Europe by Italian merchants from Florence, Genoa, and Venice. The price of the spices increased with each change of hands, accounting for the intense interest of the Portuguese in capturing a portion of this lucrative trade. When the Portuguese established an alternate route around the Cape of Good Hope directly to Europe, they began to usurp the successful and long-standing pattern of gold-for-textiles-for-spice developed by the Arab traders (Subrahmanyam 1993; Wolf 1982).

The spice merchants of the Malay Archipelago were savvy traders. They did not produce cotton textiles and favored the bright cotton cloths from India. It is possible that as the Portuguese made their way up and down the West African coast, stopping for water and supplies along the way, they recognized that merchants like the Kalabari were equally savvy and might also appreciate the Indian textiles preferred by the spice merchants. The Portuguese regularly traded a South Indian fabric called Salempores to the Spice Islanders. Salempores were described as white and dyed with indigo, possibly checkered, and measuring one yard wide and sixteen yards long. The Portuguese naturally would have selected textiles whose sales were successful elsewhere, so perhaps it was this cloth that first entered the Kalabari aesthetic. If so, the introduction of six of the thirteen primary characteristics of Real India occurred at this time. Salempores were all cotton, dyed with natural indigo with its unique color and scent, and measured one by sixteen yards. In fact, images of *pelete bite* dating from the late twentieth century feature an indigo blue and white-checkered pattern as the foundation motif (Eicher 1987: 43), suggesting an early cultural authentication of these elements. In addition, based on field observations of Real India in the process of being woven for the Nigerian market, warp-winders brushed rice starch onto the warp to ease handling. It is possible that this practice was quite ancient and might have been a characteristic of Salempores. The rice starch contributed to the special fragrance of the cloth, adding another smell to the Kalabari aesthetic concerning Real India. In any case, by the early seventeenth century, one chief market for Salempores was the Guinea Coast, as the bight of West Africa was known (Chaudhuri 1978; Irwin 1956).

Over the next 400 years, the Portuguese, the Dutch, and English who followed, usurped the successful and long-standing pattern of trade developed by the Arabs. Each of the European East India Companies engaged in extensive trade of a wide variety of Indian cotton textiles, referred to by dozens of names. Sorting through the glossaries of trade textile terms reveals some names were synonymous for the same cloth, and some names were applied to fabrics of widely varying description. Because Indian cotton textiles acted as a currency in the spice trade and later in the slave trade, the competition for control over textile sources was fierce. It is hardly surprising that primary trade documents offer only ambiguous cloth descriptions, lest these corporate secrets fall into the wrong hands. Add to this ambiguity the fact that there was little agreement on the spelling of many textile terms, most likely because Europeans interacting with speakers of many languages were attempting to phonetically duplicate the indigenous textile terms as they heard them.

Descriptions of what was actually purchased in different West African ports of call help clarify matters. For example, in the glossaries, the term Guinea Stuffs consistently identifies "the generic term for a wide range of cheap, brightly-coloured Indian calicoes, mostly striped or chequered, and very popular with the negroes" (Irwin and Schwartz 1966). Jean Barbot, writing of his voyages along the Guinea Coast in the late seventeenth century, offers useful details about color. He reports in 1678 that "Guinea Stuffs or cloths" were in demand in Sierra Leone. "Broad and narrow nicanees fine and coarse" and "narrow Guinea stuffs chequered, ditto broad" were in demand on the Gold Coast and were used to make "clouts to wear round their middles" (Barbot cited in Kingsley 1899: appendix). Barbot does not include any cloth in his discussion of New Calabar, the ancestral home of the Kalabari, but reports Old Calabar preferred "striped Guinea clouts of many colours." His references to color throughout his report indicate that more than blue and white Salempores were for sale. The Guinea Stuffs are defined by their many colors. Red dyes were very popular in East Asian markets, as were yellows, greens, and violets. All dyes were natural and, like indigo, carried unique odors. Stripes and checks were yarn-dyed until the Industrial Revolution. Thus, Barbot's report is evidence that by the end of the 1600s, the Kalabari had a wider range of colors from which to select a preferred color palette in yarn-dyed fabrics woven into a checkered or plaid design. The Kalabari aesthetic for Real India had become more defined.

Furthermore, Barbot reports in 1700 that trade goods popular in the Congo and Cabenda included "Guinea stuffs, 2 pieces to make a piece" (ibid.). The meaning of this description is unclear, but it might be evidence of the introduction of the bordered *rumal* format into the Kalabari aesthetic for Real India. North Indian Gujarati weavers wove Indian cotton *rumals* for the Islamic market. *Rumal* distribution expanded as Islam expanded throughout North India and into East Asia. The Victoria and Albert Museum has two uncut handkerchief pieces excavated at Fostat, Egypt, dating to fifteenth-century Gujarat. They are coarse compared to nineteenth-century Real India and their borders printed instead of woven, but their bordered format around a central field is unmistakable. Gujarati weavers also produced Guinea Stuffs for the East India Companies. It would have been only a matter of time before the *rumal* design made its way to the Guinea Coast. Following a devastating famine in Gujarat in the mid-seventeenth century, weavers and weaving traditions moved to South India to villages along the Coromandel Coast. It is possible that cotton *rumals* formerly woven for the Islamic market, closer to North India, worked their way into the West African trade where they found acceptance and popularity. When weaving for West Africa moved to South India, the *rumal* tradition went with it.

Meanwhile, the apogee of the Indian textile trade occurred in the years between 1670 and 1700 (Lawson 1993). Throughout the sixteenth, seventeenth, and eighteenth centuries, the East India Companies were the major purveyors of both the spice and slave trades, financed with Indian cottons (Wolf 1982). Demand increased in Europe generally and in England specifically because of the fast colors, bright prints and patterns, and overall comfort of this fascinating new textile compared to English wool and linen. When the Portuguese and Dutch introduced sugar production to Brazil and the West Indies, demand for sugar resulted in an increased demand for West African slave labor, which in turn led to increased demand for the textiles to both procure slaves and to clothe them. By the end of the seventeenth century, specific types of Guinea Stuffs (such as Callowaypoose, Chelloes, Hussanees, and Populees) appeared regularly in the records (Home Miscellaneous Series vol. 6, 1631–64). As competition intensified for ever increasing numbers of able-bodied slaves, greater efforts were made to meet West African middleman/customer tastes. The generic "anything goes" blend of available brightly colored cotton stripes and checks was no longer a successful strategy. Ever more specific textile terms would be used hereafter.

From an examination of the trade dispatches between Madras and London, evidence suggests that the progression of Real India terminology away from the generic term Guinea Stuffs to more specific terms continued. In addition, diversification in textile products expanded. For example, between 1744 and 1755, thirty-seven varieties of "piecegoods" (average-length cloths, as compared to "longcloths") were exported out of Madras for London (Dodwell 1920). Guinea Stuffs was not one of those categories, but Salempores, Callowaypoose, and four types of *rumals* were specified. Of the *rumals*, the types described as "Red & White" and "Masulipatnam" are of particular interest. Red and white implies a check or stripe and Masulipatnam is near Ventapollam, a central distribution center for the East India Company in the late seventeenth century. By 1850, the trade cloths called Ventapollam Handkerchiefs were a significant textile product exported from Madras. The height of the Handkerchief trade was 1853, with several kinds of Handkerchief fabrics exported from Madras: Ventapollam Handkerchiefs, Lunghie Handkerchiefs, and Madras Handkerchiefs.

Middlemen in the textile trade possibly simplified the terminology by grouping checkered or plaid *rumal-* or Handkerchief-style cloths into a name reflecting their port of origin. Thus, Ventapollam Handkerchiefs appear to be a link between the generic term Guinea Stuffs and the specific Real Madras Handkerchiefs. Taken together, the evidence from Fostat and Ventapollam lend credence to the idea that sometime in the late 1600s, checkered Guinea Stuffs and the *rumal* format coalesced into the Real India of the late twentieth century. A ninth Real India characteristic entered the Kalabari aesthetic with the introduction of *rumal* borders.

The steady demand for Indian cottons as currencies in the spice, slave, and sugar trades inspired the Industrial Revolution. As demand for Madras Handkerchiefs in West Africa increased, new European cotton mills attempted production of the first power-loomed imitations of Madras Handkerchiefs, using raw cotton imported from India. An early English effort at domestically producing Guinea Stuffs was attempted and abandoned in 1706, prior to the Industrial Revolution. Apparently, West African middlemen preferred East India Company goods to imitations (Irwin 1955). In other words, by the early 1700s, the intrinsic and extrinsic characteristics of Guinea Stuffs/Madras Handkerchiefs had been culturally authenticated into West African life so thoroughly that imitations were readily detected and rejected.

During the late 1700s, the English East India Company became the governing force in India, at the expense of its earlier trade activities. The Company appears to have lost focus on the tastes and needs of its customers, and private traders filled the gap because they could respond to individual market tastes more quickly. Abolition of the British slave trade in 1807 meant a sharp reduction in demand for Indian trade textiles. Competition to supply the remaining customers was fierce. For the Kalabari, however, the slave trade was replaced by trade in palm oil, used as an industrial lubricant in the textile mills of the Industrial Revolution. Private traders made every effort to retain the custom of these West African middlemen. In the early and mid-nineteenth century, once again, terms for specific types of textiles crystallize. In an appendix to his 1823 *Remarks on the Country Extending from Cape Palmas to the River Congo*, Captain John Adams listed and briefly described those cloths that sold best in particular West African ports. He included specific types of Guinea Stuffs – Chelloes, Nicanees, Calawaypores (Callowaypoose) – as well as Guinea Stuffs generally, which Adams said should be checked, without any border. This implies that Guinea Stuffs routinely featured borders, suggesting that the fusion of checked Guinea Stuffs and handkerchief-bordered *rumals* had already occurred prior to his report.

Adams also listed Lungee Handkerchiefs and Pullicat Handkerchiefs (originating on the Coromandel Coast) along with Chelloes and several types of *rumals*, all of which are "esteemed at Calabar." His context appears to refer to New Calabar, home of the Kalabari (Jones 1963). The Guinea Stuffs listed as cheap and coarse were not preferred by the Kalabari; Callowaypoose and *rumals* were Kalabari best sellers. Adams' comments suggest that by this time, if not before, a higher thread count and better quality yarn and weaving fulfilled, in part, the Kalabari aesthetic for Real India. When Kalabari artisans first created *pelete bite* is unknown (Renne 2001). One crucial characteristic of Real India, however, is a thread count of sufficient density to permit the subtraction of threads without compromising the integrity of the cloth. Adams' report documents an eleventh component of Real India.

Throughout the late 1700s, as the capabilities of power spinning and power weaving in Europe improved, mills in England, France, and Switzerland produced imitation Madras Handkerchiefs. In 1836, imitation Madras Handkerchiefs constituted the main manufacture of Montpelier, France (Brunnschweiler 1957). One example of a private trader entering the Madras Handkerchief trade at this time was A. Brunnschweiler and Co., also known as ABC. A. Brunnschweiler and Co. was a family-owned Swiss cloth manufacturing and weaving company. By 1872, it manufactured power-loom woven imitations of Madras Handkerchiefs for the West African market because of the popularity of Madras Handkerchiefs in West Africa generally (Van der Laan 1983). Imitation Madras Handkerchiefs proved popular and profitable, but not as much as Real Madras Handkerchiefs. West African customers skillfully identified one from the other. One way African customers determined authenticity was the presence of small holes along the selvage of the fabric. Weaver use of lateral tension (tentering) bars to help maintain the fabric's full width during weaving creates these small firm holes. In an attempt to add "genuineness" to early ABC imitation Madras Handkerchiefs, a member of the Brunnschweiler family designed a "hole making machine," which apparently carried out a very complicated mechanical movement involving pins set into a roller, piercing the fabric. The experiment was unsuccessful as their West African customers were not deceived (Fröhlich 1981). Thus, tentering marks became evidence of hand weaving and defined a critical component of the Kalabari definition of Real India. The meaning of the term Real India becomes clear.

At first, ABC imported Real India and other cottons from South India, then reexported their wares via a sales office in Manchester, England; but by the turn of the twentieth century the company had established offices in Port Harcourt and Lagos to better understand and to communicate local tastes directly to master weavers in Madras. Norman and D. B. Fröhlich were members of the Brunnschweiler family and acted as ABC's agent in Rivers State, Nigeria, and in Madras. During the first half of the twentieth century, innovations like the use of "artificial silk" (rayon) embroidery and chain stitch embroidery were introduced; but for the Kalabari market, "Reals," as they were by then called, remained the best-selling product.

One popular innovation to Real India involved a new way of folding the fabric that enclosed the cut edges and created a tidy square packet. In 1925, ABC introduced a line of trademarked Real India called INTORICA, from the phrase India-to-Africa. The Kalabari respected the INTORICA name for its quality Reals, which suggests that the Fröhlichs were very well versed in the Kalabari aesthetic for Real India. The fold of the fabric was modified to display the INTORICA name woven into the selvage and became a twentieth-century mark of value – and a twelfth characteristic of Real India.

In 1993, D. B. Fröhlich confirmed Norman Fröhlich's description of Real India, emphasizing the importance of hand weaving. He notes that on Real India floating weft yarns indicated where to cut apart the handkerchief squares. Indeed, an examination of Real Madras Handkerchiefs dating from 1855 held in the Victoria and Albert Museum bore this feature, a final characteristic of Real India.

D. B. Fröhlich reiterates the Kalabari specification for natural dyes. He refers to these as "running dyes." The warp was wetted and woven while moist so the colors slightly melted into each other. Moreover, he articulated the importance of the unique odor of Real India, as described earlier. Another attempt to deceive African customers with imitations included sprinkling "aromatic powders" to impart the fragrance of Reals. Again, it did not fool West African customers. Agents at one export office in Madras reported Kalabari customers went so far as to taste the fabric to verify its authenticity.

Did Real India need to "taste like a duck"? Certainly by the late twentieth century Real India carried at least thirteen discrete characteristics, color and weave being the most prominent. Tasting the fabric seems superfluous. Perhaps the agent was attempting to reenforce the idea that his customers were very particular and this export house could satisfy any demand. Perhaps this idea of tasting fabric originated with a linguistic confusion about Kalabari customers having very specific aesthetic tastes. Jasleen Dhamija (personal communication, 2005) reports that market women in many societies taste cloth for the presence of salt used to set indigo, because artificial dye processes do not use salt. Can the Kalabari be included in this practice? Tasting cannot be corroborated in published sources, so documenting this practice is a fascinating avenue for future research. In any case, tracing the history of Real India illuminates the origins of its characteristics.

Within the Kalabari aesthetic, Real India is identified by the way it looks, the way it feels, the way it smells, and some say by the way it tastes. The physical senses were a crucial set of tools in determining the authenticity of imported textiles. The sensual nature of Real India played an important role in the enculturation and perpetuation of identity for the Kalabari as they used Real India in daily and ritual life. The production and use of Real India exemplifies discussion of the role our five senses play in the aesthetics of dress (Eicher *et al.* 2000). Our aesthetic involvement with textiles creates associations profoundly linked to memory and meaning.

NOTE

1. I use the term "aesthetic" to refer to a set of characteristics that summarize an ideal informally agreed upon by a group of people. In this case, Real India is an object with characteristics that are appreciated by the senses. It captures the spirit of a people and communicates what it means to be Kalabari (Eicher *et al.* 2000).

REFERENCES

Adams, J. (1823), *Remarks on the Country Extending from Cape Palmas to the River Congo*, London: G. B. Whittaker.

Alagoa, E. J. (1970), "Long-Distance Trade and States in the Niger Delta," *Journal of African History* 11 (3): 319–29.

Amalsad, D. M. (1926), *The Development of the Madras Handkerchief and Lungy or Kaily Industry in the Madras Presidency*, Madras: The Superintendent, Government Press.

Barbot, J. (1746), *An Abstract of the Voyage to New Calabar River, or Rio Real, in the Year 1699*, London: Printed by assignment from Messrs. Churchill for Henry Lintot and John Osborn.

Brunnschweiler, A. O. (1957), "History of the Madras Handkerchief Trade," Unpublished notes held at Dakshinachitra, Madras.

Chaudhuri, K. N. (1978), *The Trading World of Asia and the English East India Company 1660–1760*, Cambridge: Cambridge University Press.

Dhamija, J. (1994), "The Geography of Indian Textiles: A Study of the Movement of Telia Rumal, Real Madras Handkerchief, George Cloth & Guinea Cloth," unpublished paper presented at the seminar on Real Madras Handkerchief: A Cross Cultural World Trade Perspective, Madras, India, February 5–7.

Dodwell, H. (1920), *Calendar of the Madras Dispatches 1744–1755*, Madras: Madras Government Press.

Eicher, J. B. (1987), "Kalabari Funerals: Celebration and Display," *African Arts* 21 (1): 38–45, 87.

Eicher, J. B. (1988), "Indian Textiles in Kalabari Funerals," *Asian Art and Culture* 9 (2): 68–79.

Eicher, J. B., Erekosima, T., and Liedholm, C. (1982), "Cut and Drawn: Textile Work From Nigeria," *Craft International* (Summer): 16–19.

Eicher, J. B., Evenson, S. L., and Lutz, H. A. (2000), *The Visible Self: Global Perspectives on Dress, Culture, and Society*, New York: Fairchild Publications.

Evenson, S. L. (1991), "The Manufacture of Madras in South India and Its Export to West Africa: A Case Study," Master's thesis, University of Minnesota.

Evenson, S. L. (1994), "A History of Indian Madras Manufacture and Trade: Shifting Patterns of Exchange," Doctoral dissertation, University of Minnesota.

Fröhlich, D. B. (1993), Unpublished notes, held at Dakshinachitra, Madras.

Fröhlich, N. (1981), "The Story of the Firm Fröhlich, Brunnschweiler & Cie," Manchester: A. Brunnschweiler & Cie.

Home Miscellaneous Series, vol. 6 (1631–64), vol. 11 (1704).

Horton, R. (1960), *The Gods as Guests: An Aspect of Kalabari Religious Life*, Lagos: Federal Government Printers.

Horton, R. (1960), "The Gods as Guests: An Aspect of Kalabari Religious Life," *Nigeria Magazine* (March).

Irwin, J. (1955), "Indian Textile Trade in the Seventeenth Century: Western India," *Journal of Indian Textile History* 1: 4–33.

Irwin, J. (1956), "Indian Textile Trade in the Seventeenth Century: Coromandel Coast," *Journal of Indian Textile History* 2: 24–42.

Irwin, J. and Schwartz, P. R. (1966), *Studies in Indo-European Textile History*, Ahmedabad: Calico Museum of Textiles.

Jones, G. I. (1963), *The Trading States of the Oil Rivers*, London: Oxford University Press.

Kingsley. M. H. (1899), *West African Studies*, London: Macmillan & Co. Ltd.

Lawson, P. (1993), *The East India Company: A History*, London: Longman Group UK Limited.

Michelman, S. (1991), "Dress in Kalabari Women's Associations," Doctoral dissertation, University of Minnesota.

Petgrave, M. D. (1992), "Indian Madras in Kalabari Culture," Master's thesis, University of Minnesota.

Renne, E. (2001), "'Our Great Mother ... tied this cloth': *Pelete Bite* Cloth, Women, and Kalabari Identity," in S. J. Torntore (ed.), *Cloth is the Center of the World: Nigerian Textiles, Global Perspectives*, St. Paul, MN: Goldstein Gallery of Design.

Schneider, J. and Weiner, A. B. (1986), "Cloth and the Organization of Human Experience," *Current Anthropology* 27 (2): 178–84.

Subrahmanyam, S. (1993), *The Portuguese Empire in Asia 1500–1700*, London: Longman Group UK Limited.

Van der Laan, H. L. (1983), "A Swiss Family in West Africa: A. Brunnschweiler & Co., 1929–1959," *African Economic History* 12: 287–97.

Vogt, J. (1975), "Notes on the Portuguese Cloth Trade in West Africa, 1480–1540," *International Journal of African Historical Studies* 8 (4): 623–51.

Watson, J. F. (1866), *The Textile Fabrics of India: Series I*, London: The India Office.

Watson, J. F. (1873), *The Textile Manufactures of India: Collection of Specimens and Illustrations of the Textile Manufactures of India (Second Series)*, London: India Museum.

Wolf, E. R. (1982), *Europe and the People Without History*, Berkeley: University of California Press.

10 PERFORMING DRESS AND ADORNMENT IN SOUTHEASTERN NIGERIA

Sarah Adams

The following focuses on the discrepancy between personal, embodied performances of dress and adornment, and external aesthetic appraisals. My interest in body theory is rooted in my study of Igbo women's *uli* painting, an ephemeral black-line body art, and body in southeastern Nigeria.[1] The pigment women use to adorn their bodies comes from the juice extracted from the *uli* pod, which is green when applied to the body, turns black overnight, and remains visible for about four days. The juice, a thin liquid, can be very hard to control on the surface of the body. Accomplished artists apply the juice in swift gestures, redirecting its flow over the curves of the body, and gracefully incorporating "mistakes" into the final composition. Once very popular in Nigeria, *uli* body painting currently is less so, but still vividly remembered.

In my search for an appropriate framework I began by surveying some of the more common theoretical frameworks African art historians have used to interpret personal adornment.[2] Many of our earlier models draw from anthropology, not surprising given that the historical roots of African art history are in anthropology. I was surprised, however, to find that the French philosopher René Descartes, who asserted an absolute dichotomy between mind and body, continues to have a profound impact on all aspects of body theory. Contemporary scholars of Western body arts still tend to start routinely with Descartes' notion of the body, and then try to undermine it by asserting its opposite. In contrast, in art historians' work on the African body, the critique of Descartes is often brief and implicit; art historians depend greatly on structuralist and semiotic models. Though scholars are rightly critical of Descartes, body theory nevertheless continues to divide between body- or mind-focused models and the two approaches are seldom used in combination.

In this essay I suggest, through a discussion of some new directions in my own research, that approaches that focus only on the body and its perceived semiotics frame the body as passive, as an object that simply receives culturally derived ornament. The application of additional theoretical approaches focused on embodiment, such as those proposed by Pierre Bourdieu and Paul Connerton, replaces the mind in the body and thus frames the body as active. In embodied models, the body does not just passively receive cultural inscription:

it actively creates culture through bodily performances of adornment. Such models also create much needed space for personal agency and resistance. I use a combination of these approaches in my work in order to collapse a persistent Cartesian mind/body binary preserved in much of the scholarship on dress and personal adornment.

Much of the writing on African arts of personal adornment relies on concepts alluded to by Marcel Mauss and Emile Durkheim, and then developed in Mary Douglas' early texts *Natural Symbols* (1970) and *Purity and Danger* (1984). Mauss first introduced the notion of *habitus*, the idea that learned bodily practice is a site of culture, which Bourdieu later takes up and elaborates in *Outline of a Theory of Practice* (1977). Mauss asserts that the body is "man's first and most natural instrument" (1979: 104). In *Purity and Danger*, Douglas builds on Mauss' work, describing the body and its humors as "a model which can stand for any bounded system" (1989: 115). In *Natural Symbols*, she expands this connection and argues that the symbolism of the body, which gets its power from social life, governs the fundamental attitudes to spirit and matter. Therefore ideas about the body reflect cultural ideas and, by extension, adornment of the body reflects cultural ideas. When we apply this idea to history of dress and personal adornment, it becomes clear why this model remains powerful and central to African art historians' analysis of body adornment, and to historians of dress in general. Though Douglas' model is drawn from Mauss, who described the body as mindful in his own work, when Douglas' principles are applied the result tends to be external visual analysis of bodily inscriptions as they relate to cultural ideas. This approach, however, denies the wearer's personal agency and power.

Michel Foucault's *Discipline and Punish* (1975) has also been a critical text in my discussions of *uli* body painting, especially in reference to the colonial body. Foucault asserted the body has inherent power, that it is the "object and target of power" (1995: 136). He argued that in the eighteenth century, for example, the physical bearing of the French soldier, the physical expression of "soldier-ness," became something not inherent to the body but *made* through silent impositions of automatism of habit (ibid.: 135). These acquired automatisms of habit ranged from how the head was held, the position of the shoulders, where the eyes looked, and how quickly the body moved. Control over such bodily movement (and, I would add, movement dictated through impositions of dress and bodily adornment) implies a "subtle coercion, of obtaining hold on [the body] at the level of mechanism itself – movements, gestures, attitudes, rapidity: an infinitesimal power over the active body" (ibid.: 137). Foucault notes "a body is docile that may be subjected, used, transformed and improved" (ibid.: 136). While Foucault's notion of the body and this notion's potential applications within discussions of the colonial body are compelling, like Douglas' model, Foucault's notion of biopower leaves little space for personal agency or resistance to assertions of power over the body.

THE FIRST LAYER: BATTLING FOR THE SOUL, BATTLING FOR THE BODY

The most productive way to demonstrate how the layering of theoretical models adds new dimensions to the study of personal adornment is to root this discussion in the specific example of the history of dress in Arochukwu, a village in southeastern Nigeria. I use both Douglas and Foucault in my own research on *uli* painting in Arochukwu, where I studied the impact a mission marriage training school had on the history of dress in that area.[3] I will first analyze that project and then demonstrate how the application of embodied models to this same material adds another layer to the analysis.

In the 1930s in Arochukwu, Scottish Presbyterian missionary Agnes Arnot established an embroidery cooperative at the Slessor Memorial Home for Girls, a mission marriage training school. In the early twentieth century, parents and prospective husbands from Arochukwu and other regions of West Africa sent young girls to Slessor to learn "domestic sciences" and receive a basic Western-style education. The girls learned, among other things, to cook, embroider, tailor clothing, do laundry, and to garden. In short, the young women learned useful vocational skills within a specific sector of the colonial economy. In the 1930s and 1940s, Arnot encouraged young Aro girls at the school to use *uli* body painting designs for embroidery on cloth (Figure 10.1).[4] The work was then sold, in Nigeria and abroad, to raise money for the mission. Arnot collected drawings on paper of body painting designs from artists who did not attend the mission school, and these drawings were then made into embroidery templates for the mission girls.[5]

Figure 10.1 Watercolor of a woman painted with *uli*, ca. 1930s/40s. Duckworth Collection, Pitt Rivers Museum, University of Oxford. 1972. 24.114. 42½ × 9⅝ inches.

In keeping with Christian concepts of the body, however, the girls who embroidered *uli* on linens were not allowed to paint it on their bodies. Another missionary, Mrs. Mackernell, actively enforced this policy. To this day she is still remembered as "Daddy" in Arochukwu because, unlike Arnot, she left the Slessor compound daily to go out into the community and do evangelical work. Mleanya Iheonyebuokwu, who attended the Slessor school during this period, remembered that young girls from Slessor who appeared at school or in church wearing *uli* were beaten by Mrs. Mackernell (interview, Arochukwu, March 2000). While other preadolescent girls not attending the mission school wore no clothing as a sign of their chastity, preadolescent girls at the mission school wore dresses, often hand-me-downs imported from mission donations in the United Kingdom. Thus, during this period in Arochukwu, preadolescent mission girls' dresses became another sign of chastity and modesty, this one rooted in European Christian concepts of the body and modesty. At another level, these dresses also signaled affiliation with the mission marriage training school.

Several drawings on paper by *uli* body painting artists during this period survive in the Pitt Rivers Museum in Oxford. Among this collection is an anonymous work, a watercolor of a woman adorned with body painting designs (Figure 10.1). The work reconstructs another aspect of the history of dress in Arochukwu during the period. While no one I spoke with in Arochukwu was able to recall who had painted the watercolor of the woman's body, the body painting itself was likely done by *uli* artists in Arochukwu in the 1930s or 1940s. The work is about four feet long, painted on four pieces of paper tied together at intervals with string, as if to make it easily collapsible for travel. *Uli* artists Grace Nwosu and Victoria Nwosu said this image was *uli* painting as it was done in the 1930s and 1940s on the bodies of *mgbede* women, nonmission-affiliated women who were coming out of their period of isolation in preparation for marriage (interview, Arochukwu, March 2000).

During the period of isolation before marriage, preadolescent, nonmission girls in Arochukwu were kept sedentary for several months and fed rich foods supplied by their families and sometimes their future husbands. The period of seclusion was a time when women in the community instructed the young, unmarried girls on sexual, religious, and domestic matters. In short, this was another form of marriage training, one for nonmission-affiliated girls. When *mgbede* girls emerged from seclusion from the fattening room, they were presented to the community, including a rapt audience of mission girls, at the height of their beauty – their hair styled in elaborate coiffures, their bodies covered in sumptuous garments of black-line body art like that depicted in the Pitt Rivers example. Wealthier girls also wore coiled brass anklets and bracelets on this occasion (Figure 10.2). In C. S. Okeke's overview essay on the history of Igbo dress, she explains that when an Igbo woman came out of the fattening room she "did not use cloth as apparel . . . If she had to wear some cloth at all, it was a narrow piece across her waist . . . to further accentuate her hip area" (1992: 789). Okeke adds that during a young woman's wedding she would tie a wrapper for the first time:

Figure 10.2   Young woman wearing *njaga*, ca. 1930.

And from then on she wore wrappers like a married woman... In traditional Igbo culture children below these ages [twenty-one for boys and fourteen for girls] did not normally require much by way of clothing... This was based on the belief that clothing could conceal their acts of licentiousness, particularly among the girls with regard to unwanted pregnancies. Nakedness was therefore a mark of purity among children. (ibid.: 790)

Therefore the adornments worn by preadolescent *mgbede* women, and their rejection of clothing, expressed concepts of purity to future husbands, in-laws, and the community at large.

Mgbede women's adornments conveyed other ideals understood and appreciated by those who attended their public outing. Specifically, Grace Nwosu and Victoria Nwosu noted that patterns clustered around the neck, legs, and stomach of the woman in the Pitt Rivers Museum drawing drew attention to important parts of a woman's body. Patterns on the neck emphasize a straight, long, and strong neck. Many in Arochukwu say the neck is a center of beauty; a long neck is very attractive. *Uli* is used to accent the neck's length and beauty, and in some cases to create the illusion that a woman's neck is longer than it actually is. *Uli* on the neck of a woman from the fattening room also advertises to her future husband its straightness and strength, which means she can carry a heavy load on her head, and implies she can work hard and will therefore bring wealth to the home. To support this explanation, Maazi Ogbonnaya Uku Ivegbunna, a member of the *Ekpe* society, a powerful secret society in Arochukwu, said children in this area are sometimes named Olujie, meaning "bent neck" (interview, Arochukwu, March 2000).[6]

Another proverb illuminates the artists' focus on the neck, "If the neck breaks, the head falls." To be a human being one's head must sit squarely on one's shoulders. This quality separates humans from animals, so *uli* is also used to emphasize humanity, as Susan Vogel put it, as a "mark of civilization" (1988).[7] To have a bent neck is to be in some way less than human and therefore clearly less than desirable. Victoria Nwosu also pointed out that to kill anyone you cut the neck, especially for sacrifice. Although the neck is a location of beauty, strength, and humanity, it is also vulnerable as it connects the heart and the head. To emphasize this idea of the neck as a place of potential vulnerability, Grace Nwosu added, "When you are sick, the trembling voice tells that the body is weak." She explained that when you visit a sick person and they can speak well you do not worry; it is only when their voice (and she implied neck here) trembles and is weak that you are concerned for their health. If the neck and therefore voice are strong, the person is strong. John Umeh, a *dibia* (Igbo doctor/diviner/psychologist) brings up a related proverb, "if one remains silent, unconcerned or aloof, one's Chi [personal god or protector] would also remain silent, unconcerned and aloof" (1997: 43). Strength of voice, in other words, equals strength of character. So the use of *uli* to draw attention to a woman's straight, strong neck focuses attention on her health, her essential humanity, her potential for financial success, and her ability to speak clearly and loudly to determine her destiny.

Uli artists in Arochukwu said legs, emphasized through pattern concentration over the knees, are important for some of the same reasons that the neck is important. A woman's legs must carry her back and forth from home to the market or farm; a woman who cannot hold a load on her head (and neck) and carry it with her legs to the market will not bring much wealth to her husband and family. Straight, strong legs emphasized by *uli* advertise both beauty and potential for creating wealth for herself, her husband, and her family. One woman said, "if your legs move fast you will get what you want."

Pattern clusters on the stomach draw the eye to a woman's clean, lush, black pubic hair, which an *mgbede* woman would have displayed as a sign of fertility when she came out of the fattening room. Maazi Ivegbunna commented that in Arochukwu a "big" (meaning wealthy) woman has "a well-developed pubic area." "People fear a big woman for this," he said, "and these women are called *ikpu ukwu*," which means great or large vulva. In addition to these meanings mapped onto *mgbede* women's bodies through *uli* body art in the 1930s and 1940s, this form of adornment also indicated the wearer was more than likely not attending the Slessor marriage training school.

During this period in Arochukwu, both *uli* body painting artists and expatriate missionaries recognized and employed women's bodies as powerful sites for cultural inscription. As Linda Arthur explained, "While a person's level of religiosity cannot be objectively perceived, symbols such as clothing," and I would add here body adornment, "are used as evidence that s/he is on the 'right and true path'" (1999: 1). During the 1930s and 1940s in Arochukwu, two systems for preparing young girls for marriage coexisted: the fattening room and the mission marriage training school. Each approach had its own way of creating visual evidence on the body that those encompassed by those systems were on the "right and true path." The religious, cultural, and social philosophies behind each method of preparation were expressed through dress or personal adornment. Women in Arochukwu today remember it as the time of a visually polarized period in the history of dress in this area, a "divided market."

THE NEXT LAYER: EMBODIMENT AND RESISTANCE

My initial analysis of the history of dress in Arochukwu during this period does not address the fact that these varying inscriptions upon the body certainly affected what Bourdieu calls *habitus* or, learned, but unconscious, repeated culturally derived bodily practice in response to surroundings or, in this case, to adornment. Rather than ask how culture was mapped onto docile bodies during this period of intense interculturation, we might also address how modification of the body and adornment on the body affect *movement*, and how it is learned and becomes unconscious or *habitus*, and finally how culture then grows out of these learned, repeated, unconscious movements. These questions restore the sense of a personal and active body that creates culture rather than simply passively receives it. This approach returns a degree of agency to the individual.

If we add the embodied experience to our semiotic analysis of adornment, we bridge the Cartesian split in our theoretical approaches and move toward a personal, mindful body that acts and resists. Andrew Strathern neatly summarizes this leap in his discussion of Paul Connerton's work on the body and memory: "emphasizing habit and habit memory brings us closer to lived experience than other approaches of a semiotic kind that see cultural meanings inscribed on the body and on clothing that different categories of people wear. Connerton argues that clothing not only conveys messages that can be decoded; it also helps to actually mold character by influencing the body's movements" (1996: 29).

When preadolescent mission girls in Arochukwu who had not worn clothing, an expression of bodily purity, donned dress, did it affect the way they moved their bodies? Did their daily bodily performances in response to these often ill-fitting, hand-me-down dresses in turn create cultural ideas about young women who attended the mission marriage training school? Of interest, many women I spoke with in Arochukwu, who were and were not affiliated with the mission, said mission girls were not as physically strong as nonmission girls. "The [nonmission] girls felt the mission girls were not strong enough to mix with them," Slessor graduate Iheonyebuokwu recalled (interview, Arochukwu, March 2000). The nonmission girls thought mission girls were weak and Iheonyebuokwu seemed to concur, "Sometimes we would carry firewood with them but our load would not be as much as theirs" (ibid.).

Part of this perceived discrepancy in relative physical strengths of mission and non-mission girls had to do with the fact that the mission school placed a great deal of emphasis on training girls for careers that were more sedentary, such as being seamstresses. Might it also be possible, however, that these ideas also grew from repeated bodily performances of the dresses? Did people in Arochukwu start to think of mission girls as slow walkers because they couldn't see their legs move under their dresses? Did the mission girls in turn internalize these observations? It is also likely many of the dresses young mission girls wore during this period were hot and cumbersome, as mission records indicate that many wore dresses that were donated by churches in England and Scotland and were therefore made of materials that were not necessarily ideal for the climate.[8] Might we suggest, then, that this also slowed some of the mission girls down in their daily activities?

In terms of restoring an embodied perspective to my analysis of *uli*, I can also talk about my own experiences of wearing *uli*. Though an outsider, I still think some of the things I experienced when I wore *uli* shed light on an embodied perspective of this art. While my white skin generally makes me a spectacle in Nigeria, when I wore *uli*, I was more aware of my body and its movements. I was also aware *uli* controlled and directed other people's gaze. When I wore *uli* it was one of the few times when in Nigeria I felt I had a degree of control not over whether people looked at me but *how* people looked at me, where they looked, and focused their attention. When I was not wearing *uli* most people looked at my face, but when I wore *uli* people looked openly at my entire body. Though I wore a dress over most of my body patterns, once people saw one pattern, women in particular would crouch down to inspect my legs, then take my hands and turn my arms around to look at the patterns. *Uli* invited touch. *Uli* functions similarly to a tattoo, in the way it draws people to you. In short, it changes your relationship to the world.

Body painting is often a collaborative process, with patterns chosen and placed on the client's body through conversation between patron and *uli* artist. Accomplished *uli* artists, however, often choose to paint themselves, but after they paint the parts of their bodies they can reach, they leave their backs and the backs of their legs to a trusted friend to decorate. Focusing of this creative process, in which the woman adorned has some control over how she is adorned, further underscores the idea that a woman can actively manipulate *uli* to control where and how people look at her. Foucault talks about docile bodies, and my initial analysis spoke to the way in which *uli* makes the body docile, locks it into a cultural moment. In contrast, the embodied perspective, how *uli* is performed, actually suggests that the wearer's use of *uli* makes the viewer's body or, at the very least their gaze, docile and controlled. In this perspective, the wearer is in control. When we consider the image of the woman wearing *uli* using this embodied perspective, we start to see ways in which she is no longer just passively inscribed with culture, but actively controls public appraisal of her body. This embodied perspective on *uli* restores some agency to the wearer.

Though this is an embodied analysis of *uli*, I would not describe a woman's performance of *uli* as *habitus*, because the term *habitus* refers to repeated, *unconscious* bodily behavior. This is still the *conscious* aspect of bodily behavior because *uli* is an ephemeral art, it lasts on the body only four or five days, so there is not enough time for repeated, unconscious bodily behavior to develop in response to it. We can address the embodied aspects of *uli* in isolation, but adornments worn with *uli* also shape bodily experience, which allows us to deal more directly with unconscious bodily practice derived from performances of adornment over time. In Arochukwu in the 1930s and 1940s, just before, during, and just after the period of premarital seclusion, young women often wore pairs of heavy spiral anklets called *njaga* that spanned from the ankle to just above the knee (Figure 10.2). These anklets were paired with elaborate *uli* at the final public outing. At the purely aesthetic and semiotic level, *njaga* were paired with *uli* to draw further attention to the straightness of the legs, which, as I already noted, conveyed ideas of physical strength and potential for economic success. Because *njaga* were made of brass they were also quite expensive and not every woman could afford them, so they were also a sign of wealth. Most important to this discussion is that *njaga* were very heavy and, therefore, they changed the way a woman walked. Walking became slow and somewhat awkward. Though a woman usually packed cloth around her ankles to keep the *njaga* from rubbing and making sores, over time sores nevertheless usually developed, and these further mediated movement.

In Arochukwu, women noted variously that the practice of isolation before marriage can be interpreted as a period of ritual gestation or ritual death before becoming an adult woman. *Njaga* restrict bodily mobility, which suggests the state of gestation or ritual death. We might ask then if connections between the period of isolation before marriage and ideas of gestation and rebirth are simply mapped onto a passive body, or if these ideas grew out of the wearer's use of these ornaments? More likely, these ideas derive from some combination of the two. If we consider how these ornaments were used by the women who wore them, and how cultural ideas about women's bodies are born from those usages, we restore agency to the young women who wore these adornments.

Similar ideas can be drawn out through analysis of sets of wide brass anklets once commonly worn by wealthy women in what is now the Anambra State region of southeastern Nigeria (Figure 10.3). Again, we can discuss these anklets in terms of cultural ideas mapped onto the body; that is, we may analyze the meanings of the motifs and discuss the anklets as expressions of wealth. Those who observed women who wore these anklets, however, most commonly talk about how the anklets informed bodily behavior. To keep the disks from striking against each other, women swung their legs out and to the side as they walked. Many

Figure 10.3   Woman wearing brass anklets, 1898–1902.

travelers who passed through southeastern Nigeria in the late nineteenth and early twentieth centuries, when these anklets were in fashion, wrote about this manner of walking.

In a handwritten caption next to Alexander Braham's photo of a woman with the brass anklets (Figure 10.3), which dates from between 1898 and early 1902, Braham describes the woman's gait:

> This woman is wearing one of the most valued of native ornaments… None but a woman of position, the favored wife of a chief may wear them. They are fourteen inches in diameter, and weigh on an average four to five lbs each. They cause the wearer to walk with a most peculiar gait: leg over leg as you see in the picture. Yet the woman becomes expert in the arrangement of them and can walk or run with them on with speed and ease. Once fastened on they are never removed night or day.[9]

Unlike *uli* painting or *njaga*, these ornaments were worn permanently, so as Braham suggests here, the ways in which they affected bodily behavior must eventually have become unconscious, an excellent example of *habitus*. How did cultural concepts grow out of women's performances of these adornments? As John Mack noted in his study of adornment, "Movements, gestures, and general deportment are also relevant. Indeed, these may be so characteristic that they may be reproduced so as to suggest the presence of adornment even when it is not in fact being worn" (1988: 10). In this same discussion Mack includes a captivating aside, in which he notes that Igbo women who could not afford these wide anklets nonetheless walked in a way that suggested they were accustomed to wearing them. In some cases, especially with historical materials such as these anklets, embodied analysis of personal adornment requires imagining yourself into another person's skin, a process that acts as a constant, and important reminder of one's status as an outsider on many counts. I also have found that this approach begins to bridge that chasm between mind- and body-focused models, between docile and active bodies, between those who wear these adornments and those who analyze them from the outside.

NOTES

1. *Uli* patterns are also used in mural painting, which I study too, but for the purposes of this essay I will focus only on body painting.
2. A good collection of early articles on African arts of personal adornment can be found in Arnold Rubin (1988).
3. In Arochukwu, body painting is pronounced *uri*, but I use *uli* here for the sake of continuity within this essay.
4. Of interest, though girls from all over West Africa attended Slessor, Arnot limited participation in this project to young girls from Arochukwu.
5. Some women reported that the drawings were made into embroidery templates at the mission school in Arochukwu, while others said the drawings were sent to Scotland and made into templates there. Because the project developed over several decades, and was revived again during the Biafran War (1967–70), it is likely that both accounts are true.
6. Because there was, and to some extent still is, a high rate of infant mortality in this area, mothers who had lost many children would name a child Olujie to mark the newborn as undesirable to the spirits. Such a name is meant to trick the spirits into leaving the child in this world, as spirits would reject an imperfect child. A child with a bent neck will grow to be a weak adult without the physical means to accumulate material success.
7. This interpretation is especially interesting in light of the comments of one Slessor graduate who recalled that she thought the *mgbede* women painted with *uli* "looked like beasts."
8. National Library of Scotland, MS 7686 (1922).
9. Alexander Braham, photo album, Rhodes House Library, University of Oxford, MSS. Afr.S.2288.

REFERENCES

Arthur, L. B. (1999), "Dress and the Social Control of the Body," in L. B. Arthur (ed.), *Religion, Dress, and the Body*, Oxford, New York: Berg, pp. 1–7.
Bourdieu, P. (1977), *Outline of a Theory of Practice*, Cambridge, New York: Cambridge University Press.

Connerton, P. (1989), *How Societies Remember*, Cambridge: Cambridge University Press.

Douglas, M. (1970), *Natural Symbols: Explorations in Cosmology*, New York: Pantheon Books.

Douglas, M. (1984), *Purity and Danger: An Analysis of the Concepts of Pollution and Taboo*, London, New York: Ark Paperbacks.

Foucault, M. (1995), *Discipline and Punish: Birth of a Prison*, A. Sheridan (trans.), New York: Vintage Books.

Mack, J. (1988), *Ethnic Jewelry*, New York: Abrams.

Okeke, C. S. (1992), "Igbo Textiles, Costumes and Apparel," in A. E. Afigbo (ed.), *Groundwork of Igbo History*, Lagos: Vista Books, pp. 789–90.

Rubin, A. (ed.). (1988), *Marks of Civilization: Artistic Transformations of the Human Body*, Los Angeles: Museum of Cultural History, UCLA.

Strathern, A. (1996), *Body Thoughts*, Ann Arbor: University of Michigan Press.

Umeh, J. (1997), *After God is Dibia: Igbo Cosmology, Divination, and Sacred Science in Nigeria*, Vol. 1, London: Karnak House.

Vogel, S. (1988), "Marks of Civilization," in Arnold Rubin (ed.), *Marks of Civilization: Artistic Transformations of the Human Body*, Los Angeles: Museum of Cultural History, pp. 97–105.

11 WOMEN, MIGRATION, AND THE EXPERIENCE OF DRESS

Mary A. Littrell and Jennifer Paff Ogle

WOMEN, MIGRATION, AND THE EXPERIENCE OF DRESS

In his seminal work, *The Experience of Place*, Tony Hiss describes multisensory perceptions of the built environment that contribute to rich experiences of place.

> This underlying awareness – I call simultaneous perception ... is more like an extra, or a sixth, sense: [i]t broadens and diffuses the beam of attention evenhandedly across all the senses so we can take in whatever is around us – which means sensations of touch and balance, for instance, in addition to all sights, sounds, and smells. It's simultaneous perception that allows any of us a direct sense of continuing membership in our communities. (1990: xii–xii)

Hiss elaborates that as any one of the senses is heightened, diminished, or eliminated, the holistic perception of place can change such that the overall experience is altered. Through the transformed commingling of senses, a new intersensoriality or synesthetic experience emerges (Feld 2005; Howes 2005; Tuan 1993). Hiss' conceptualization served as the launching point for our exploration of the *experience of dress* among women from India living in the United States. More specifically we examined how women's senses, sentiments, and symbolic experiences of dress remained stable *and* changed as they migrated across cultures and forms of dress.

India provides women with a wide range of multisensory dress experiences as they advance from childhood to adulthood, foster ties within the family, establish new relationships at school and in the workplace, prepare for weddings, and participate in daily and seasonal rituals (Banerjee & Miller 2003; Edwards 2003; Huyler 1999; Tarlo 1996). As women adopt forms of dress, whether Indian styles or Western attire, they forge associations and create memories that provide "valued feelings" or sentiments associated with appearance (Stone 1965: 229). Across the life span, a richly layered identity tells of a woman's marital status, social class, economic status, political viewpoint, and religious practice. It is these sensual experiences, sentiments, and meanings of dress that provided the context for our study of Indian women who grew up in one culture, but migrated to another.

Our interpretive study draws from interviews with seventeen Indian women who were reared in India and have resided in the United States for a minimum of three years. The women ranged in age from mid-twenties to mid-fifties and lived in US communities with vibrant Indian populations. All but two were married and all held postsecondary degrees. Twelve were employed in positions ranging from teaching to information technology, lab science, and social work. Three were graduate students. Throughout the text, we use quotations to illustrate emergent themes from the interviews. Each informant has been given a number (e.g., P1, P2) to demonstrate our use of multiple informants' responses in developing our analysis.

In this essay, emergent themes from the interviews are integrated into a *grounded progression of the experience of dress* within cultural context. Components of the model include: a multisensory self and associated sentiments brought from India, sensory challenges experienced upon arrival in the United States, US-based influences on dress, and negotiations of senses and sentiments while settling in the United States. The progression culminates in a transnational self in the US context (Figure 11.1). As such, the model of progression illustrates Steven Feld's perception that as "place is sensed, senses are placed; as places make sense, senses make place" (2005: 179).

MULTISENSORY SELF BROUGHT FROM INDIA

Our initial interview questions about the sensory components of Indian dress elicited rich and emotionally laden descriptions of a dress gestalt centered on eight sensual components: color, fabric textures, embellishments, sounds, smells, the jeweled body, skin enrichment,

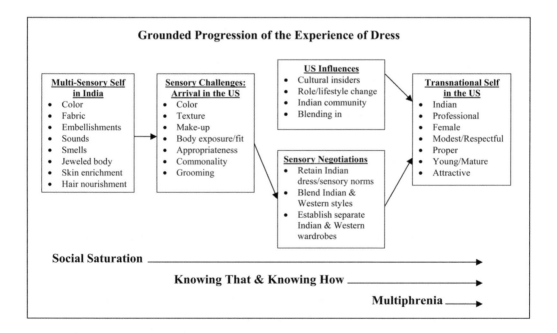

Figure 11.1 Model of the experience of dress.

and hair nourishment. We draw on a sampling of women's descriptions to highlight their emotional attachments to a multisensory self initiated with requisite ear piercing as infants; monitored in the home by parents and siblings; and further honed as young adults among friends and co-workers in India.

When speaking of color in dress, women intermingled their nuanced descriptions with sentiments of beloved family members and friends in India:

> I think of beautiful pastels. Beautiful pastel *bandhani* [tie-dyed small dots] saris from Gujarat waving in the breeze on a clothesline outdoors, with their beautiful dot designs of birds and other things. I never did like bright colors and that is probably due to my mother who, as a widow, wore pastels. I used to feel badly that my mother had been deprived of wearing bright colors. Her life with me was in pastels. (P6)

For other women, weddings evoked sensual memories of color and emotional attachments to their Indian homeland: "The marigold flower... We use those for weddings, and there are so many colors in one flower. I associate India with these colors. That's India, that's me, that's my home" (P1). Still others spoke of color in metaphoric tones:

> When you are talking about the Indian people they are very colorful people. The homes are colorful. Color is something not just used literally but metaphorically – color is a word that I always think of India. Food, the way it is colorful in the intermingling of the bursts of color in the spices. Even the national bird, the peacock, is colorful. You have all the traditional sweets, very colorful – oranges and yellows. The saris lined up on the street [in shops] are all very colorful. The people walking around have a very colorful personality. Even the way they talk and the way I talk [with many gestures]. Colorful is the word not just for clothing, but all across the board. (P13)

Women paired their color associations with strong attachments to particular fabrics. Silk, georgette, chiffon, and starched cotton, along with fabric embellishments, emerged repeatedly in descriptions. As one woman noted, Indian fabric draws you in, "You want to look at clothes again to see some other things" (P12). Another woman elaborated:

> To me it's the fabrics. It's the colors. It's an amazing quality of fabrics and generally handmade ones. So it's block prints on silk. It's silk georgette – the saris and the beading. The handwork is just phenomenal. The sense of color, the industriousness of people, just the ability to create beautiful fabrics. I think it tells a lot about a country. I do worry if Walmart goes to India. What will happen? (P9)

The women's multisensory conceptualization expanded from the sight and feel of fabrics to sounds.

> If you're wearing bangles ... they make certain sounds. So, I always like the glass bangles, the more traditional. They break very easily, so I started buying metal ones, but they don't make the sound like a glass bangle. I always like to wear long earrings. It has to move. You can feel something moving. Something that enhances the contours, again. The bangles showing your wrist, a little bit, even if you have a small bracelet. The anklets,

I loved when I got married. And that lets you know that there is a new bride in the house. (P1)

Several women also spoke of the rustle and smell of the sari: "[A s]ilk sari has a smell when you open it, and when I open my own saris and get that smell I get very excited. It makes you homesick. That smell stays when you walk and you pull the *pallu* [decorative end-piece of the sari] and you get that smell" (P5). Other women waxed fondly on sentiments associated with the fragrances of jasmine, rose, and henna.

As women talked about treatments for the hair and the skin, the close physicality among mothers, grandmothers, aunts, and sisters was valued by many, but begrudged by a few, particularly when they were young girls. Fathers also played a role in attaching value to grooming. A woman remembered, "It was my father who said, 'A girl's beauty is in her hair.' I will never forget that" (P10). Sentiments, both positive and negative, emerged from grooming rituals:

> When I was a girl, my mother would put oil [in my hair] and wash it and braid it and put flowers in it. They, my mother and my aunts and sometimes friends, for fun, would play with my hair. They would oil my hair once a week … Sundays, everybody puts oil in their hair, waits for one or two hours and … goes for shampooing. It was a ritual kind of thing – almost a ceremony. Everybody, my sisters too, would put oil and then one by one you would go to the bathroom and your mom or somebody would help you … shampoo. Once you got into the bathroom the whole body would be massaged with oil. I miss that now but then I didn't like it. I thought it was boring but now I see the benefits. When you came out the skin would feel soft, the hair would feel soft. (P12)

Natural products abounded in India for body waxing, hair oiling, and massaging the skin: "I used to put egg and henna, and those grandmotherly kinds of remedies. And, I still believe in those. Natural things. Chick pea flour is always a remedy for many things. It's like 409 – in the *Big Fat Greek Wedding*" (P1).

Singling out a solitary sensory experience proved difficult for some women who exemplified Hiss' simultaneous perceptions in their dress descriptions (1990):

> When I imagine sari, I always imagine nice silk saris. With a beautiful color and border. Those are the very important things for us, like if the sari is nice, but the border is wrong, then we are not going to buy the sari. So it has to be a combination of border, material, color, and the designs. I don't know when we put on the saris and the jewelry, it's like a romantic mode, yeah you are in honeymoon. When you wear a very nice sari and you dress up and that whole thing, your mind is very different, like you are in a dream world when you put it on. (P5)

SENSORY CHALLENGES UPON ARRIVAL IN THE UNITED STATES

Clothed in a multisensory self derived from dress experiences in India, the women arrived in the United States as new brides or students. The women faced a variety of sensory challenges, undergirded for many by the familiarity of already wearing jeans, pants, and Western-style shirts in India. For these women, alteration of even one sensual norm common in India transformed their former holistic conception of self (Hiss 1990). Dress challenges for many women centered on colors, textures, make-up, fit, body exposure, appropriateness, and what they observed as a boring commonality, along with lack of attention to grooming. Some women remembered issues of garment fit and appropriateness that challenged their sensual norms upon arrival:

> I felt that body size did not define what one was expected to wear. In India, if you are overweight you would never be expected to wear jeans or skirts. But here, for me it was initially very surprising to see really overweight people wearing shorts. It took me some time to digest the fact that shorts are common here and it is not only an outfit to be worn by people with good bodies. (P2)
>
> I couldn't believe how much emphasis there was on little girls to look grown up and wear make-up. The other thing was seeing older women trying to look so young. Why were people not wanting to look their age? (P6)

With color assuming such a pivotal role in defining Indian sensibility, not surprisingly some women expressed confusion when facing a new color palette: "[At] Christmas, I remember how people dressed in reds, greens, blacks, and maybe off-white and that's it, and … I was really surprised at that. Now I know that those are Christmasy colors" (P15).

For other women, perceptions of a lack of interest in grooming sparked comparisons with their homeland. Sentiments of Indian pride surfaced.

> You would never be seen in India in the way that we might run down to the grocery store to get some milk [in the United States]. You just have to look presentable [in India]. Even poor women will have crisp pressed sari at home even if it is old. The men who are poor and out selling food are well groomed. You would look at a hot dusty train and every shirt is pressed and starched. There is a lot of pride in looking a certain way. (P9)

SENSORY NEGOTIATIONS

As the women began their roles as students, professionals, or wives in the United States, they experimented with new forms of dress, make-up, hairstyles, and body exposure. In some cases, negotiations led to maintenance of certain Indian norms. For example, women echoed over and over, "I'd feel naked without my earrings, just naked." Likewise, few women adopted the brighter make-up they observed in the United States.

While many women adopted a neutral color palette for their everyday attire in the United States, bright colors were hard to forgo among a few women.

> I am always in bolder colors… When I started working that was the first thing that somebody noticed, saying "You sure wear different colors. I would be afraid to try those colors. I've just always worn pastels my whole life. I feel like it [bright color] won't go with my hair color. It just looks so nice on you." I couldn't be in pastels. I'm very happy with my bright colors. (P10)

In other cases, women blended their old and new preferences, often joining an Indian embroidered *kurta* (thigh-length tunic top) with jeans while adding a *dupatta* (long neck scarf) as a light wrap. One woman, tired of wearing plain t-shirts in the United States, added her own Indian element, "I did some mirror work [tiny mirrors encircled with embroidery] on one of my t-shirts to make it look very different and somewhat Indian. I was just getting tired of wearing simple t-shirts and wanted to do something different" (P2).

In contrast to women who blended Indian and Western styles, other women maintained separate sensory selves both in their closets and in their dress choices for work, domestic life, and Indian events.

> When I wear Indian dress, I do wear brighter colors. For Western clothes, I don't wear the bright colors, but more natural colors, maybe with a splash of color. In India, I would never wear black but I do here. If you look at my closet I have a lot of black and white but the Indian part is very bright – reds, blues, pinks, and greens. The other section is more neutral. (P5)

Particularly when wearing Indian dress to an Indian event, women called forth their multi-sensory experiences from India when judging the dress of their peers: "When you meet people in the community [Indian party] you always want to be as Indian as you can be and dress that way with the jewelry and the clothes. People will even say, 'I see that it has been awhile since you have been to India. You are repeating [what you are wearing to an Indian function]'" (P10).

LIVED EXPERIENCES IN A NEW CULTURAL CONTEXT: US INFLUENCES

A variety of lived experiences within the United States informed the symbolic meanings that the women came to associate with both Indian and Western appearances. In many instances, the women's reflections upon these experiences contributed to a reworking of meaning, which, in turn, was invoked to guide future self-presentations.

For instance, through careful observations of cultural insiders and their traditions, the women gained an accumulated understanding of the meanings associated with varied US cultural motifs and forms of dress. This learning process was an incremental one in which the women gradually assembled an increasingly nuanced understanding of a new cultural sensory and meaning system: "Sometimes it is hard for me to keep track what goes when. There was a shirt that I really like – it has a scarecrow on it. For the longest time, I didn't realize it was a fall [shirt]. I wore it all the time because I really liked the colors. But slowly, I learned what goes when" (P1).

Social feedback produced through interactions with cultural insiders also informed the women's meaning-making processes and their attendant revisions in meanings ascribed to their own dress and appearance as well as those of others. In some instances, these cultural insiders included assimilated members of the local Indian community who had preceded the women in their move to the United States, and who were perceived by the newcomers to possess a reliable stock of knowledge about Western dress mores and norms. The newcomers readily accessed these insiders through tight-knit networks of Indian families, intently seeking and following their sartorial guidance as a means by which to navigate the subtleties of unfamiliar dress and appearance codes. The women valued this brand of gentle sisterly counsel, frequently invoking it to plan their self-presentations: "Initially, having a sister-in-law who was already here and who was very Americanized helped. She would say, 'Oh, you cannot wear that' or 'That's too low.' I would always pull my hair up with little barrettes, and she would say, 'Oh, that looks too cutesy'" (P10).

In other cases, social feedback from Americans contributed to the women's interpretations of dress symbols and their resultant revisions of the meanings they came to associate with dress. Perhaps the most poignant and emotionally laden account of such an interaction was Participant 5's recollection of some rather distressing interpersonal interactions that occurred shortly after her arrival in the United States in the early 1970s. These experiences alerted her to new cultural meanings of her dress and appearance and challenged her sense of self in a palpable way.

> At that time the economy there [United States] was doing very bad and there were a lot of racial problems. So, I was more comfortable in pants than sari. I could hear some of the slurs when I went out. [Americans] could pinpoint us, and we were targeted very badly. When I first came, that one thing motivated me to wear pants really fast. (P5)

Although the sentiments produced through Participant 5's interface with unknown cultural insiders certainly diverged from those created through Participant 10's fondly recollected interactions with her sister-in-law, it is significant, to note in both cases, the women invoked their newly reworked meaning systems to meet a similar sartorial goal – that of successfully blending in to their new cultural surroundings.

Finally, for many women the move to the United States entailed not only a physical relocation, but also a variety of role and lifestyle adaptations. As noted, a number of women came to the United States as new brides or students, and, in many cases, their migration to the United States represented the first time they had lived away from their families of origin. These role and lifestyle adaptations necessitated yet further revisions of the meanings invoked to guide appearance management decisions. In the following comment, one woman elucidated the ways in which her new lifestyle set a context for her revised associations with Western and Indian dress:

> I feel comfortable wearing Western dresses; they're very practical. You're very mobile here. You don't have a lot of help, like in India. There, you have people come clean your house, and you have people take your garbage out, and if you wore sari, maybe you could get away with it, because you're not doing a lot of physical stuff there. But, here, when you have to go grocery shopping with a two-year-old, I would *never dream* of wearing a sari. *Absolutely unthinkable.* Even on weekends I prefer to wear a short and a t-shirt in summer and do my gardening. It's the practicality of the situation. (P3)

CONSTRUCTING THE TRANSNATIONAL SELF IN THE US CONTEXT

Insomuch as identity "establishes what and where a person is in social terms," it can be conceptualized as the self in context (Stone 1965: 223). Identity is made apparent to others through the use of dress and "is intrinsically associated with all the joinings and departures of social life" (ibid.). Thus, it is perhaps not surprising that throughout their interviews, the women alluded to the ways in which their departure from their native Indian culture and their subsequent immersion within US culture contributed to their construction of multifaceted, transnational identities. Of particular interest was the process through which they integrated a rather sophisticated understanding of sensory and dress norms and expectations within both India and the United States to guide the ways in which they made varied identifications of themselves as Indians, as professionals, as females, as modest or respectful persons, as proper persons, as young or mature persons, and as attractive persons.

The narratives of three women illustrate well the complex ways in which the women manipulated dress to construct varied identities within their new cultural context. One woman spoke to considerations relevant to the communication of a professional identity. Of interest here was the way in which her views on this topic changed over time, paralleling her increased depth of experience in varied cultural roles (e.g., cultural outsider, professional) as well as corresponding shifts in how she imagined others may review varied appearances and related self-identifications.

> The first day I was supposed to meet my new boss I pulled out a *shalwar kamiz* [loose pants and tunic top], and my husband said, "No, no … you want to maintain a professional appearance." So, we went to Marshalls and picked out a jacket. He said, "You can wear *shalwar kamiz* later, when you have established your role, but when you are first going to see her, it will be better if you dress the way that everybody does." Now I feel like I have grown enough personally and professionally that wearing *shalwar kamiz* would not be a hindrance, and I would be able to communicate. At that time, if she had her biases come up and she had seen me in my outfit, it may not have given me that opportunity to join the group. (P10)

Another newly married woman also addressed the logic she used in selecting Indian versus Western dress in constructing a given, often multifaceted, identity. In particular, she explained the varied ways in which she used dress either to convey materially her commitment to Indian mores regarding womanhood, marriage, and propriety or to facilitate her desire to move comfortably between Indian and Western cultures.

> In India after marriage, I want people to think of me as a good girl. So, I prefer to wear saris and *shalwar kamiz* in front of my in-laws and my parents. If I go to India, I'll wear Indian dresses, and I'll want people to think that I'm still Indian, not a Westernized version of myself. I don't want people to think that [my husband] is molding me into this Western culture. I think I should be comfortable in both the cultures. If I'm going to India, I prefer to wear Indian dresses, if I'm here I prefer to wear Western dresses. (P11)

From both sensory and esteem perspectives, this young woman clearly delighted in following and adapting selected Western fashion trends, at least in certain contexts. She found pleasure in viewing televised style programs and took cues from these American programs as she constructed her Western-dress persona. She also acknowledged the sense of confidence she gained from using her dress to convey an affiliation with her new culture. At the same time, however, she spoke to the ways in which her relocation from India to the United States had stifled opportunities for her to experience the sensual nature of her Indian dress and to make identifications of the self as a new bride. For her, this opportunity lost was laced with sentiments of regret: "I miss wearing saris. Every new bride is supposed to wear good saris, dressed up nicely with jewelry and everything. After coming here, I never got a chance to wear all my Indian dresses, my jewelries. They are just in the locker" (P11).

A third woman's comments provided understanding about the ways in which immersion within a new culture set a context for the exploration of varying constructions of identity as a modest woman. Of interest are the multiple, context-bound ways in which she conceptualized "modesty."

> I had seen Western movies. So, I knew what people wore in the US. Still, sometimes I would be shocked… Like some tank-tops, you'd see stuff hanging out, and I'd be like, "Wow! I mean, that's not nice." But then the other day, I got a swimsuit for myself, and I thought, I couldn't imagine wearing that in India. It's not like stuff was hanging out, but it was not modest according to what standards I had before. So, my standards definitely have changed a lot. Just to give you an example, when my in-laws were here when my son was born, there were some things in my closet that I didn't feel like wearing in front of them. Not that they would say anything; they're really nice people. But, I knew that my perception had changed. I just felt I shouldn't look *that sexy* in front of them. (P8)

CONSTRUCTING TRANSNATIONAL IDENTITIES IN A POSTMODERN REALITY: SOCIAL SATURATION

Hiss' 1990 work on the sense of place became the theoretical launching point for this chapter. As we move through the data analysis process, however, the meanings that emerge lead us to integrate a second theoretical perspective into our interpretations: Kenneth Gergen's scholarship on the self (1995). Taken together, Hiss' and Gergen's perspectives offer a holistic lens through which to gain understanding about the women's cross-cultural negotiations of the senses, sentiments, and meanings associated with dress, and the ways in which these negotiations informed the women's self-presentations.

In seeking to situate our findings within this expanded theoretical context, it is instructive to consider the following reflection.

> My husband likes me wearing skirts, nice tops, *kurtas*. Nice jeans, low-rise jeans, saris also. He says, "Whatever you wear, it should be good for the occasion. If you are going for an Indian get-together, wear sari or *shalwar kamiz*. If you are going to meet my American friends, wear something decent, but Westernized." And, if we both are going

> alone for any vacation, or some place out of the town, he insists me to wear some sexy
> clothes. He just likes that. So, it's according to the occasion. (P11)

Underpinning this comment was a keen recognition of the role of social context and audience in guiding one's lines of dress behavior and corresponding identifications of self. Implicit here was not so much the question, "Who am I?," but rather, the query, "Who can I be with you?" (Cahill 1995: 231).

In the words of Gergen, then, the women experienced social saturation, or a "dense" population of the self in which one considers numerous significant and generalized others whose "voices" represent diverse and often incompatible perspectives. Gergen uses the term "multiphrenia" (many minds) to refer to this pattern of self-consciousness. According to Gergen, the saturation of the self is produced within a postmodern cultural context that affords individuals virtual access to multiple, often faraway realities resulting in what Joshua Meyrowitz refers to as the notion of a "generalized elsewhere" (1989: 327).

Although the women frequently referenced the role of Western media in shaping their constructions about life in the United States prior to their arrival, it was their actual immersion in this culture rather than their virtual one that seemed to be most salient in their acquisition of a language of self that allowed for "multiple and disparate potentials for being" (Gergen 1995: 233). Implicit here were two learning processes, which Gergen refers to as "knowing that" and "knowing how." Through their observations and interactions within the United States, the women acquired and honed a working knowledge of the sensory and symbolic elements of dress patterns associated with people of various social locations. This, then, is "knowing that." With time, the women learned to "know how," or to put into practice their new knowledge about US dress norms when the appropriate circumstances for doing so arose.

The seeds of social saturation were sown long before the women arrived in the United States. It was within their native India that the women first were socialized to master a complex system of social norms that provided sensory and symbolic prescriptions regarding what, when, and how clothing should be worn. Although many of these considerations focused upon the wearing of Indian attire such as the sari or *shalwar kamiz*, early socialization processes also addressed the wearing of Western dress.

> We were going to the silver market in Bombay, and I came out of my bedroom in shorts.
> My mother said, "You will not come out like that." So there was an expectation that
> you could wear shorts and go to the swimming pool, but you didn't want the unwanted
> attention in the market, nor did you want to offend anybody. (P9)

Thus, by the time they arrived in the United States, many of the women had formed initial impressions about the sensory and symbolic experience of wearing Western dress, impressions that would be further transformed by their immersion within the US culture, and had developed an appreciation for the significance of audience and context in shaping appearance management decisions.

Gergen suggests that social saturation and multiphrenia can induce feelings of inadequacy in those who try to satisfy multiple and sometimes incompatible constructions about how one "ought" to be or behave (1995). Although the women certainly acknowledged that forging identity in shifting cultural contexts can be a slippery slope, they also spoke of this experience as positively expanding their opportunities for identity construction.

> We are the lucky generation here. [We have] the opportunity to blend the best of both. You are not letting go of that which is India. There was a previous generation who either completely let go or completely held on to India. We are in between. For our generation, especially for my kids, you bring the best of both worlds. My son, who is three and a half, will ask me, "Are you Indian or are you American?" It is hard to answer. I will say, "You were born here so you are American, but your mommy is from India. Those are your roots and this is your reality." I also struggle when I go back to India because you don't completely fit in there nor do you completely fit in here. Here you are different, physically or whatever. There you are different; action-wise, you have changed. Your dress styles have changed; your attitudes have changed. You're in that in-between. It will really be curious to see what my children turn out to be, their attitudes. They are like little American kids in Indian bodies. I personally think that the things that will hold them to the culture ... one is food and the second is clothing. (P10)

In sum, the experiences of these Indian women provide an apt example of Gergen's supposition that personal identity is not fixed, but, rather, is constructed and reconstructed in concert with the contextual demands of everyday life (1995). Likewise, the women's experiences support Steven Feld's notion that as new meanings arise, the formerly unfamiliar intersensoriality becomes familiar (2005). As part of their geographical relocation between two cultures, the women experienced shifts and challenges in relation not only to the multisensory experience or simultaneous perception of dress but also in relation to the sentiments and meanings associated with varied forms of dress. For these Indian women, their expanded *experience of dress* ultimately was instrumental in supporting the development of a new, multifaceted, and transnational sense of self.

REFERENCES

Banerjee, M. and Miller, D. (2003), *The Sari*, Oxford: Berg.

Cahill, S. E. (1995), "Postmodern Social Reality," in S. E. Cahill (ed.), *Inside Social Life: Readings in Sociological Psychology and Microsociology*, Los Angeles: Roxbury Publishing Company, pp. 230–31.

Edwards, E. (2003), "Marriage and Dowry Customs of the Rabari of Kutch: Evolving Traditions," in H. B. Foster and D. C. Johnson (eds), *Wedding Dress Across Cultures*, Oxford: Berg, pp. 67–84.

Feld, S. (2005), "Places Sensed, Senses Placed: Toward a Sensuous Epistemology of Environments," in D. Howes (ed.), *Empire of the Senses: The Sensual Culture Reader*, Oxford: Berg, pp. 179–91.

Gergen, K. (1995), "The Dissolution of the Self," in S. E. Cahill (ed.), *Inside Social Life: Readings in Sociological Psychology and Microsociology*, Los Angeles: Roxbury Publishing Company, pp. 231–7.

Hiss, T. (1990), *The Experience of Place*, New York: Alfred A. Knopf.

Howes, D. (2005), "Introduction: Empires of the Senses," in D. Howes (ed.), *Empire of the Senses: The Sensual Culture Reader*, Oxford: Berg, pp. 1–17.

Huyler, S. P. (1999), *Meeting God: Elements of Hindu Devotion,* New Haven, CT: Yale University Press.

Meyrowitz, J. (1989), "The Generalized Elsewhere," *Critical Studies in Mass Communication* 6 (3): 323–34.

Stone, G. P. (1965), "Appearance and the Self," in M. E. Roach and J. B. Eicher (eds), *Dress, Adornment, and the Social Order*, New York: John Wiley & Sons, Inc., pp. 216–45.

Tarlo, E. (1996), *Clothing Matters: Dress and Its Symbolism in Modern India*, Chicago: University of Chicago Press.

Tuan, Y.-F. (1993), *Passing Strange and Wonderful: Aesthetics, Nature, and Culture*, Washington, DC: Island Press.

12 HANDMADE TEXTILES: GLOBAL MARKETS AND AUTHENTICITY

Victoria L. Rovine

> Styles went ethnic everywhere this summer, from Saks Fifth Avenue to the 99-cent store.
>
> N. Bernstein, *The New York Times*

A recent article in *The New York Times* focusing on a merchant in Astoria, Queens, described the fad for Indian tunic blouses with sequined embroidery. The article offered a vivid illustration of the phenomena that characterize many contemporary fashion markets: (1) the globalization of clothing styles and fashion manufacture; (2) the changing identities associated with garments, textiles, and styles of dress; (3) the revival and re-creation of forms associated with "tradition"; and (4) the adaptation of new production techniques to suit changing markets. This essay focuses on one element that remains constant in the midst of fashion's global markets and shifting terrains: the role of texture, both literal and conceptual, in the production of "authentic" styles of clothing.

The markers of authenticity in dress, the features that signify distinctive cultural characteristics and practices, are often preserved or imitated as garments move between markets. By exploring one of these markers, texture, I seek to elucidate the construction of authenticity in the realm of dress. How does texture communicate authenticity, and what information does it encode? What does this information reveal about the expectations that are attached to garments in various markets, both Western and non-Western? After introducing the issues through the case of Indian blouses sold in the United States, I will turn to African garments, which vividly illustrate the shifting markets and meanings of garments associated with "authentic" cultures. I will also detour into classic Western haute couture, a market in which authenticity has distinct connotations, many of which are also connected to texture. These worlds come together through discussion of contemporary African haute couture design, in which textiles associated with "authentic" cultures are employed, drawing on the histories out of which these associations emerge to create entirely new forms.

This investigation addresses the literal as well as the figurative meanings of texture, both of which are at play in the production of authenticity. The literal meaning of texture in the realm of fabrics and clothing is determined by factors including the type of fibers, the manner in which they are spun or otherwise prepared for the loom, and the nature of the weave. These variables produce a quality that can be perceived through the skin. The figurative texture of a fabric, the *feeling* it evokes, is also closely related to the techniques and circumstances of its manufacture, but it is the stories that reverberate from a textile's manufacture that lend it authenticity in this second sense, as I will describe. In order to address these multiple incarnations of texture, this exploration of the production and the perception of authenticity combines technical analysis with discussions of the emotional impact of clothing and textiles. Understanding texture requires a range of methodologies, from the "hard data" of manufacturing techniques to the ineffable realm of "feelings."

"AUTHENTIC" FASHIONS AND GLOBAL MARKETS

The Indian- or Pakistani-style shirts featured in the *New York Times* article are part of an international system whereby a garment's association with local "tradition" propels it onto global markets. The change in markets often relocates the manufacture of garments to completely new contexts where new populations are drawn into the production, in this case, to China and to a small factory in Brooklyn which is "staffed primarily by Latin American immigrants" (Bernstein 2005: 21). The identities that are attached to particular clothing styles, "Indian," "African," or any other cultural or regional designation, may have little to do with their actual provenance, for the idea of "Indian-ness" or "African-ness" is preserved through key features. In this case the fabrics and adornments create their recognizably "Indian" style when reproduced and readjusted, as are the production techniques such as "shortcuts like ready-made rolls of sequins instead of the kind sewn on one-by-one" (ibid.). Yet the value of handmade production is preserved, if only through the efforts made to imitate it: "And though Chinese factories now have the technology to mimic handwork, [one wholesaler] said he sometimes turned back to India for real handwork" (ibid.). The garments may also be produced for several distinct markets, from inexpensive outlets aimed at local South Asian immigrants to $3,000 designer versions sold at Saks.

The meanings of these tunics shift in global markets, their reception among new consumers affects their significance for their original audience. Thus, the South Asian immigrant owner of the boutique in Astoria noted a change in her own attitude: "I felt embarrassed with these clothes... Now I feel proud, because everybody's wearing them" (ibid.). Such cycles of authenticity and fashion complicate the classifications of clothing. As Joanne Eicher and Barbara Sumberg noted, ethnic dress can be defined in opposition to fashion: "Often known as traditional, ethnic dress brings to mind images of coiffure, garments, and jewelry that stereotypically never change... In other words ... the terms 'traditional' and 'ethnic' imply non-fashionable dress..." (1995: 300–301). Yet, garments shift between categories, sometimes propelled by their aura of authenticity.

TEXTURE, MANUFACTURE, AND AUTHENTICITY

Although customarily separated, the realms of high fashion and of non-Western dress often intersect and overlap, as the Indian tunics illustrate. Exploration of the role of texture as a marker of authenticity reveals a striking consistency between the markets for high-fashion and for non-Western attire. In both markets, texture serves as a barometer of the expectations attached to authenticity. In the realm of dress and adornment, our eyes may tell us if something is beautiful, but we rely on our hands to tell us if fabrics are "genuine," if a garment is "authentic." Touch is the sense most deeply used in questions of authenticity.

Texture provides information about production, a key factor in the evaluation of authenticity. Handmade manufacture is key to the creation of authenticity in the worlds of both Western haute couture and "ethnic" attire associated with non-Western cultures, though for very different reasons. Handmade manufacture is, in fact, the key defining feature of haute couture fashion. Official designation by the French fashion syndicate requires that a design house employ at least twenty people, with the presumption that all their work will be by hand. This handwork produces a sense of exclusivity through high price. In a feature on the fashion industry *The Economist* pointed out a designer dress can require "700 hours of painstaking labour" and cost more than $100,000 ("Fashion's Favorite" 2004: 5).

In a discussion of the development of the fashion system in the early decades of the twentieth century, Ellen Leopold notes haute couture long has had a special role as a bastion of handwork, with garments "presented as one-off style 'creations' that enhanced the originality and individuality of the consumer in a world of increasingly mass-produced goods" and further that "the imagery of advertising sought to play down if not conceal entirely the contribution of machinery to the production of clothing" (1992: 109). Handmade manufacture has become an ideal as much as it is an actual method. In the 1950s, Angela Partington observes, Christian Dior "pioneered the system through which manufacturers and retailers could sell an 'Original-Christian-Dior-Copy'" (1992: 151). In the high-fashion economy, thus, the hand of the designer has been abstracted, signified by a name on a label that continues to represent their identity. The originality of the handmade is translated into the conceptual realm, a move echoed in African textiles and fashion.

Production by hand has powerful implications in the market for non-Western garments and textiles as well as in high fashion, for it carries associations with authenticity, tradition, and local cultures. In his discussion of the success of Oriental carpets in Western markets, where they are associated with "authenticity," Spooner notes: "[T]he fact of their being hand-made became a significant characteristic, and as the craft was gradually drawn into the world economy the survival of traditional relations of production became an additional factor [in their success on the international art market] – the rug was an exotic product made in its own exotic production process for its own exotic purpose" (1986: 222). Ronald Waterbury describes a similar focus on the handmade as a central element of the globalization of the market for Oaxacan embroidery, noting that for many consumers "a handcrafted object evokes the aura of human tradition, the sweat and skill of its individual maker, and – since craftsmanship avoids the repetitive precision of a stamping machine – uniqueness and originality" (1989: 245).

As these examples demonstrate, the value of handmade manufacture lies in its evocation of lives and stories, offering consumers a means by which to partake physically in those narratives. The power of the handmade to evoke such stories crosses cultural boundaries. Just as the detailed stitches of a high-fashion garment may allude to the so-called "little hands" of the seamstresses in Dior's atelier, so too may carpets call to mind the Central Asian nomads to whom they are often attributed, or as a Mexican blouse evokes Oaxacan villagers.

AFRICAN TEXTILES/AFRICAN AUTHENTICITY

Turning to Africa, a strip-woven, indigo-dyed wrapper embodies the physical presence of weavers and dyers in a Malian village. Adam Levin, a dealer, art promoter, and author of the recent book *The Art of African Shopping*, encapsulates this animation of the handmade: "Like all handmade textiles, this cloth 'lives'" (2005: 98). The cloth in question, an indigo-dyed cotton wrapper, epitomizes the texture, both literal and symbolic, that results from handmade manufacture (Figure 12.1). Levin purchased the cloth quite close to its point of

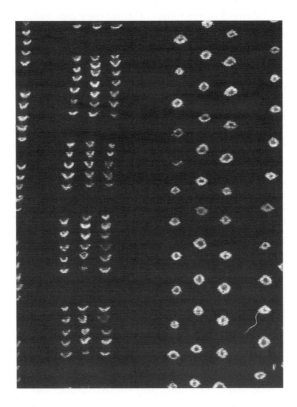

Figure 12.1 Indigo-dyed cloth, strip-woven cotton, Dogon region, Mali, late-twentieth century. Private collection.

production and he evoked the hands (in this case, the arms) of the maker in his description of the fabric: "I bought my favorite piece of cloth on the cliffs of the Dogon in Mali, from a woman whose brown arms gleamed a deep, iridescent blue in the Sahel sunshine" (ibid.). The cloth and its maker are, thus, intimately linked, to the point of being the same color. The life out of which this cloth emerges is, by implication, the life of this Dogon woman, working in her rural village.

While the texture and color of specific handmade textiles and garments might evoke the circumstances of their production, this elision of African culture and handmade production has in some instances been broadly generalized and applied to African artistic production as a whole. Thus, in a popular publication on the adaptability of African textiles and other art forms to American home décor, Sharne Algotsson and Denys Davis declare: "African art ... evokes a time when fabric dyes were derived from plants, earth, and minerals; when cloth was produced from the pounding of tree bark; and when wooden objects were carved with rudimentary tools" (1996: 10). African-ness itself thus evokes the technology of the handmade.

Feel, a broad, ineffable term that encompasses texture, is also implicated in the determination of authenticity. It is the "feeling" of garments that allows consumers to insert themselves into the stories the clothing evokes. Such was the case for one male, African American consumer of a *bogolan* (mudcloth) suit who described the impact of the ensemble on his own sense of identity as he tried it on: "So what if the shop didn't have a mirror? I didn't need one to tell me how wearing the African clothing made me feel. The weight and regal cut of the cloth made me feel, well, reconnected" (Marriott 1997: section 9, 1). Or, as cited in the exhibition catalog, *Wrapped In Pride*, on the changing roles of Ghanaian *kente* cloth in global markets, one American wearer of the cloth explicitly connected her feelings with its handmade manufacture: "Having been there and actually watched the weaving ... gives me a special feeling, and I think I do feel a little different" (K. Smith-Phillips in Quick 1998: 262). The texture and weight of the garment evokes feelings in the wearer; feelings produced at the intersection of texture and authenticity.

MASS PRODUCTION OF THE HANDMADE

The connection between texture and authenticity is reflected in the mass production of cloth and garments that retain the stylistic signifiers of the handmade. *Kente* cloth is but one prominent example of factory-produced textile reproductions wherein the strips of woven patterns mechanically printed in a variety of media are marketed as "authentic." *Bogolan*, the Malian textile, offers another example (Rovine 2001). In its original form, this cloth is woven on narrow strip looms using locally spun cotton. It is then dyed using a labor-intensive process that involves applying a mineral pigment to the areas around the geometric patterns, darkening the background so that the motifs remain white.

As *bogolan* has been adapted to new, international markets, the elements that mark it as handmade have been carefully preserved or reproduced. The application of dyes has been accelerated by the reversal of the positive/negative space, so that cloth can be quickly adorned by painting simple linear patterns. Even stencils have been adapted to *bogolan* production, so that patterns can be even more efficiently applied. Yet, such streamlining of technologies has only minimally impacted the texture of *bogolan*, which is, along with its geometric patterns, crucial to its authenticity. The vast majority of the cloth made for sale in both domestic tourist markets and in international markets as "ethnic" textiles and clothing is made of the same strip-woven fabric that has long given *bogolan* its distinctive texture.

In a revealing twist on the many adaptations of this textile in diverse markets, American designer Daryl K. recently took a strikingly different approach to the use of *bogolan* by literally inverting the cloth in order to emphasize its handmade production (Horyn and Armstrong 2002: 81). Daryl K. created pants made of *bogolan* that appear to focus entirely on its handmade texture, to the exclusion of the patterns that usually define the cloth. The designer turned *bogolan* inside out, revealing the strips and the saturated browns and yellows that bleed through the seams along with a shadowy echo of the linear patterns. This reversal of the cloth's orientation (the side that has been adorned is now invisible) dramatically accents the strips, and the stitches that hold them together are the most important elements for the designer.

In a fascinating exception to this preservation of *bogolan*'s strip-woven texture, the textile's distinctive patterns have been adapted to factory-printed textiles, severing the patterns from the textured support of the strip-woven cloth. Yet, the handmade cloth is still referenced even in the mass-produced fabric. Patterns are surrounded by an "aura" of the handmade in the form of an encircling ring of "smudged" edges, reproducing the imperfection of the hand-painted cloth. In one prominent example of this phenomenon, leading Malian fashion designer, Chris Seydou, designed a *bogolan*-inspired textile produced by a Malian factory in 1991 (Rovine 2001: 116) (Figure 12.2). The pattern incorporated subtle variations in color saturation and soft edges around the linear patterns. Thus, Seydou hints at manual production, a crucial element of *bogolan*'s popularity both at home and abroad, even as he initiates industrial production of the cloth to meet new demands and find new markets.

Other fabrics, too, have been translated from literal to symbolic references to the handmade. Along with the woven patterns of *kente* and the carefully painted motifs of *bogolan*, the vast array of effects that result from tie-dye and other resist dyeing techniques from many West African textile traditions have been painstakingly replicated in the medium of screen printing and other technologies of mass production. The factory-printed versions of resist-dyed fabrics also reproduce key markers of the handmade, such as fuzzy edges and uneven seams. Thus, through visual cues, these textiles allude to the handmade production crucial in the perception of authenticity. In a dramatic example, a Senegalese factory print, purchased in the early 1990s, imitates the explosion of rippling color that is the result of tie and dye techniques used with multiple plunges into dye vats of diverse colors (Figure 12.3).

Figure 12.2 *Bogolan* or mudcloth, strip-woven cotton, Bamako, Mali, late twentieth century. Private collection.

A particularly rich discussion of the visual re-creation of texture is provided by Leslie Rabine, who describes the work of designers in the SOTIBA textile factory in Dakar, Senegal. These designers employ a variety of techniques in their efforts to reproduce the visual cues of handmade wax resist (batik). Their work is part of a long history of global markets and technical innovations that began with Indonesian batiks and continued with European reproductions of batiks intended solely for African markets. Thus, these designers partake in a multilayered production and reproduction of authenticity, as Rabine describes: "Sotiba fabric began not simply as a copy of Indonesian batik, but as the French copy of the English imitation wax" (2002: 139). Rabine describes the efforts of designers to ensure that the markers of handmade manufacture are reproduced in the factory cloth, including elements such as "Le misfit," which "imitates the leaky border between motif and background that results from the wax-resist dyeing technique" (ibid.: 145). The final step in the printing process is the application of "Le crack," a design element that imitates the cracking effect of wax-covered cloth that has been crumpled as it is submerged into the dye vat. The complexity of effectively reproducing what was an accidental, even an undesirable,

Figure 12.3   Factory-printed reproduction of resist-dyed cotton fabric, SOTIBA textile company, Senegal, late twentieth century. Private collection.

by-product of the handmade batik required intense effort on the part of the designer: "It took him a whole month and many frustrating tries to produce a realistic representation of dye bleeding through a wax crack" (ibid.: 146). Of a cloth that had been carefully designed to incorporate "certain irregularities," "the designer said, 'You feel the African in it'." Thus, the cloth's authentic African-ness is located in the deliberate imperfections that mark manufacture by hand.

Adding yet another layer to this nexus of the handmade and the mass-produced, Rabine notes that, in fact, factory production need not eliminate the human element. In an ironic twist, "almost all the work, from beginning the design to mounting it on the print cylinders, *is* done by hand – with the help of huge rolls of cellophane tape, themselves symbolic of the workers' efforts to keep the old factory equipment patched together" (ibid.: 147). Thus, the SOTIBA workers who use elaborate machinery to imitate closely the appearance of the handmade must manipulate those machines by hand. Yet this element of hand manufacture does not lend the cloth the texture of authenticity so desirable on the market.

The manipulation by hand of outdated or broken machinery is not compatible with the notion of handmade as authentic. That is, not all work by hand carries connotations of authenticity.

ISISHWESHWE AND THE SCENT OF AUTHENTICITY

Along with the use of carefully designed patterns to communicate the tactile attributes of authenticity visually, in at least one case *smell* features in the sensory reproduction of the handmade. The iconic South African textile *isishweshwe* (or *shweshwe*) has a rich local history dating back more than a century (Leeb du Toit 2005). The cloth, also known as "German Print," and characterized by its small, neatly ordered geometric patterns, was originally made using indigo dye and, in the late nineteenth century, a synthetic form of indigo developed in Germany (Figure 12.4). In South Africa, its status as imported (arriving with German settlers in the nineteenth century) and, until recently, its foreign manufacture, has precluded its inclusion in conventional conceptions of "authentic" South African attire.

Since the late 1990s, however, *isishweshwe* has become a symbol of national identity and, as such, the market for *isishweshwe* and *shweshwe* imitations has grown. Only one

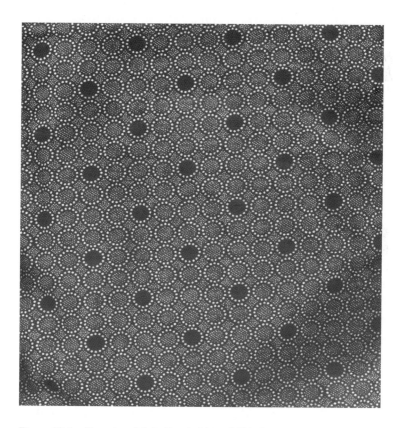

Figure 12.4   *Shweshwe* fabric, South Africa, 2001. Private collection.

manufacturer, Da Gama Textiles, still produces the cloth using the nineteenth-century process associated with "authentic" *isishweshwe*: copper rollers etched with patterns that are used to apply an acid solution to blue-dyed cotton percale, bleaching out white patterns. Several experienced textile consumers in South Africa told me they can smell the difference between the Da Gama technique and other printing technologies. The sound and texture of the cloth offer other clues to its authenticity – the name *isishweshwe* itself is said to be a reference to the sound the stiff-textured cloth makes when its folds rub together. At least one *isishweshwe* imitator was trying to reproduce the cloth's authentic smell! Thus, authentic production, whether by hand or by machine, can be communicated – and imitated – through several senses.

Isishweshwe brings us back to the realm of fashion trends in which handmade manufacture is a key feature. Numerous South African designers have made use of *isishweshwe*, and many have been inspired to use it because of its "authenticity." In the words of one young design student, "shweshwe is the celebration of a cultural heritage that embraces the new" (Counihan 2005: 63). Or, as Adam Levin describes it, the cloth has been transformed from the attire of matrons who have little access to fashion trends into the garb of choice for trendsetters: "*Shwe-shwe* fabric – once the domain of overweight aunties – is now a favorite of young black and white women" (Levin 2005: 173). In South African fashion, the texture of the past is thus melded with the cutting-edge styles of the present.

COMING FULL CIRCLE?

In Western fashion markets, the association between handmade manufacture and authenticity is embodied by the handwork of haute couture. Parisian fashion designer Jean Paul Gaultier frequently borrows from African and other non-Western dress practices, but without concern for their cultural authenticity. In his winter 2004 collection, he presented an entire African line with a richly beaded dress as the crowning ensemble. The dress is authentically haute couture in its complex handwork, creating multiple layers of texture and color. But it is culturally inauthentic; that is, elements from everywhere have been cut and pasted into Gaultier's personal aesthetic vision without acknowledging their cultures of origin. A spread in *The New York Times* magazine in March, 2005, offered another view of these distinct versions of authenticity (Hirshberg and Barnes 2005). Pairs of bags, one by a named designer, one identified only by the non-Western culture from which it originated, emphasized the apparent synchronicity between these two distant realms, creating a contrast that seems aimed at lending the Western designs a veneer of authenticity. One of those bags, of a type used by Yoruba diviners in Nigeria, appeared in both realms, stripped of its authenticity in one culture to be literally stitched into another. The desire to produce and reproduce authenticity drives these transpositions of form and translations of meaning. Texture plays a crucial role in negotiations over authenticity in the realm of dress, providing a sensitive barometer of shifting local identities and changing perceptions of other cultures.

REFERENCES

Algotsson, S. and Davis, D. (1996), *The Spirit of African Design*, New York: Clarkson Potter Publishers.

Bernstein, N. (2005), "In Craze for Tunic Blouses, It's See and Be Seen in Sequins," *The New York Times* (September 11): 21.

Counihan, H. (2005), "Shweshwe: The Long History of the Latest Trend," *Urban Fabrics* (July): 63–4.

Eicher, J. B. and Sumberg, B. (1995), "World Fashion, Ethnic, and National Dress," in J. B. Eicher (ed.), *Dress and Ethnicity: Change Across Space and Time*, Oxford: Berg, pp. 295–306.

"Fashion's Favorite." (2004), *The Economist* (March 6–12) 370 (8,365): 4–5.

Hirshberg, L. and Barnes, R. (2005), "The Things They Carried," *The New York Times Magazine* (March 20): 72–9.

Horyn, C. and Armstrong, D. (2002), "She Wears the Pants: Daryl K. is back in charge" and "Oh, K!" *The New York Times Magazine* (September 22): 77–83.

Leeb du Toit, J. (2005), "Sourcing Amajamani/Isiswhweshwe and Its Indigenization in South Africa," Unpublished paper.

Leopold, E. (1992), "The Manufacture of the Fashion System," in J. Ash and E. Wilson (eds), *Chic Thrills: A Fashion Reader*, Berkeley: University of California Press, pp. 101–17.

Levin, A. (2005), *The Art of African Shopping*, Cape Town: Struik Publishers.

Marriott, M. (1997), "Meaning in a Suit from Mali," *The New York Times* (October 26) section 9: 1, 5.

Partington, A. (1992), "Popular Fashion and Working-Class Affluence," in J. Ash and E. Wilson (eds), *Chic Thrills: A Fashion Reader*, Berkeley: University of California Press, pp. 145–61.

Quick, B. (1998), "Pride and Dignity," in D. Ross (ed.), *Wrapped in Pride: Ghanaian Kente and African-American Identity*, Los Angeles: Fowler Museum of Cultural History, pp. 203–65.

Rabine, L. W. (2002), *The Global Circulation of African Fashion*, New York: Berg.

Rovine, V. L. (2001), *Bogolan: Shaping Culture through Cloth in Contemporary Mali*, Washington, DC: Smithsonian Institution Press.

Spooner, B. (1986), "Weavers and Dealers: The Authenticity of an Oriental Carpet," in A. Appadurai (ed.), *The Social Life of Things: Commodities in Cultural Perspective*, New York: Cambridge University Press, pp. 195–235.

Waterbury, R. (1989), "Embroidery for Tourists: A Contemporary Putting-Out System in Oaxaca, Mexico," in A. B. Weiner and J. Schneider (eds), *Cloth and Human Experience*, Washington, DC: Smithsonian Institution, pp. 243–71.

13 GROWING OLD AND DRESSING (DIS)GRACEFULLY

Annette Lynch, M. Elise Radina, and Marybeth C. Stalp

The cultural meaning of female aging in the United States strongly affects the domination of the mass media with ideals of youthful beauty and fashion products primarily designed for young bodies and young lifestyles. Older women do not see themselves or their lifestyles depicted in the fashion system, which leads to feelings of being marginalized and invisible. In addition, aging for women, in contrast with that for men, has been made more difficult in the United States due in part to a culturally maintained reliance on attractiveness as a measure of female accomplishment throughout the female life cycle (Kaiser 1997).

Our research investigates the emergence of Red Hat Societies (RHS) as an empowering means of managing identity for aging American women. We used Erving Goffman's symbolic interaction framework of managing stigma to analyze the behavior of women within RHS chapters as a response to the stigma surrounding aging for women (1963). Our research also explored the theoretical reclaiming of fashion by RHS members, an area explored by scholars working on younger populations who argue fashion is an important part of women's culture that can function as a form of self-expression, agency, and transformation (Chideya *et al.* 1993; Scott 1998).

The RHS chapters studied were all located in the rural Midwest. While isolated women of color were active in some chapters included in the study, the majority of members in all chapters were white. Our qualitative research approach included participant observation by all three researchers, interviews, and focus groups. All three researchers shopped together to buy pink hats for a statewide meeting, wearing the hats when eating out together, and presenting at academic meetings. While this behavior gave us entry into the study groups, perhaps more significantly it helped us understand their responses to wearing the hats as a group, and the amusement that happened as a result.

BACKGROUND AND BEGINNINGS: RED HAT SOCIETY

The RHS began in 1997 when Sue Ellen Cooper, a midlife, white, Californian bought a red fedora on a whim in an Arizona thrift shop while on vacation. She discovered wearing the hat made her feel free to have fun again as she did when she was younger. Cooper wanted to share this experience with her friends, so she started a tradition of buying her female friends red hats for their fiftieth birthdays, and sharing with them the Jenny Joseph poem

Figure 13.1 Red Hat Society women posing in their flamboyant apparel.

"Warning," with its linkage of aging to having fun and wearing red hats (see Figure 13.1). Cooper's group of friends named themselves the RHS and began meeting in public spaces wearing their red hats. Their activities quickly earned them public and media attention, and e-mail interest from women across the country. The RHS grew to include both chapters officially registered on Cooper's RHS website (36,000) and regionally based unofficial chapters, for a total official membership of 850,000 (Walker 2005).

Chapters are typically small (under fifteen) in order to make restaurant dinner reservations for meetings easily and to ensure bonding between the group members. When assembling, a chapter elects a Queen Mother and selects a name for their group, often incorporating the color red as well as adjectives describing the attitude of the group. Examples of group names not in this study include: Red Hat Rubies, Diamonds in the Red, and Red Foxes (Cooper 2004). Activities, meeting times, and frequencies of gathering vary by chapter. Some chapters meet for lunch, high tea, wine-tastings, travel regionally to cultural exhibits and events, and even meet to quilt or knit. The enjoyment each group experiences depends upon the make-up of the chapter.

RHS official membership is restricted to women who are fifty or older. Those younger than fifty interested in being involved in the chapters can wear pink and lavender, and are referred to as "pink hats." Pink hats are Red Hats in training, and in more formal groups undergo at fifty what is called a "red-uation." A red-uation occurs when women graduate from pink and lavender to red and purple. Important to note, Red Hat women are rewarded for their rising age, instead of being punished, as typically occurs in mainstream society (Calasanti and Slevin 2001; Cooper 2004).

As RHS membership has grown, Rob Walker (2005) observed a group's subversive ability to make the surrounding culture look at female aging differently has grown proportionately. Walker also noted youth subcultures that challenge existing normative standards of behavior and appearance have received scholarly attention (for example, Hite 1988; Kennedy 1993; Riordan 2001; Scott 1998; Wilson 1990), and one of the groups most dramatically marginalized in current American culture, aging women, has been largely ignored. This essay examines RHS membership as an appearance management strategy for older women experiencing the stigma related to stereotypes of female aging in American youth-oriented society. Appearance management, fashion alienation as related to aging, and aging as stigmatized identity emerge in attitudes toward older women.

REVIEW OF LITERATURE

APPEARANCE MANAGEMENT OF AGING

Gregory Stone declared the dressed body establishes a two-way communication system, with the wearer creating a program of dressed appearance that an audience reviews, creating a discourse on the meaning of dress (1965). As a result of this communication exchange, the wearer may alter to achieve a more positive review, or maintain the dress to challenge existing norms or standards. Research on appearance management done with a sample of female college students indicates young women practice appearance management behaviors in order to meet cultural ideals of beauty, despite differing attitudes toward gender roles and differing levels of self-esteem (Lennon and Rudd 1994).

Studies of management of dress identity indicate older women respond to society's negative review of their aging female attractiveness by using cosmetics, undergarments, and custom-tailored garments to try to appear younger, and hide the aging process (Bartley and Warden 1962; Ebeling and Rosencrantz 1961; Jackson and O'Neal 1994). John Schouten found individuals use plastic surgery most often during periods of personal transition or movements from one phase of life into another, such as movement into perceived old age (1991).

FEMALE AGING AS STIGMATIZED IDENTITY

Research shows women's attractiveness to men decreases significantly with age, while men's attractiveness to women is not impacted significantly by the aging process (Mathes *et al.* 1985). Related research found age plays a fundamental role in ratings of female attractiveness, with older fashion models receiving lower ratings than younger models in image-based quantitative studies (Korthase and Trenholme 1982; Lennon 1988; Nowak 1975; Sorell and Nowak 1981). Studies show aging as a fundamental component of physical attractiveness for aging women, with middle-age women describing thin and young as the ideal of beauty (Lennon 1997).

The research results may in part be explained by using Susan Kaiser's gender role dichotomy (Table 13.1), which establishes key differences in how males and females in the United States are socialized to measure accomplishment. On the one hand, boys and men learn to measure themselves based on an agonic standard of active definitions of self that are used to mark success, and which allow men to gain power and attractiveness as they age. Girls and women, on the other hand, perceive physical attractiveness as the key to positive reviews, leading to heavy reliance on youthfulness and beauty, and a related loss of attractive power with aging. Women therefore experience higher degrees of negative stereotyping and stigma related to aging than their male contemporaries.

Table 13.1 Coding of gender ideology: "Doing" versus "Being"

Doing	Being
Emphasis on achievement and action	Emphasis on appearance and attraction
Physical effectiveness	Physical attractiveness
Adventure script in popular media	Romance script in popular media
Agonic (aggressive and active) power	Hedonic (indirect and attracting) power
Ideology of building character	Ideology of maintaining character

Source: Susan Kaiser's (1997) gender role dichotomy.

Susan Kaiser and Joan Chandler's work concludes that aging relates positively to feelings of fashion alienation for women (1984). Women over fifty reported frustration regarding finding suitable and/or unique dress styles available for their age group. Older women also expressed a lack of understanding or identification with fashion symbols used in the mass media. This research indicates that as a result of the natural aging process and the related inability to follow fashion trends due to sizing and availability issues, older women become stigmatized with little access into the mainstream arena of fashion culture.

Using Goffman's 1963 early work, stigma has been defined within the dress literature as "possession of an attribute that is undesirable or difficult to understand" leading to classification of an individual as "different from others" (Feather *et al.* 1989: 289–90). Goffman's definition of stigma as an attribute with the power to marginalize individuals, making them feel separated from mainstream culture, aptly fits older women in current American culture. According to Goffman, one of the methods individuals use to manage stigmatized identity is to join together with other members of the stigmatized group and present a positive image to others, often through shared dress and appearance styles.

METHODS AND DATA COLLECTION

We collected data using ethnographic methods from multiple sources and types of data (Emerson *et al.* 1995). These included in-depth interviews with twenty-five participants, a focus group interview with seven participants,[1] participant observation at RHS events and meetings, and examination of RHS publications and merchandise. Both the in-depth and focus group interviews followed a semistructured format. We analyzed data using an inductive approach. All members of the research team read each interview in its entirety, noting perceptions of common themes. The research team then discussed these common themes and came to agreement on them. One of these common themes, management of aging identity, forms the focus of this essay.

Three distinct bodies of data form the results sections. This includes data supporting the use of Goffman's management of stigma through group bonding behavior and data that explore the reinforcement of bonds in the group due to shared life-span experiences. Data summarizing specific behaviors recounted by group members that challenge traditional female aging stereotypes, with specific attention paid to the relationship of women in the RHS to fashion and the hedonic power it can create then follows. The section concludes with a discussion exploring what red hats symbolize or mean to RHS women and why they were selected as the dress item giving rise to this movement.

RESULTS

RHS AS MANAGEMENT OF STIGMA

As stated earlier, one method of managing stigma is to bond with other stigmatized individuals and create a group that shares symbols and behaviors to help all members transcend the negative traits ascribed to the group by others (Goffman 1963). This theme appears throughout all the interviews, and consequently is discussed in many different forms in this section.

When asked about aging stereotypes women typically narrated how they experienced their own grandmothers. "I remember when we looked at our grandmas and they were OLD people! My kids and grandkids don't think of me as old! And it isn't like we are not at the age they were, but all they did was make cookies and stay home" (RHFG1-04).[2] General distancing of participants active in RHS from being classified as "old" or "gray-haired" was extremely common. As a typical example, one interview subject retorted, "Old, gray-haired and old, that just doesn't fit anymore... We are changing that attitude!" (RH03-04). Most women frankly admit their age early in the interview and stress RHS is not about hiding or masking aging, but is rather a celebration of the freedom and joys that come with the aging process. As one woman stated, "We are admitting to our age, but we are saying we don't care about our age, we are old people who are having fun!" (RH06-04). A stubborn streak also reflects women being written off by the younger generation. One woman quipped at the end of an interview, "Hey, don't write us off yet, we're not gone. We can still have fun!" (RH07-04).

Some women discussed the fashion industry and their experiences trying to buy clothing or follow fashion. One woman experienced age stereotyping as she was trying to order a Red Hat jacket using a direct mail supplier:

> Once I sent for a coat and jacket from a catalog. It was a medium, but it was huge. So I called up and ordered a small, and I said to the man on the phone, "is this jacket sized right?" and he said "that's Red Hat [merchandise], they are usually larger." I didn't say anything, but this must mean that he thought that older women are larger. And I don't believe that, but you know the stereotype. When you get to be 50, they say you are an old woman. I don't feel old. (RH03-04)

In many cases the women distance themselves from fashionable behavior with claims such as "I am not fashionable, I do my own thing" (RH14-04). This comment demonstrates reservations about how current fashion reflects older consumers and also exemplifies a confidence in her own personal style as expressed in Red Hat regalia.

Dress is clearly the most powerful symbol of cohesiveness for group members. Women repeatedly brought up how critical dress was to making the group fun and cohesive:

> The same group can go out and there is not an air of giddiness at the breakfast without the outfit. When we have the red hat and purple on there is an air of fun. I don't know how to explain it, but it is there, it is the common thread, and everybody's there for the same reason. Wearing it makes the difference. (RH12-04)

Many women emphatically declared the hats are only worn when the group gets together, with very few women claiming they wear their red hats in other situations. One interview subject went as far as to say, "I don't think any one of us would choose to dress in purple and red hats. The only reason we do it is because it is part of being in the group" (RH10-04). Some chapters we interviewed get together to buy and decorate matching outfits or hats:

> We look for inexpensive, then we embellish, go to old stores and go shopping, look for feathers, boas, go to the dollar stores. It's kind of fun to see how you can embellish a bargain. Because none of us want to put twenty to fifty dollars into a hat, we are all retired, we can't spend that kind of money … but part of the fun is the search. (RH14-04)

Negotiations take place ahead of time within these chapters resulting in shared dress styles for particular activities: "We have different outfits. We have a t-shirt that has our name on it. It just depends on how you want to dress or where you are going. Like the tram ride. We all wore our purple t-shirts and our hats, not our fancy hats, cowboy hats, straw hats, something simple. Not one with flowers or feathers" (RH03-04). That Red Hat members gain security from all being dressed in like colors and similar styles permeates the interviews, "Well some people, when they put on that red hat their ego gets a little big, more ego, more outgoing. Some people really change when they are dressed up. But it is fun when everybody has on the red hat, then you don't feel singled out" (RH21-04).

While the group may be interpreted as coming together to battle aging stereotypes as a collective group rather than individually, a strong secondary adhesive holding the group together is common stage of life and shared histories. The majority of women stress for most of their lives they took care of others and that the RHS presented the opportunity finally to focus on the self, "Oh, I just like the idea that we can be free. And I guess I am of that generation where I did a lot for my kids all the time, and now it is kind of time to sit back and just relax and have fun" (RH01-04). Many bring up that RHS creates bonds as women joining together do more for themselves. "It really spurs them to think in new directions. Do more for themselves. One gal in our chapter comes to tears every time she talks about the fact that this is the first time she has ever done something just strictly for herself" (RH12-04). Thus, while the RHS is a response to stigma through group behavior, the strength of the bonds holding the women together is deepened by a set of shared experiences drawn from the time they all played the invisible but critical roles of raising children and doing community service.

ANTI-AGING BEHAVIOR AND DRESS

Interviewed RHS members continually reference the Jenny Joseph poem as they explain their dress and behavior. In particular women refer to the poem's opening lines linking growing older to dressing (dis)gracefully:

> When I am an old woman, I shall wear purple,
> With a red hat which doesn't go, and doesn't suit me.
> (2001: 29–30)

The poem links the wearing of what one Red Hat member referred to as "bodacious" dress to behavior that challenges aging stereotypes which assume older people are serious, slow moving, largely invisible, not very fun, and always well behaved:

> It is the poem with the outfit, the poem dictates to make up for the sobriety of your youth and then you decide how you are going to do that. At the picnic, we brought watermelons so we could learn to spit. That is part of the poem. The poem to me is huge. The poem dictates that you wear the colors and have a good time. It always goes back to that. (RH12-04)

Ignoring ladylike manners and having the freedom to be visibly loud in public are central to the feeling of youthfulness RHS women experience. The customary invisible role older women often play in this culture is set aside by RHS members as they go out together wearing their hats with pride and zip, "We can be very loud and kind of obnoxious because we do just have fun and act goofy and laugh" (RH17-04).

Part of the fun of the public events is the violation of proper dress rules they had learned as young adults. Women describe being overdressed, overdone, and over the top in terms of accessories, colors, and behavior as if to visibly announce: we will not be ignored! For example, one woman stated, "People my age love being ourselves, being able to wear clothes that don't necessarily match" (RH04-04). Another recounted, "I never wore red. I had red hair growing up; I never wore red. This is the first red article that I have ever purchased, but I am over fifty and I am proud of it. I do wear red now, and I don't care!" (RH04-04). For RHS members, membership allows them to feel young and to have fun again; some made reference to their childhoods. Women give central importance to the group, stating that without it they would not feel the same freedom from rules and responsibilities:

> I think it just empowers us to be more free. And maybe do some things that we normally wouldn't do. I think when you are in a group, a large group like ours, where everybody else is doing these silly things, you can do things and not feel like everybody's just sitting there staring at YOU because you are being silly. But there are so many of us doing it, that you know, it is accepted. (RH02-05)

Another aspect of youthfulness emerged as a theme in the interviews, namely a renewed power to attract hedonistic attention, particularly from men. Many women noted how delightful it was to get compliments on their appearance when they appeared as a group. Some expressed amazement men would be complimenting them on their appearance at their age:

> a lot of times it will be the men that will come up and make a comment about it. Which, I don't know, in a way it is kind of amazing. I mean, you know, it is kind of like, they like to see that feminine side again ... a lot of times they will come up and just have that comment. That, "you look so nice in your red hat." (RH02-05)

Revealing the feminine side through the wearing of hats and accessories, and the public recognition they receive for the behavior, gives RHS members feelings of hedonistic power many had not experienced in a long time, "We went out to eat at a restaurant you know and that is a lot of fun to do because like I said, you go in and you definitely get noticed because you've got there eight or ten women sitting around with their hats on" (RH06-04). Regaining power to attract positive attention from their appearance, particularly from men, is cited repeatedly as part of RHS fun. One woman stated, "There is something about women in red hats I guess. Men will come up to us and say, 'how do I join this group?' Oh they just love it" (RH07-04).

Older women expressed delight with the growing availability of Red Hat fashion items through catalogs, the internet, as well as in retail environments. RHS conventions feature prominent displays of Red Hat merchandise for sale as a part of the proceedings, and "shopping, shopping, shopping" is often a feature of the RHS chapter meetings. For these older women, accustomed to seeing special merchandise created for youth markets, to be granted so much attention by retailers, direct mail organizations, and local businesses gives positive feelings:

> The businesses were actually the ones to organize this Red Hat event. I think they are all catching on that Red Hatters are becoming a very large group of people. Certain places you go into they will name sign ups [raffle tickets] or punch cards. Then at the end you turn in your name and the businesses give away prizes. They have all these stores that have Red Hat items! (RH08-04)

At the conclusion of the event, Red Hatters turn in their raffle and punch cards, which are then drawn for prizes. The freedom from conventional fashion is clearly expressed in comments like, "when you get older you don't have to stick to the norm, and you don't have to follow fashion" (RH01-05), thus opening up the possibility for this market segment of older women demanding a more active and enjoyable set of products to embody their Red Hat identities.

WHY RED HATS?

The choosing of hats to symbolize group identity for women in this age group must be analyzed in light of their history with hats as they were growing up and at earlier stages of their adult lives. These women grew up and came of age during an era when women commonly wore hats in public. For them, the wearing of hats during these earlier stages of their lives had to do with following rules, being proper, and in many cases dressing up and going to church:

> We wore hats. We were Catholic and had to wear hats to church. And so we wore hats a lot, we wore hats when we dressed up even the people who weren't Catholic. And I mean we had to wear them to church and our three daughters all had to wear them to church. We thought it would be terrible if they did not keep their hats on in church. (RH03-05)

For these women the symbolic meaning of hats relates to following the rules and wearing the "proper" matching dress and gloves. So for this generation of women, the violation of the rules, so central to the fun of being an RHS member, is ideally expressed in the wearing of improper and ostentatious hats.

Another reason red hats work well as a symbol for this group is that hats are easy to put on and take off. In observing the arrival and departure of RHS members from meetings, members frequently put on their hats either in the parking lot, as they enter a restaurant, or as they sit down for the meeting. It is easy to decide when to "announce" your identity as an RHS member, with some less outgoing women choosing to do it when they are with the rest of their chapter. Once placed on the head, however, the red hats are extremely visible to others, thus affording women the attention from others that is so central to Red Hat activities.

Other forms of dress used to announce Red Hat identity are similarly portable and easy to take on and off. Some women wear red feather boas, which they often don after connecting with their group. Similar meaning is associated with these items, "It's perfectly permissible to be bodacious, so when I am feeling bodacious I wear this boa to the meetings" (RH10-04). Even in the case of jewelry women sometimes add it to the outfit once they arrive at the meeting location, and tone it down if they have to go somewhere else before or after the meeting. For example, in discussing the fact that she often breaks the rules and overdoes her dress for the meetings, one woman explained why she was more subdued the day of the interview, "We are definitely not perfect; we wear as much jewelry as we want. I didn't wear any today because I had to go to the store before this, [but usually] the more the better!" (RHFG1-04).

A final reason for choosing the red hat is because of the poem, and the fact that the poem speaks so clearly to women in this age group. For almost all women interviewed, they circled back to the poem as being central to what the organization means to them and the meaning they derive from wearing the Red Hat regalia in community with other women:

> I think the poem explains what the women are really trying to do. When we get on our purple and our red, we are allowed to be silly … we all still have this little girl inside of us … society says you are supposed to be prim and proper, you are supposed to use your quiet voice inside … society says you are old enough that we have taught you your manners, [but when] we put on our red hats and we can be the little kid again, just like the poem dictates … I shall sit on the street … I will learn to spit… (RH12-04)

CONCLUSION

Results from our study largely reinforce research literature in terms of describing how older women in American culture experience aging. Substantial interviews confirmed women feel stigmatized and marginalized by the aging process due to the cultural emphasis on physical attractiveness and youthfulness as measures of female worth. Our research also provides an up-to-date utilization of Goffman's work, and aptly illustrates the positive impact of stigmatized individuals bonding together and using symbols and behavior to reinvent themselves in a more positive guise.

Perhaps most significantly our research broadens the research done on the use of fashion to reinvent female identity in youth subcultures by examining the less visible population of older women. Older women responded to negative reviews of the female aging process by using cosmetics, dress, and surgery to make themselves appear younger. In contrast, our participants used dress to make older women visible and interesting again, and to gain the power to attract positive attention from others. The priority placed on youth in America influences scholarship as well as popular culture. As the American population continues to age, it becomes imperative that we focus attention on older as well as younger groups. In our research much was gained in terms of understanding the redefinition of aging in America through a study of this particular organization and its dress and behavior. In addition, it challenges us to reconsider our use of Kaiser's gender role dichotomy, which is often interpreted as women losing hedonistic attention as they age. These Red Hat women seem to be successfully waging a battle to regain that attention, and with it feelings of self-worth and value.

In terms of fashion alienation literature, the impact of the RHS on American perceptions of female aging needs to be recognized as going beyond the creation of RHS merchandise.[3] RHS members certainly feel affirmed and delighted by the range of merchandise created just for them and to fulfill their desire for fun and fashionable looks. Perhaps of more significance, the presence of the Red Hats on the public stage in tandem with other active older Americans is redefining what it looks like to age in America.

NOTES

1. Trained undergraduate and graduate students conducted the majority of interviews and focus groups.
2. Interviews are coded throughout using RH (red hat), participant number, and year. Focus group interviews are coded throughout using RHFG (red hat focus group), focus group number, and year.
3. The recent opening and closing by GAP Inc. of Forth and Towne, a chain store focused on providing interesting fashion for the mature female market, is symptomatic of the fashion industry's attempt to dress this growing market of older women looking for interesting apparel.

REFERENCES

Bartley, L. and Warden, J. (1962), "Clothing Preferences of Women Sixty-five and Older," *Journal of Home Economics* 54: 716–17.

Calasanti, T. and Slevin, K. F. (2001), *Gender, Social Inequality, and Aging*, Walnut Creek: AltaMira Press.

Chideya, F., Rossi, M., and Hannah, D. (1993), "Revolution, Girl Style," in L. J. Peach (ed.), *Women in Culture*, Oxford: Blackwell Publishers.

Cooper, S. E. (2004), *The Red Hat Society: Fun and Friendship After Fifty*, New York: Warner Books.

Ebeling, M. and Rosencrantz, M. L. (1961), "Social and Personal Aspects of Clothing for Older Women," *Journal of Home Economics* 53: 464–5.

Emerson, R., Fretz, R., and Shaw, L. (1995), *Writing Ethnographic Fieldnotes*, Chicago: University of Chicago Press.

Feather, B. L., Rucker, M., and Kaiser, S. B. (1989), "Social Concerns of Post-Mastectomy Women: Stigmata and Clothing," *Home Economics Research Journal* 17 (4): 289–99.

Goffman, E. (1963), *Stigma*. Englewood Cliffs, NJ: Prentice Hall.

Hite, M. (1988), "Writing – and Reading – the Body: Female Sexuality and Recent Feminist Fiction," *Feminist Studies* 14 (1): 121–2.

Jackson, Hazel O. and O'Neal, G. S. (1994), "Dress and Appearance Responses to Perceptions of Aging," *Clothing and Textiles Research Journal* 12 (4): 8–15.

Joseph, J. (1992), *Selected Poems*, Tarset, England: Bloodaxe.

Kaiser, S. B. (1997), *The Social Psychology of Clothing*, New York: Fairchild Publications.

Kaiser, S. B. and Chandler, J. L. (1984), "Fashion Alienation: Older Adults and the Mass Media," *International Journal of Aging and Human Development* 19 (3): 1,984.

Kennedy, D. (1993), *Sexy Dressing Etc: Essays on the Power and Politics of Cultural Identity*, Cambridge, MA: Harvard University Press.

Korthase, K. M. and Trenholme, I. (1982), "Perceived Age and Perceived Physical Attractiveness," *Perceptual and Motor Skills* 54: 1251–8.

Lennon, S. (1988), "Physical Attractiveness, Age, and Body Type," *Home Economics Research Journal* 16: 195–203.

Lennon, S. (1997), "Physical Attractiveness, Age and Body Type: Further Evidence," *Clothing and Textiles Research Journal* 15 (1): 60–64.

Lennon, S. and Rudd, N. A. (1994), "Linkages Between Attitudes Toward Gender Roles, Body Satisfaction, Self-esteem, and Appearance Management Behaviors in Women," *Family and Consumer Sciences Research Journal* 23 (2): 94–117.

Mathes, E. W., Brennan, S. M., Haugen, P. M., and Rice, H. B. (1985), "Ratings of Physical Attractiveness as a Function of Age," *Journal of Social Psychology* 125 (2): 157–68.

Nowak, D. A. (1975), "The Appearance Signal in Adult Development," Unpublished doctoral dissertation, Wayne State University, Detroit.

Riordan, E. (2001), "Commodified Agents and Empowered Girls: Consuming and Producing Feminism," *Journal of Communication Inquiry* 25 (3): 279–97.

Schouten, J. W. (1991), "Selves in Transition: Symbolic Consumption in Personal Rites of Passage and Identity Reconstruction," *Journal of Consumer Research* 17: 412–25.

Scott, L. M. (1998), "Fresh Lipstick, Rethinking Images of Women in Advertising," in L. J. Peach (ed.), *Women in Culture*, Oxford: Blackwell Publishers, pp. 131–41.

Sorell, G. T. and Nowak, C. A. (1981), "The Role of Physical Attractiveness as a Contributor to Individual Development," in R. M. Lerner and N. A. Bush-Rossnagel (eds), *Individuals as Producers of Their Development: A Life-Span Perspective*, New York: Academic Press, pp. 389–446.

Stone, G. (1965), "Appearance and the Self," in M. E. Roach and J. B. Eicher (eds), *Dress, Adornment, and the Social Order*, New York: John Wiley and Sons, pp. 216–45.

Thompson, S. M. (1999), *Mother's Taxi: Sport and Women's Labor*, Albany, NY: SUNY Press.

Walker, R. (2005), "Middle-Age: Bring it on," *The New York Times Magazine* (Web archives, January 30).

Wilson, E. (1990), "Deviant Dress," *Feminist Review* 35: 68–74.

14 EMBODYING THE FEMININE: MALE-TO-FEMALE CROSS-DRESSING

Jane E. Hegland and Nancy Nelson Hodges

This essay highlights and interprets connections found among cross-dressers' desire to cross-dress as expressed through their personal experiences. Based on narratives of thirty male-to-female cross-dressers posted on their websites, we examine sensory responses and sentimental associations with regard to dressing the body as "feminine."[1] Such responses include the waxy taste of lipstick on the lips, the donning of a wig or a high-heeled shoe while stepping into womanhood, the constriction of hosiery on the lower body, and the swish of a skirt against the thigh. Through their websites, these cross-dressers also tell readers of feelings evoked by such memories as a mother's pair of shoes, grandmother's perfume, or a sister's dress as influential in their decision to cross-dress. Because cross-dressing from male to female necessarily involves dressing the body, whether through clothing, accessories, cosmetics or even prosthetics, these are but a few responses and personal sentiments that reflect cross-dressers' efforts to embody femininity.

We used an interpretive methodology to explore the cross-dressers' websites as texts of lived experience (Kvale 1996; Mann and Stewart 2000; van Manen 1990). Looking across the narratives, common themes emerged that point to the importance of sensory reactions to, as well as sentimental associations with, dress as crucial to the development of the individual's identity as a cross-dresser. The internet is a common means of expression used by members of this marginalized community and research establishes the ways the internet functions as a safe space to share ideas and experiences (Armitage and Roberts 2002; Porter 1997). The internet also allows for a certain amount of anonymity, which is particularly important for those cross-dressers who have yet to make their identities public. Exploring cyberspace as a venue used by the cross-dressed individual opens a wealth of opportunities for investigating issues of gender, identity, and dress. Creators of the websites often utilize them as forums for describing their personal histories, for posting the latest photos of themselves "dressed" and for sharing tips and advice on how to achieve the right look. This essay elucidates the ways dress, whether in visual or verbal form, plays a dominant role within such forums.

BACKGROUND

CROSS-DRESSING ON THE INTERNET

As a popular means for discussion of appearance the internet has become a tool during the late twentieth and early twenty-first centuries to establish and even to alter gendered identities. The seamless realm of the internet allows such identities to cross cultural boundaries instantly and without regard for real physical space (Joinson 2003; Jordan 1999; Kardas and Milford 1996; Kolko *et al.* 2000; McKie 1997; Miller and Slater 2000). Marginalized groups have turned to the internet to communicate their own unique attitudes and behaviors (Bell 2001; Jones 1997; Nakamura 2002). Through the internet, these individuals in general, and cross-dressers in particular, have found a way to express the most intimate details of their lives while remaining completely anonymous. Thousands of websites are devoted to experiences of individual cross-dressers and the "Transgender Web Ring" functions as a search tool for locating individuals, support groups, electronic magazines, and management resources recommended within the transgender community. As indicated by the myriad electronic discussion groups frequented by cross-dressers, "the internet is not just an information repository; it is also a community" (Cohen 1998: 16).

Personal websites of cross-dressers typically include photographs and textual descriptions of the individual, along with sound, video, and links to other cross-dressers and cross-dresser-friendly events and activities. Photographs, however, are one of the most important elements of the webpage. As Marissa explains: "When we spend an entire afternoon to dress up, the moment of shooting a picture is the crowning, the sublimation of our work. That's why our masterpieces must not remain in a drawer! That's why we have to seize ... the opportunities offered by the internet!" (Marissa 2000: 8). These personal webpages will often have links to commercial websites that sell products and services focused on developing the cross-dressed appearance. Such commercial sites include access to products used to modify the body through hair removal and make-up. In addition, sites sell such body supplements as shoes and clothing that accommodate the larger size of the male-to-female cross-dresser. Another commonality among these commercial sites is the inclusion of a list of tips for creating a passable transgender appearance, and often an additional link to a live expert who can provide personal assistance.

DEFINING THE (CROSS-)DRESSED BODY

Labels used by cross-dressers to explain their activities include such terms as *transgender*, *transvestite*, *cross-dresser*, *across-gendered*, and even *gender gifted* and *expressing the feminine self*. The term *cross-dresser* is used predominantly throughout this essay, and is a more behavior-specific term commonly used to refer to someone who dresses in the manner of the opposite gender, rather than someone undergoing surgical processes that lead to a biological change from one gender to another (Tewksbury 1995).

Within this essay, *dress* is defined as a combination of modifications made to the body itself along with supplements placed on the body (Eicher *et al.* 2000). Modifications can be temporary or permanent and may include products that alter the physical form of the body, whether via cosmetics, hair color, nail polish, tanning or lightening cream. Supplements are characteristically temporary in nature and consist of such items put on the body as garments, shoes, and accessories.

Use of dress to establish, and in the case of cross-dressing, to alter one's appearance according to social dictates of gender has been explored in a number of different ways (Bullough and Bullough 1993; Garber 1992; Hegland 2005; Hegland and Nelson 2002). Because we focus on personal experiences of cross-dressers in their use of dress to alter the appearance of gender, it is necessary to discuss the distinction between the terms *female*, *feminine*, and *femininity*. Within the websites there is a clear motivation on the part of the cross-dressed individual to create a finished appearance that comes as close as possible to resembling a biological female. Though we are cognizant of the fact that the terms female and feminine (and *male* and *masculine*) are not synonymous, the definitions become muddled when discussing biological males who take on feminine trappings in order to create an appearance that is persuasively female. While the term female results in biological categorism, femininity is continuously variable and is underpinned only by prevailing definitions of masculinity and femininity. By exploring the concept of femininity through the perspective of cross-dressers, our purpose is twofold: to examine the meanings of dress within the daily lives of cross-dressers and to explore the ways they use dress to achieve an individual, yet clearly gendered, identity.

METHODOLOGY

THE WEBSITES

After careful study of numerous websites, we developed criteria for those ultimately selected for analysis. In the selection process, we excluded websites of individuals who self-identified as preoperative and postoperative transsexuals, and those who described themselves as *female*-to-male cross-dressers or transgendered individuals. Each of these categories has its own unique characteristics, but for this study we focused on male-to-female cross-dressers who are not currently exploring the option of sexual reassignment surgery. Additional criteria included photographs of the website owner in her female persona, along with testimonials of personal experiences with cross-dressing.

Upon establishment of these basic criteria, we worked independently to locate and to select 100 websites that fulfilled our criteria. A total of thirty cross-dresser sites were then culled. Although not part of our initial criteria, most of the cross-dressers' sites include a listing of the individual's likes, dislikes, favorite places to shop, body measurements *en femme*, and female celebrities or idols. All sites have an e-mail address link, and many have links to other transgender individuals, resources such as support groups, wig suppliers, transgender cosmetics, and even "passing consultants" – people who are known for their skill in helping cross-dressers achieve as realistic a feminine look as possible. Narratives along with the photographs contained within the websites formed the "texts" which constituted the primary source of data for the study (Jones 1999).

THE CROSS-DRESSERS

A variety of demographics surfaced. Ages of the individuals at the time of posting the webpage span from early twenties to late fifties, with the majority being in their mid thirties. All state they are heterosexual men, though a few claim feelings of bisexuality or sexual ambiguity while dressed *en femme*. Most are married or are in a monogamous heterosexual relationship. The cross-dressers live in Brazil, Japan, Taiwan, Australia, Russia, Germany, Austria, Italy, England, and the United States. Their education ranges from high school diplomas to college degrees. Employment includes plumbers, retail salesmen, musicians, computer analysts, and information technology specialists. Four of the thirty refer to past military experience, particularly in the United States navy, while three are Vietnam War veterans. Reasons for cross-dressing range from the sexual or fetishistic, to those of comfort, or achieving a feeling of "rightness" about dressing as a woman. For example, Liz reveals a strong sense of comfort in her cross-dressing. She writes, "For me, it's not a sexual issue, but one of comfort. I feel, well, comfortable dressed as a woman. My mental frame is comfortable and that is all that matters to me" (2001: 9).

The thirty sites also reflect varying degrees of participation: from dressing one or two times a month, to living full-time as a woman. All have female names and refer to themselves as such when dressed. Barbie Lanai provides a fairly representative explanation of her experience: "I'm a totally heterosexual male to female cross-dresser. I think most CD'ers are very private, dressing only in the bedroom or at home and would never mention their crossdressing in public. I dress almost every evening and weekends, but only at home and only in private" (Biography 1999: 1). Most had not openly communicated their desire to cross-dress to others, and therefore for much of their lives have had to deal with the tension between their need to express themselves and the fear of being caught.

THE ANALYSIS

Since there is minimal research on cross-dressers' use of the internet, our objective is to attempt to understand the ways male cross-dressers seek to shape their identities through dress. To do this, analysis and interpretation of the texts follow a hermeneutic process, in that each website was analyzed as a part within the larger whole (Nelson 2000; Thompson *et al.* 1989). We interpreted both written and visual content within the websites. Each part within a website was read alone and then read as part of the entire site. Likewise, each website was read alone and then read again as part of the entire set of websites. This iteration allowed for full development of the interpretation as well as connections within and across the websites. As a result of this process we established inductive categories and inferences to specific themes from the texts as narratives (Spiggle 1994). Each theme is then illustrated through excerpts from the websites.

Our study of the narratives focused on the genesis of the individual's desire to cross-dress, which resulted in two thematic areas of meaning: sensory reactions to dress and personal sentiments regarding dress. Both areas demonstrate the importance of dress in achieving a female identity. We were also interested in an exploration of how these sites help individuals to establish their own unique cross-dressed identity. Through our interpretation of the form and content common across the thirty websites, we examine what it means to embody femininity from the perspectives of the cross-dressers themselves.

INTERPRETATION

Descriptions of early experiences with cross-dressing on all the sites revealed a deeply rooted connection to the experience of women's dress and intense associations with dress of female relatives and role models. Such experiences range from being dressed as a girl by a female family member, to borrowing a female family member's clothing covertly, such as underwear and hosiery, just to see what it would be like to wear these items of apparel. Many participants begin their personal page with an account of the first time they cross-dressed. The earliest age at which most can remember wanting to cross-dress ranges from four to fifteen years of age, with many recalling their first experience at around age five. Often, early experiences led to an attraction to certain forms of dress, as was the case with Barbara Ann:

> One of my earliest childhood memories is of trying to walk in my aunt's high heeled shoes while visiting at her house. I was probably 4 or 5 years old, and I must have looked rather comical as I stumbled and shuffled in her shoes, but she thought it was very cute. She is still my favorite aunt . . . and I still adore high heeled shoes. (Beginnings 2000: 1)

SENSORY RESPONSE: THE LOOK AND FEEL OF FEMININE DRESS

According to many cross-dressers, the ongoing fascination with women's forms of dress can be traced back to positive feelings brought on by the way a piece of clothing felt or the sound it made. Over time, these feelings become part of the individual's overall identity as dressed, taking on critical importance within the process of dressing as a female. Frequently, a particular body supplement will be described as the key piece that bridges the gap between the real and the ideal self. For Amanda (Figure 14.1) it is a wig: "The moment I slip on my wig is when I become a woman. It's like stepping into an alternate universe. I leave my male self behind and Amanda walks the earth" (2004: 3).

Stockings, however, are by far the most popular body supplement to function as a cross-dressing catalyst. Karenanne reveals how she became attracted to stockings around the time of her mother's death:

> I was 12 when my mother passed away. As the oldest of 6 children, I assumed the responsibility of assisting with the meals, laundry, cleaning and general raising of my brothers and sisters. This was a time of a lot of anxiety for me and I began collecting

Figure 14.1   Amanda. Reproduced with permission.

and wearing more articles of women's clothing. I loved the feeling of stockings and originally collected ones which had been discarded. Soon, I began acquiring stockings and undergarments from clotheslines. (My Journey! Chapter One 2001: 2)

Yvonne (Figure 14.2) also writes about the importance of hosiery in her early days of cross-dressing:

You could say that my story begins almost thirty years ago. That would be around the age of twelve or so, the first time I snuck into my parents' bedroom and slipped a pair of my mother's nylon stockings from the dresser and tried them on in the bathroom. I used a slightly large T-shirt as a short dress and immediately fell in love with femme image and the feel of nylon on my legs. (Meet Yvonne, A Cross-dresser's Story 2005: 1)

Figure 14.2   Yvonne. Reproduced with permission.

Panty hose, and indeed, lingerie in general, is often cited within the narratives as more than just an important component of a cross-dresser's appearance; it is of critical significance to her overall identity as a female. That is, wearing lingerie in and of itself invokes a feeling of femininity. Debra Helen makes this point quite clear in the following excerpt: "What I really loved most, of course, was lingerie – the lacier, the sexier, the tighter, the better. I couldn't have been happier coming home from work and slipping into something slinky and sexy" (2004: 5).

Nicole Asahi's (Figure 14.3) early experiences follow suit, as evidenced by this recollection on her website: "When I was 16, I got my introduction to wearing pantyhose. It happened when some female guests left some of their pantyhose hanging up to dry in the bathroom. I sneaked into the bathroom, locked the door and tried on a pair. I can still remember my surprise at the delicious feeling of the pantyhose gliding over my legs" (How It All Started 2005: 3). For these cross-dressers, being dressed as a female goes beyond simply donning clothing assigned to women. It is critical to the experience of transformation sought by the cross-dresser, who seeks to become a woman via dressing in a manner that allows her to *feel* feminine.

Figure 14.3   Nicole Asahi.
Reproduced with permission.

Different types of modifications used to dress the body as feminine are also discussed within the narratives. Cosmetics are topmost on the list of temporary means and, for those who venture out in public dressed *en femme*, are a requirement in order to create a passable appearance. For many, the use of cosmetics allows them actually to see the transformation and to experience it through the sensations of applying lipstick, foundation, and eyeliner. Cláudia writes about how the introduction of cosmetics has amplified her cross-dressing routine:

> [For the past few] years, I've been wearing make-up when I cross-dress, which took me to another level of "womanhood." The very act of making-up brings to my mind thoughts I don't have as a man, and it's very interesting to see my face changing in the mirror (although I can't get rid of the shadow of my beard, no matter how well I shave). (2000: 6)

Modifying the body via shaving, whether the legs, the face, or both, is important to the cross-dressing process, at least according to Jillian, who writes: "I shaved my legs and I feel like they are my legs now not just rented or borrowed" (Part of My Story 2000: 5).

SENTIMENT AND MEMORY: THE INFLUENCE OF ROLE MODELS AND RELATIVES

Through their websites, cross-dressers often tell readers of feelings evoked through childhood memories about powerful responses to items of dress worn by relatives or women who held influential roles in their lives. For example, during an online interview, Amanda traces her lifelong fondness for hair back to childhood:

> One of my very vivid childhood remembrances is of playing with my hair, and that of my sister. I would twirl it around my fingers for hours and hours. I had very curly red hair as a child, and always seemed fascinated by it. I'm still in love with hair. I could sit in front of a mirror styling my wigs for days. (KC's Top Ten Interview 2004: 12)

Female family members have substantial influence on the development of urges to cross-dress in childhood. The nature of the influence, however, differs widely depending on the individual. Siobhán (Figure 14.4) expresses a multifarious early childhood memory that associates her beginning attraction to cross-dressing with her mother's clothing; the following excerpt gives special insight into the connection between motivation and sentiments of cross-dressers:

> My earliest recollection [of "dressing"] is of finding one of my mum's ballerina tutus, from when she was young, and dressing up in it. Everyone laughed, at first. However, after repeated incidences, they became serious. It became obvious to me that they weren't happy with me doing this … so it was at this point that I went "underground."
>
> During a telephone call, later in 1997, I was asking my mother questions about my early childhood, particularly with regard to my transgenderism. I had been voluntarily attending psychiatric sessions, and had been asked some questions, to which I didn't know the answers. My mother told me that at a very young age, as early as two, I used to climb out of my cot and get her nightie. She'd often find me, in the morning, wearing it. (Siobhán 2005: 2–5)

A few cross-dressers connect more abstract memories with their motivations for cross-dressing. Teresa Ann wanted to be a girl after seeing a film in childhood: "The first movie I ever remember seeing as a child was 'Peter Pan.' The minute the film ended, I knew that I wanted to grow up to be just like Wendy! I just didn't identify with Peter (or Michael or John for that matter) … At a very early age, five or six, I started to explore the idea of 'being a girl'" (n.d.: 1). Barbie Lanai was similarly inspired by a Miss America Pageant:

> One of my first memories along this line is when I was probably 5 or 6; my parents were watching a Miss America Pageant on television. Girls are always so cute and pretty and beautiful as compared to boys. The contestants wore such wonderful looking clothes with skirts swishing around their nyloned legs, their feet in high heels, their

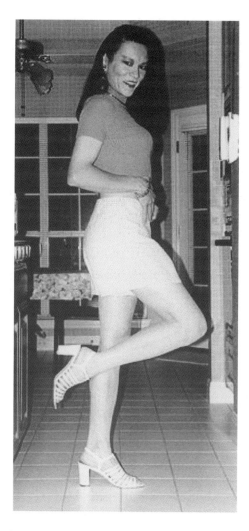

Figure 14.4 Siobhán.
Reproduced with permission.

tiny hourglass waist, their flaring hips, their rounded breasts, their fingernails so long and nicely painted, their hair long and flowing, their faces all dolled up. I thought how nice to look so special and that maybe someday I could be a pretty Miss America too. I mentioned something about this to my parents; and they told me that I could *never* be a Miss America, because I was a boy. Not a girl! Ergo: boys can never be pretty, they can only be boys. If you want to be pretty you must be a girl first. The seed had been planted. (Biography 1999: 1, 2)

DISCUSSION AND CONCLUSIONS

Dress is critical in the lives of cross-dressers, as it allows them to become what they believe they should be and to therefore express their ideal self. But dress is more than just a tool to facilitate the masculine-to-feminine transformation. Dress carries with it the desires, motivations, and goals of cross-dressers. Powerful connections can be seen between the senses, feelings, and dress within each narrative. A range of body modifications and supplements are imbued with significance beyond measure for cross-dressers, functioning as the key to their interest in exploring, at a very young age, how it would feel to be a female. Dress also acts as a catalyst for their discussions of what it means to be a woman within society. For the cross-dressers in this study, dress helps them to embody that which they were not given in either biological or social terms – femininity.

Although the narratives clearly point to interconnections between dress and gender within the cross-dressers' desire to achieve the embodied feminine, it is difficult to reconcile fully their use of dress to express "woman" as a state of being with feminist concerns about the female body. This is particularly the case given the content that surfaces within and across the websites. Many, if not all, cross-dressers in this study boldly embrace the trappings of objectification. Though many of them are clearly conscious of the messages they send, they nevertheless prefer to dress to express age-old stereotypes that conflate femininity with an overt sexuality. Barbie Lanai includes a comment that reflects this preference: "Real women just don't seem to wear dresses very much any more, and any girl wearing a short dress and heels is bound to be looked over closely" (Barbie's first shopping *en femme* 1999: 18). Creating an identity that is meant "to be looked over closely," and solely for purposes of consumption by the male gaze, does little to erase the imprint of male desire on the female body so deeply rooted in culture, history, and social convention. It also does little to facilitate the struggle against the objectification of the embodied feminine that both women and men have been participating in for decades.

Just as the concepts of male and female and masculinity and femininity are complex and a mixture of physicality and enculturation, there is nothing innately feminine about hosiery or a slinky dress. An interesting argument that surfaces often on the websites is that cross-dressing allows men to "get in touch with their feminine side." By reflecting upon the development of their desires to cross-dress, these individuals are perhaps better able to understand and explore what they perceive as a more nurturing side of themselves. Coreen puts it this way:

> I had always felt confused about my identity, because I was unknowingly trying to maintain an unreal male façade that wasn't natural. I have changed my attitude. I am very aware now of being drawn into macho stancing and competitiveness ... I have tried more and more to let my natural female mannerisms flow, which is hard to do, due to so many years of keeping that guard up. A lot of this has to do with not caring so much of what people think of you, and just being yourself. (More recent attitudes 2005: 14; State of the art at the end of '98, 2005: 10)

Websites by and for cross-dressers are increasing at an exponential rate, generating an enormous amount of information on the topic. As an anthropological study of human behavior and dress, this research not only has important implications for furthering our understanding of the connections between the senses, emotions, and dress, but also for understanding how cyberspace functions as its own sociocultural realm. In particular, this study illustrates the depth and richness that can be found within electronic personal narratives, and how such narratives can be used to anchor an approach to the study of dress and gender in everyday life. These narratives are essential to understanding not just the *what*, but also the *why* at the core of cross-dressing.

Looking at the experiences of these thirty individual cross-dressers, there is indeed much to be learned about how we all must manage the tension between expressing the self and the dictates of society. These narratives provide insight into the variety of ways dress functions to facilitate assumptions about the gendered self in society. Objects of dress stimulate the senses and spark sentiments that reveal the true complexity of human action. Exploring the role of dress within the cross-dresser's world is much like peeling an onion; with each layer comes a deeper understanding of how a cross-dresser, like each of us, relies upon dress to make manifest the diverse desires of the self in the quest for a unique identity.

NOTE

1. In a previously published paper (Hegland and Nelson 2002), these websites were explored through three areas of content: (1) an analysis of cross-dressers' use of the website as a journal, wherein they reveal such experiences as their first incidents with cross-dressing, the common fear of being caught, their relationships with friends and family, discussions of sexuality, and whether they are successful at passing in public; (2) a description of their attempts at communicating a feminine identity primarily through dress and posture; and (3) their discussion of the importance of the internet as a tool and a forum for dialogue – for individuals and for the global transgender community. In the present study, we explore the first content area in more depth by examining recollections of early desires to cross-dress. This essay focuses on fourteen of the thirty websites. The total collection offers a diversity of perspectives on the topic of cross-dressing. For a full citation list of the thirty websites, refer to Jane Hegland and Nancy Nelson (2002). The following include a few additional websites that may also be of interest to the reader: Andee (2004), Debbi (2005), Joanne (2005), Juliana (2005), Robin (2005), and Sharon (2005).

REFERENCES

Amanda. (2004), *Amanda's Transgender Garden*, retrieved August 8, 2005, http://www.amandarichards.com/index.html.

Andee. (2004), *Andee's home page*, retrieved August 8, 2005, http://members.tgforum.com/andeew/Andee's_Page.html. (Initially retrieved March 13, 2000, http://members.tgforum.com/andeew/Halloween2.html.)

Armitage, J. and Roberts, J. (eds). (2002), *Living with Cyberspace: Technology and Society in the 21st Century*, London: Continuum.

Barbara Ann. (2000), *Barbara Ann's Page*, retrieved August 8, 2005, http://hometown.aol.com/bobbi418/index.html.

Barbie Lanai. (1999), *Barbie Lanai's Home Page*, retrieved April 4, 2000, http://www.geocities.com/WestHollywood/Heights/6262.

Bell, D. (2001), *An Introduction to Cybercultures*, London: Routledge.

Bullough, V. L. and Bullough, B. (1993), *Cross-Dressing, Sex, and Gender*, Philadelphia: University of Pennsylvania Press.

Cláudia. (2000), *Cláudia's Corner*, retrieved August 8, 2005, http://www.geocities.com/WestHollywood/ Cafe/9247/.

Cohen, L. B. (1998), "Searching for Quality on the Internet: Tools and Strategies," *Choice* 35 (Supplement): 11–27.

Coreen. (2005), *Coreen's Corner*, retrieved August 8, 2005, http://www.geocities.com/RodeoDrive/1967/index. html.

Debbi. (2005), *Debbi Richard's Home Page,* retrieved August 8, 2005. http://www.debbirichards.com/.

Debra Helen. (2004), *Debra Helen's Web World*, retrieved August 8, 2005, http://www.geocities.com/ FashionAvenue/Mall/5508/indexdh.html.

Eicher, J., Evenson, S., and Lutz, H. (eds). (2000), *The Visible Self*, New York: Fairchild Publications.

Garber, M. (1992), *Vested Interests: Cross-Dressing and Cultural Anxiety*, New York: Routledge.

Hegland, J. E. (2005), "Drag Queens, Transvestites, Transsexuals: Stepping Across the Accepted Boundaries of Gender," in M. L. Damhorst, K. A. Miller, and S. O. Michelman (eds), *The Meanings of Dress,* 2nd ed., New York: Fairchild Publications.

Hegland, J. E. and Nelson, N. J. (2002), "Cross-dressers in Cyberspace: Exploring the Internet as a Tool for Expressing Gendered Identity," *International Journal of Sexuality and Gender Studies* 7 (2/3): 139–61.

Jillian. (2000), *Jillian B's page*, retrieved March 14, 2000, http://www.geocities.com/WestHollywood/ Salon/3467/.

Joanne. (2005), *Joanne's world*, retrieved August 8, 2005, http://www.geocities.com/joanne_tgirl/. (Initially retrieved April 27, 2000, http://members.xoom.com/ XMCM/joanneray/.)

Joinson, A. N. (2003), *Understanding the Psychology of Internet Behaviour: Virtual Worlds, Real Lives*, New York: Palgrave Macmillan.

Jones, S. G. (ed.). (1997), *Identity and Communication in Cybersociety*, Thousand Oaks, CA: Sage.

Jones, S. G. (ed.). (1999), *Doing Internet Research: Critical Issues and Methods for Examining the Net*, Thousand Oaks: Sage.

Jordan, T. (1999), *Cyberpower: The Culture and Politics of Cyberspace and the Internet*, London: Routledge.

Juliana. (2005), *Juliana's Secret Garden,* retrieved August 8, 2005, http://www.geocities.com/WestHollywood/ Village/4618/index-e.htm. (Initially retrieved March 16, 2000: http://www.geocities.com/WestHollywood/ 8576/.)

Kardas, E. P. and Milford, T. M. (1996), *Using the Internet for Social Science Research and Practice*, Belmont, CA: Wadsworth.

Karenanne. (2001), *Karenanne's Journey*, retrieved August 8, 2005, http://www.geocities.com/WestHollywood/ 8298/.

Kolko, B. E., Nakamura, L., and Rodman, G. B. (eds). (2000), *Race in Cyberspace*, New York: Routledge.

Kvale, S. (1996), *Inter-Views*, Thousand Oaks, CA: Sage.

Liz. (2001), *Lurkin Liz's*, retrieved August 8, 2005, http://www.geocities.com/WestHollywood/4549/.

Mann, C. and Stewart, F. (2000), *Internet Communication and Qualitative Research: A Handbook for Researching Online*, London: Sage.

Marissa. (2000), *Marissa's Home Page*, retrieved March 29, 2000, http://www.geocities.com/WestHollywood/ Stonewall/9536.

McKie, C. (1997), *Using the Web for Social Research*, Toronto: McGraw-Hill Ryerson Ltd.

Miller, D. and Slater, D. (2000), *The Internet: An Ethnographic Approach*, Oxford: Berg.

Nakamura, L. (2002), *Cybertypes: Race, Ethnicity, and Identity on the Internet*, New York: Routledge.

Nelson, N. J. (2000), "Listening to Jane Cunningham Croly's 'Talks with Women': Issues of Gender, Dress, and Reform in Demorest's Monthly Magazine," *Clothing and Textiles Research Journal* 18 (3): 128–39.

Nicole Asahi. (2005), *Nicole Asahi's Cozy Corner*, retrieved April 6, 2000, http://www.nicoleasahi.com.

Porter, D. (1997), *Internet Culture*, New York: Routledge.

Robin. (2005), *Robin's nest*, retrieved August 8, 2005, http://members.tgforum.com/robinno2/. (Initially retrieved March 14, 2000, http://www.geocities.com/WestHollywood/Cafe/2854.)

Sharon. (2005), *Sharon Rebecca Persky's home page*, retrieved August 8, 2005, http://freespace.virgin.net/sharon. persky/welcome.html. (Initially retrieved May 3, 2000, http://freespace.virgin.net/sharon.persky/welcome. html.)

Siobhán. (2005), *Siobhán's Home Page*, retrieved August 8, 2005, http://www.siobhansplace.co.uk/.

Spiggle, S. (1994), "Analysis and Interpretation of Qualitative Data in Consumer Research," *Journal of Consumer Research* 21: 491–503.

Teresa Ann. (n.d.), *Teresa Ann Thompson's Home Page*, retrieved April 4, 2000, http://www.members.tgforum. com/terriann/biopage.html.

Tewksbury, R. (1995), "Cross-dressing: Changing from Him to Her," in P. C. Rollins and S. W. Rollins (eds), *Gender and Popular Culture*, Cleveland: Ridgemont Press.

Thompson, C., Locander, W., and Pollio, H. (1989), "Putting Consumer Experience Back into Consumer Research: The Philosophy and Method of Existential-phenomenology," *Journal of Consumer Research* 16: 133–46.

van Manen, M. (1990), *Researching Lived Experience: Human Science for an Action Sensitive Pedagogy*, New York: State University of New York Press.

Yvonne. (2005), *Yvonne's Place*, retrieved August 8, 2005, http://www.yvonnesplace.net/.

15 VIRTUAL SENSATION: DRESS ONLINE

Suzanne Loker and Susan P. Ashdown

Opportunities for virtual sensations in online interactive environments increase each day. We *see* one another using visual CAMS hooked to the top of our computers, sophisticated video conferencing, and even 3D, tele-immersion that "allow[s] people in different parts of the world to submerge themselves in one another's presence and feel as if they are sharing the same physical space" (Ananthaswamy 2000). We *talk* with others using e-mail, instant messaging (IM), text messaging, and internet-powered audio conversations. Haptic devices for *touching* during internet sessions being developed will add *touch* to the list of virtual sensations available for enhancing our lives (Isdale 2001; Kim *et al.* 2004). There are even devices under development that will add smell and taste to virtual reality (VR) environments (Ananthaswamy 2003; Knight 2004).

What do these advances mean for the way we select, wear, and ascribe meaning to dress? This essay describes the variety of virtual dress expressions available online today, the sensing functions it fulfills, the reactions and expectations of users, its role in defining one's self, and its prospects for the future. Specifically, virtual dress is analyzed in relation to:

- the body through virtual view and virtual fit;
- the perceptions of our 3D self images generated from body scans;
- dress in avatars and the symbolization of self in virtual reality games, video games, and movies.

Technologies currently under development for seeing, hearing, touching, and smelling clothing in online virtual environments will also be described. The roles we might take in understanding, creating, using, and playing with virtual dress and the senses evoked by it will be proposed.

DRESS AND THE BODY THROUGH VIRTUAL VIEW AND VIRTUAL FIT

Computer technology creates many visualizations of dress and the body never before available. Commercial websites offer a location for advertising clothing and other products to consumers (B2C) and businesses (B2B) so that location becomes irrelevant. These commercial sites primarily take the form of regular online retail or wholesale stores where products can be shown as static images. Technology exists for even more elaborate images, showing models swishing down virtual runways (see www.optitex.com).[1] Virtual showrooms replace buying trips to fashion centers by offering apparel lines and systems for purchasing the garments that are totally online. Yard sales or tag sales have been moved online through auction houses such as eBay, sell.com, and amazon.com's Sell Your Stuff.

Even more sensational are the virtual try-on commercial sites that offer customers the interactive process of creating their own virtual model based on their choices of body characteristics such as body type, height, skin and hair color, and facial details (e.g., landsend. com; mvm.com). Once your personal model is ready, you can select apparel from the virtual store, try it on the model and decide to purchase or not (Figure 15.1). Some personal models look more like the customer than others and many are cartoon-like. Nonetheless, they offer a virtual experience that represents the fitting room try-on in traditional retail shopping.

Several research groups and commercial ventures are working on turning this virtual try-on experience into a virtual fit experience. Using body scan technology, it is possible to create personal models that reflect the person's actual measurements. The models can be dressed virtually using a 2D to 3D process starting with pattern shapes of the garments and wrapping the body scan image. Pattern shapes for the selected style and size are imported

Figure 15.1   MVM screen print provides an example of My Virtual Model parametric models to demonstrate leading edge technology for marketing multichannel apparel. MVM allows customers to create a virtual model by entering their body dimensions and "try on" various retailers clothing to establish their best fit before ordering online. Source: MVM.com. © My Virtual Model Inc ("MVM").

and wrapped around the body scan (e.g., www.optitex.com). Others are developing a 3D to 2D process where scans are modified to create a garment layer with proper fitting and styling ease and then unwrapped (e.g., www.tpc.com.hk).

Fit analysis and research is another use for virtual images developed using body scanning. The Cornell Body Scan Research Group has been studying body scan measurements of both minimally clothed and clothed participants for several years (Ashdown *et al.* 2004a,b; Loker *et al.* 2004a,b, 2005). The research group's focus has been on improving apparel fit in existing ready-to-wear; that is, to adjust existing sizing systems to fit the target population better. Using the Human Solutions TechMath scanner and specialized Polyworks software to process the scans, we have developed a method to merge the scan data for each participant in minimal clothing and the test garment: a pair of pants. Figure 15.2 presents scanned images of a participant in minimal clothing and test pants. Notice how clearly the fit is displayed in the image. The software allows us to rotate the image, zoom in for a close view, and display any number of still views of the image.

The research group analyzed *xyz* scan data to determine the distance between the body and clothing, or ease, using linear circumference measures as well as surface area, slice area, and volume measurements only possible with three-dimensional data. Results were applied to adjust existing sizing systems to improve fit of a particular target market.

More relevant for this essay is our study of the virtual images for the analysis of fit (Ashdown *et al.* 2004b). Viewing the clothed scans, we can evaluate the fit, identify specific problem areas, and relate fit issues to the 2D pattern specifications. Scans of many, even hundreds, of people can be easily collected and analyzed, offering a new method for evaluating fit based on multiple fit models in a target market. Indeed, this method could

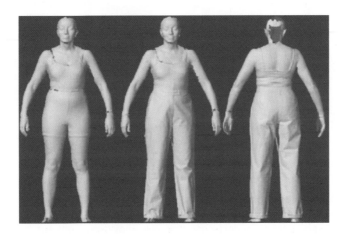

Figure 15.2   Scanned images in minimal clothing and test pants
(Cornell Body Scan Research Group).

revolutionize how fit analysis is conducted in the apparel industry. What we call *target market sizing* could replace the current standard for developing ready-to-wear sizing in the apparel industry – a single fit model and proportional sizing principles that extend the sizes up and down from the model's base size. Target market sizing could use multiple fit models in each size, more realistically developing apparel products that fit the target market and including body shapes as well as linear measurements in pattern development. Sizes could reflect the variety of shapes existing in different age cohorts, ethnic groups, and small- to large-framed persons.

Our research group has explored various fit analysis protocols using the scanned visualizations in Figure 15.2. We identified a set of body locations that a group of experts rated: front and back and overall. We found that it was important to see the minimally clothed body scan next to the clothed scan in order to evaluate what part the body itself played in the acceptability of the clothing fit. For example, when a person has body fat located above the waist either in the front or the back, it can affect how the pants fit at the waist and just below the waist. Being able to see the minimally clothed body scan helps the fit evaluators see or distinguish the pant fit from the body variations.

A second protocol that aided us in the visual assessment of fit was the ability to return to the scan many times, over a period of time, and to compare our fit ratings across scans. Not only has the number of unique bodies extended the validity of the fit analysis process, but the permanence of the scans has as well. The scans are an enduring record of the fit of a garment and can be revisited by apparel technicians and designers as the adjustments to the pattern specifications are being discussed and implemented. Designers can look at the garment fit as they prepare to use the sizing and pattern specifications in the next line or one five years from now. The usefulness of the fit analysis is extended in time and across multiple bodies with scans.

We are currently studying the actual process of fit analysis, evaluating the optimal number of experts necessary to achieve reliable and valid fit analysis results. This too has been easier with scan images than in a traditional fit analysis session. The five experts could conduct their electronic evaluations individually at any time and in any place. Indeed, two members of the expert panel loaded the images on their laptop computers and completed the analyses in another state. Preliminary analyses suggest that only two experts are needed to achieve reliable results, leading to important recommendations about how to conduct fit analyses (Ashdown *et al.* 2006).

Intellifit (www.intellifit.com) has deployed technology that scans the body for its measurements right through street clothing. This option even further decreases the objectionable invasiveness of determining body measurements for apparel sizing systems and pattern development. The technology uses low power radio waves to capture three-dimensional data about the surface of the body. It is being deployed through retail stores and mall locations and it provides size selection advice for a variety of apparel styles. Once technology for virtual fit is commercialized, a number of possibilities may be realized. The oft-verbalized idea of personal smart cards holding an individual's body scan will have a variety of uses. Businesses will be developed to: (1) take scans and put data on smart cards; (2) create software that integrates with the virtual try-on software using personal scans; (3) prepare apparel brand lines for applications such as virtual dressing of scans; and (4) offer these services to consumers virtually. Retailers can use virtual fit technology to test out brands on their target markets, evaluating virtually how well certain brands and garments fit and look on customers of various ages, ethnicities, and body types. Advertising and promotions can be focused on target markets selected by the acceptable fit of garments rather than by demographic and lifestyle variables that often have very little to do with fit. The fashion industry will have products that look good on all sizes and shapes of people and will be able to create more realistic visual images for advertising, helping to offset the ubiquitous skinny, emaciated models who can contribute to the incidence of eating disorders. In this way, virtual fit can empower socially responsible advertising practices.

DRESS AND PERCEPTIONS OF VIRTUAL 3D SELF IMAGES: COMFORT WITH BODY SCANNING

The Cornell Research Group has conducted several preliminary studies that evaluate how people react to seeing their 3D body scan images (Loker *et al.* 2004, 2005a). After 203 women, aged 35–54 years, were each scanned twice, once in minimal clothing and once in test pants, and were shown their minimally clothed scan rotating on the computer monitor, they completed a written questionnaire about their scanning experience. We found participants generally were quite comfortable with the scanning process on a five-point scale (73 percent very comfortable, 15 percent comfortable, 7 percent neutral, 2 percent uncomfortable, and 3 percent very uncomfortable) (Table 15.1). Nearly all (98 percent) said they would be willing to be scanned again though not all participants accepted the offer to take home a disk with a movie file of their scan. Questions relating to specific parts of the process also indicated high comfort levels: 80 percent comfortable or very comfortable

Table 15.1 Consumer Comfort with Scanning

Category	Comfort with Scanning Process (%)	Comfort Viewing Computer Screen (%)	Comfort Viewing Movie File (%)	Comfort Showing Family and Friends (%)
All (*N* = 203)	88.7	54.6	57.9	38.4
Misses Sized (*n* = 155)	89.0	57.4	60.9	40.6
Women's Sized (*n* = 48)	83.3	45.6	48.9	31.2

Note: Comfort indicated by scoring 4 (comfortable) or 5 (very comfortable) on a five-point scale.

with the Lycra scan suits, 82 percent with the eye-safe laser lights, 77 percent with the scan position, and 89 percent with standing stationary for the twelve-second scanning period.

Participants were less comfortable with viewing their scans. Only 55 percent of participants were comfortable or very comfortable seeing their scan on the computer screen, and 58 percent were comfortable seeing their scan as a movie file. The larger-sized women were slightly less comfortable than those wearing misses' sizes. Only 38 percent of all those scanned were comfortable or very comfortable showing their scan to family and friends, with 31 percent of the larger women expressing comfort. Most interesting to this discussion is that 68 percent of the participants preferred to look at their body scan as a movie file rather than as a stationary image on the computer screen. The rotating movement and/or the unique view that participants saw of themselves in the 3D image may explain this finding.

During the scanning study (Loker *et al.* 2005a), we observed a variety of participant reactions before, during, and following the scans. To take advantage of this opportunity to study participants' reactions to scanning, we conducted a second study on a subsample of twenty-two participants. We framed this study in symbolic interaction theory and recorded verbal responses, facial expressions, and body language describing the anticipation, process, and reflection on body scanning and viewing one's scan on the computer screen. Two interesting trends emerged from the observations: (1) participants were somewhat unsure or unsettled about the process before the scan and became noticeably more comfortable after the scan; (2) participants conceptually distanced themselves from their file image, an unfamiliar and yet highly personalizing technological output.

Several examples of verbal comments from participants 333, 308, and 307 illustrate.

Before scan process: *I had a root canal this morning, so I can do this.* (333)
After scan process: *It was a piece of cake.* (333)
After viewing scan: *I look better on there than in real life.* (333)
After scan process: *The process was so painless.* (308)
After viewing scan: *Oh Yeah. Make it real big ... I think it was really cool to see my body scan. I just didn't like what I saw.* (307)

When offered a disk with movie file, several expressed their reactions to having records of their scans, ranging from "I don't want anybody seeing it," to "I should put it on the fridge at home," and "It would be neat to do a comparative scan between now and when you get older."

We concluded from these results that "being" scanned and "viewing" your scan present two different comfort reactions. While the scanning process was considered easy and most participants were willing to do it again, viewing one's own scan was more likely to create some uneasiness. Although the scans the participants were shown were in minimal clothing, the results suggest that seeing an exact 3D image of your self may contribute negative perceptions of self for some people. The fact that the participants were seeing never-before-seen views of their own bodies (i.e., newness leading to surprise or disappointment) certainly explains some of the unease. The knowledge that these views could easily be transmitted to others electronically through e-mail or the internet may have contributed more unease. A third explanation is that we don't want to define ourselves using *xyz* data points that show every detail of our bodies, but that we would rather view a modified, if not idealized, image of ourselves. The virtual try-on systems now available at some online retailers offer images that are meant to be similar to your body type, skin and hair color, rather than to be an exact replica. An accurate but not highly detailed replication of our own bodies may be more comfortable for us to look at when we view virtual dress.

DRESS AND SYMBOLIC AND IMAGINARY SELF IN VIRTUAL WORLDS

Virtual worlds offer opportunities to create self images even further from the realistic 3D body scan data – a symbolic or imaginary self (Kushner 2004). Virtual worlds are created in a number of 2D, cartoon-like formats that are loaded separately by each player and more realistic 3D formats where players move more continuously through a building or landscape (Book 2004; Kushner 2004). Players are often represented by avatars or virtual images of a person, animal, or imaginary thing that communicates to other virtual players by typing text into a chat window or speaking to others with a live voice (Figure 15.3).

Figure 15.3 Avatars chat in a virtual environment in Secondlife (www.secondlife.com). Copyright 2006, Linden Research, Inc. All Rights Reserved.

Virtual worlds such as Second Life (www.secondlife.com), There (www.there.com), and Sims Online (www.thesimsonline.com) offer seeing and hearing sensations through these symbolic or imaginary visual images. Players create their own avatar by choosing from those offered (e.g., Sims Online and Second Life), create them from components offered or, if skilled technically, create them using online tools. Players name their avatar, select a clothing wardrobe from online shops, pay with online currency, and buy real estate (land, houses, and landscaping) to store/locate/keep their avatar. Betsy Book describes how avatars and their dress are used in virtual worlds to define a symbolic or imaginary self.

> As representations of each visitor, avatars play a pivotal role in a virtual world's community formation and social structure. Many activities in virtual worlds foreground the avatar, including avatar customization classes, avatar clothing sales, costume contests, and fashion shows. A great deal of time, energy, and even money is spent on these virtual bodies. Some people like to create avatars that are extremely different from their real bodies, personalities, or even gender while others prefer avatars that more accurately represent their offline appearance. No matter how closely an avatar mirrors its creator's offline physical appearance, the act of creating an avatar can be an experience of self-discovery for its creator. Virtual worlds typically offer a default "starter" avatar, which most users immediately change to avoid the dreaded stigma of looking like a "newbie." (2004: 2–3)

Some sites offer stereotypical body types and clothing fashions, such as VZones where hypermasculine or hyperfeminine avatars are dressed in combat or sorceress clothing (www.vzones.com). Others such as There and Second Life offer many customization options to design your own avatar, even sliders for adjusting shape and size. Both the look and name of an avatar are used to define a player's online self.

Another recent development in virtual worlds is the designing and selling of products, including clothing, to other players (Weir 2005). This is done with advertising billboards in the virtual landscape that can be clicked to take you to the designer's space. Online currency is used for the purchase. Many sites give players a small amount of currency with subscription and they can buy more with real US dollars that they eventually can cash in for a profit. Some brands, including Nike and Levi's, now offer clothing for avatars using advertising within virtual worlds to establish their brand with this new target market of players (Book 2004). Other real-world firms pay to have their logos appear within the virtual world landscapes; for example, the Intel logo appears on computer screens and the Coca Cola logo in restaurants but not for purchase.

To design and sell avatar clothing, online designers create their own clothing with design tools offered on There, Second Life, and other virtual worlds. They create their own online personalities represented by avatars, designer names, and shops to sell their clothing. For example, Chip Matthews designs and sells clothing and "skins" – new bodies or body parts to put on players' avatars. He goes by his real name, Chip Matthews, in the virtual world and is a freelance artist and animator in real life. Tim Allen and Jennifer Vatza are represented by avatars, FlipperPA and Jennyfur Peregrine, as they run a chain of stores in Second Life that sell Jennyfur's designs. They are planning to launch a real-world business website to sell these designs for virtual worlds but outside of the gamescape (Weir 2005).

These symbolic or imaginary representations of self are only popular with certain segments of the population. But as technology is introduced to children earlier, and as the opportunities and sophistication of virtual worlds continue to diffuse and reach into our everyday lives, virtual sensations will become more prevalent as a means to explore and define ourselves through avatar clothing choices, design options, and appropriate names.

TOUCHING, SMELLING, TASTING

Some very interesting exploratory new research considers tactile senses, or haptics, in virtual reality situations; that is, environments simulated by a computer. Some of these may have implications for dress. Virtual reality environments consist of visual and aural experiences displayed on a computer screen or special displays. Haptic devices (Figure 15.4) are being developed using vibration, sound, or spatial aspects of tactile sense that will someday add more sensory stimuli to these environments (Isdale 2001). Vibration induced through the computer mouse or attachments to the body such as an arm sleeve can generate texture-like feelings during a VR session. Sound, another form of vibration, is used in chairs during VR simulations to provide a tactile sensation. Small pins in an array can be signaled electronically to move and change to render a tactile sensation.

Figure 15.4   Trisenx digital Scent Dome (Copyright 2006, Linden Research, Inc. All Rights Reserved) and a virtual reality headset and tactile device from the Human Interface Technology Lab at Washington University (Image courtesy of the University of Washington Human Interface Technology Lab).

The Advanced Telecommunications Research Institute in Kyota, Japan, developed an air cannon that tracks a player's eyes during a VR activity and shoots an aroma at the player on cue (Knight 2004). For example, during a car simulation, the smell of gas might be emitted during a fast and curvy driving excursion. Or the smell of bread being baked might be emitted during an architectural walk-through by a prospective home buyer. Telewest Broadband, a UK internet service provider, has teamed up with Trisenx to develop a scent-generating device for online users (www.trisenx.com) (Figure 15.4). The advantage of such systems for a virtual fashion show, shooting perfumed fragrances to symbolize elegance or funky or "green," may be another future option for virtual dress.

Even taste is being addressed online with a device called the food simulator (Ananthaswamy 2003). It is now being developed in Japan to replicate the force of chewing while being augmented with a squirt of flavorings on the tongue. More development of these sensing devices and technologies is needed for online dress applications, but the foundation has been laid for these sensory experiences.

WHAT ROLES SHOULD WE TAKE IN CREATING AND USING VIRTUAL DRESS?

Dress created, presented, and played with in virtual environments offers many novel and provocative opportunities for clothing and textile professionals. Not only can we use virtual dress to enhance and extend teaching and research, but we can also use virtual environments as a new venue for delivering education and expressing creativity. Many possible future scenarios can be imagined to fulfill these purposes.

UNDERSTANDING VIRTUAL DRESS

The first step is to understand virtual dress in terms of reading the visual images and understanding any symbolic meanings. In the cases of clothed body scans and virtual fit applications for trying on and selling clothing, we need to learn how to look at the relationships between the virtual dress and the body to understand fit. For skilled apparel designers, reading the virtual images is probably very similar to seeing real-world clothing on the body and evaluating fit. Flare and other silhouette definitions can be clearly depicted in the virtual scans or scans wrapped with virtual clothing. Tightness can be presented as wrinkles and very smooth clothing, while looseness can be presented as fabric standing away from the body and/or overlapping and vertical folds in the fabric.

Consumers less skilled at critically evaluating clothing fit will have more difficulty in first figuring out what defines good fit and then interpreting wrinkles and rolls and tightness to indicate good or bad fit. We can develop guidelines for evaluating fit and fit preference and some specific indicators of good fit and fit problems. We can also prepare introductions for viewing virtual dress that include both technical navigation suggestions as well as a virtual reality "walk-through" of virtual dress locations on which to focus when evaluating fit.

One view unique to virtual dress is the 360-degree view of one's own body that none of us is used to seeing. We have grown up viewing ourselves in the mirror, in photographs, and home videos. But we have never watched a 3D image of ourselves revolving on a screen like a third person. We have only seen our front, side, or back view in 2D as we crane our neck to the right, left, or over our shoulder or view ourselves in a three-way mirror. Clothed scans and virtual try-on using one's own scan offer us this novel view of ourselves. The biggest questions are whether we really want to see an accurate view and how it can be manipulated to be comfortable for us to look at while still giving us the information (e.g., fit evaluation) we are seeking. Our preliminary research suggests there is still work to be done to make people want to view their own scan. Perhaps as scanning becomes more widespread and routine, we will get used to seeing a 360-degree view of our clothed body and even prefer it. Until then, we can conduct research that informs the development and incremental adoption of virtual fit through greater understanding of the psychological effects of virtual dress.

USING VIRTUAL DRESS IN EDUCATION, RESEARCH, AND COMMERCE

We have described several research and commercial uses of virtual dress such as virtual try-on for fit and visual fit assessments. It is easy to imagine additional applications of virtual dress for education, research, and commerce.

The virtual environment is already being used to enhance educational opportunities through course websites, interactive simulations, real-time video conferences, and online course offerings. As technologies continue to be developed that connect computer-assisted design and pattern making, pattern making and virtual visualizations, and virtual visualizations and meaning, the possibilities for the use of virtual dress in teaching apparel design, pattern making, and the symbolic meaning of dress vastly increase. Examples are VR for design walk-through with consumers to simulate retail buying experiences with personalized services, experimentation with dress styles and hair color to test reactions of others in VR environments before trying in real-life, and using VR for role-playing activities that explore socially constructed meanings of dress. Technologies that simulate tactile sensations can be combined with sight and sound to create the "presence" of dress for virtual classroom activities and fashion shows.

Research is needed to evaluate the salient variables that influence the acceptance of virtual dress in educational and commercial situations. Are the realistic images of clothed scans too detailed? How can virtual images be modified for greater viewer comfort? Are the avatars used in virtual worlds realistic enough to be used in simulations to teach clothing design principles and explore the meanings of dress? Why do people enjoy virtual worlds and spend time and money creating and clothing symbolic and imaginary avatars? What are the relationships between dress created for virtual worlds, reality shows on television, and the real world?

CREATING AND PLAYING WITH VIRTUAL DRESS

Technology under development can start with a 2D pattern for a garment and wrap or dress a scan in it. When wrapping technologies are perfected and on the market, we will be able to connect Computer Aided Design (CAD) pattern making to previewing virtual dress. This computer-driven process will revolutionize the creation of apparel, shortening the time involved and reducing the necessary technical skills for sample production. Made-to-order production will be feasible and accepted by consumers. Wrapping technology that demonstrates the fit of a garment accurately on one's own scan will help a consumer in online apparel purchases where real-life try-on is not feasible as well as set reasonable standards for good fit. Virtual dress offers a 3D view of apparel fit not previously available.

The act of creating dress will be offered to consumers with online mass customization tools where style, color, and fit choices can be selected and tested on screen. Consumers become designers and their unique style can be displayed on models and eventually their own 3D scans for view. Some adjustment to this role of co-designer will be necessary as consumers shift away from ready-to-wear clothing options that they can touch and try on. Offering practice sessions, virtual try-on using one's own scan, and generous return policies for garments that turn out to be unflattering will help effect a successful transition to this new consumer-involvement model for designing clothing.

Creating virtual dress for online virtual worlds for hobby or financial gain is another option. For some it is a technical and creative challenge. It is also a way to engage the youth of today as we educate the next generation. Teaching creativity requires engaging the imagination. Setting a design problem within a virtual world, defining a target customer by an imaginary or stereotypical avatar, and teaching technical skills for creating online images hold great potential for encouraging the creative process through imagination and intriguing technology.

NOTE

1. All websites mentioned in this chapter were accessed in August 2005, unless otherwise stated.

REFERENCES

Ananthaswamy, A. (October 2000), "Being There," retrieved June 6, 2006, http://www.newscientist.com/article/mg16822615.000.html.

Ananthaswamy, A. (July 2003), "Virtual Reality Conquers Sense of Taste," retrieved June 6, 2005, http://www.newscientist.com/article.ns?id=dn4006&print=true.

Ashdown, S., Loker, S., and Adelson, C. (2004a), "Use of Body Scan Data to Design Sizing Systems Based on Target Markets," *National Textile Center Annual Report*, retrieved July 15, 2006, www.ntcresearch.org/pdf-rpts/AnRp04/S04-CR01-A4.pdf.

Ashdown, S., Loker, S., Schoenfelder, K., Lyman-Clarke, L. (2004b), "Using 3D Scans for Fit Analysis," *Journal of Textile and Apparel, Technology and Management* 4 (1), retrieved July 15, 2006, http://www.tx.ncsu.edu/jtatm/volume4issue1/articles/Loker/Loker_full_103_04.pdf.

Ashdown, S., Loker, S., and Rucker, M. (2006), "Improving Apparel Sizing: Fit and Anthropometric 3D Scan Data," *National Textile Center Research Brief*, retrieved June 1, 2006, www.ntcresearch.org/pdf-rpts/Bref0606/S4-CR01-06e.pdf.

Book, B. (July 2004), "These Bodies are Free, So Get One Now! Advertising and Branding in Social Virtual Worlds," retrieved June 6, 2005, http://papers.ssrn.com/sol3/papers.cfm?abstract_id=536422.

Isdale, J. (March 2001), "Haptics," retrieved September 24, 2004, http://vr.isdale.com/vrTechReviews/ Haptics2001/Haptics_March2001.html.

Kim, J., Hyun, K., Tay, B., Muniyandi, M., and Srinivasan, M. (2004), "Transatlantic Touch: A Study of Haptic Collaboration over Long Distance," *Presence* 13 (3): 328–37.

Knight, W. (March 2004), "Where's That Funny Smell Coming From?" retrieved September 24, 2004, http://www.newscientist.com/news/news.jps?id=ns99994834.

Kushner, D. (April 2004), "My Avatar, My Self," retrieved June 6, 2005, http://cache.technologyreview.com/articles/04/04/kushner0404.asp.

Loker, S., Ashdown, S., Cowie, L., and Schoenfelder, M. (2004), "Consumer Interest in Commercial Applications of Body Scan Data," *Journal of Textile and Apparel, Technology and Management* 4 (1), retrieved July 15, 2006, http://www.tx.ncsu.edu/jtatm/volume4issue1/articles/Loker/Loker_full_100_04.pdf.

Loker, S., Ashdown, S., Cowie, L., and Lewis, V. D. (2005a), "Female Consumers Reactions to Body Scanning," *Clothing and Textiles Research Journal* 22 (3): 1–8.

Loker, S., Ashdown, S., and Schoenfelder, K. (2005b), "Size-specific Analysis of Body Scan Data to Improve Apparel Fit," *Journal of Textile and Apparel, Technology and Management* 4 (3), retrieved July 15, 2006, http://www.tx.ncsu.edu/jtatm/volume4issue3/articles/Loker/Loker_full_136_05.pdf.

Weir, L. (April 2005), "Games Without Frontiers," *East Bay Express*, retrieved June 17, 2005, http://www.eastbayexpress.com/Issues/2005-03-23/news/feature_print.html.

INDEX